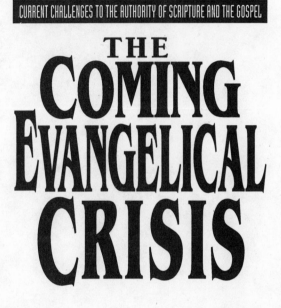

CURRENT CHALLENGES TO THE AUTHORITY OF SCRIPTURE AND THE GOSPEL

THE
COMING
EVANGELICAL
CRISIS

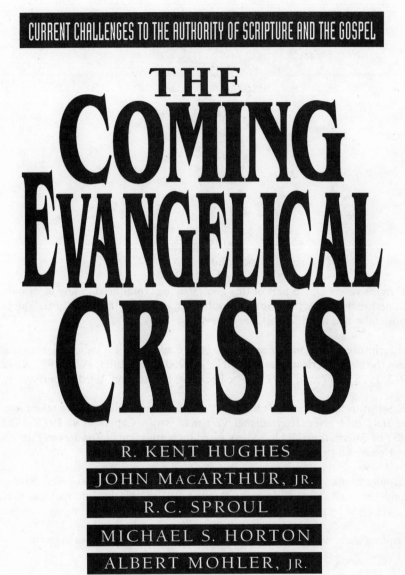

CURRENT CHALLENGES TO THE AUTHORITY OF SCRIPTURE AND THE GOSPEL

THE COMING EVANGELICAL CRISIS

R. KENT HUGHES

JOHN MacARTHUR, JR.

R. C. SPROUL

MICHAEL S. HORTON

ALBERT MOHLER, JR.

JOHN H. ARMSTRONG, GENERAL EDITOR

MOODY PRESS
CHICAGO

136626

ISBN: 0-8024-7747-X

1 3 5 7 9 10 8 6 4 2

For the reformation of the church
and the revival of biblical Christianity
in an increasingly dark time in history
when integrity in both life and doctrine
is the crying need of evangelical Christianity.

And for my daughter, Stacy,
who quietly loves God,
displays real zeal for life
and amazing devotion to her father.
Her commitment to serve her dad
in the ministry to which God has called him
is a continual source of encouragement.

CONTENTS

PART 4: FLASH POINTS IN THE CRISIS

PART 5: RESPONDING TO THE CRISIS

ABBREVIATIONS

BAGD   W. Bauer, W. F. Arndt, F. W. Gingrich, and F. W.
Danker, *Greek-English Lexicon of the New
Testament*. Chicago: Univ. of Chicago Press,
1979.

DOJATG   *Dictionary of Jesus and the Gospels*. Edited by Joel B.
Green, I. Howard Marshall, and Scott Knight.
Downers Grove, Ill.: InterVarsity Press, 1992.

DOPAHL   *Dictionary of Paul and His Letters*. Edited by Gerald
F. Hawthorne, Ralph P. Martin, and Daniel G. Reid.
Downers Grove, Ill.: InterVarsity Press, 1993.

EDOT   *Evangelical Dictionary of Theology*. Edited by Walter
A. Elwell. Grand Rapids: Baker, 1984.

LXX   Septuagint (Greek Old Testament).

TDNT   *Theological Dictionary of the New Testament*. 10
vols. Edited by G. Kittel and G. Friedrich. Grand
Rapids: Eerdmans, 1964–1976.

TWNT   *Theologisches Wörterbuch zum Neuen Testament*.
Edited by G. Kittel and G. Friedrich.

CONTRIBUTORS

John H. Armstrong (B.A., M.A., Wheaton College; D.Min., Luther Rice Seminary) is founder and director of Reformation & Revival Ministries in Carol Stream, Illinois. He served as a Baptist pastor for twenty-one years before becoming a conference speaker and editor of *Reformation & Revival Journal*, a quarterly publication for church leadership. He was general editor of *Roman Catholicism: Evangelical Protestants Analyze What Unites & Divides Us* and the author of *Can Fallen Pastors Be Restored?* and *A View of Rome*. He frequently contributes to various publications and book projects.

W. Robert Godfrey (A.B., M.A., Ph.D., Stanford Univ.; M.Div., Gordon-Conwell Theological Seminary) is president and professor of church history at Westminster Theological Seminary in California. He was the editor of *Westminster Theological Journal* for several years and has contributed to several books: *John Calvin: His Influence in the Western World; Reformed Theology in America; Scripture and Truth; The Agony of Deceit; Christ the Lord, Discord, Dialogue and Concord;* and *Roman Catholicism: Evangelical Protestants Analyze What Unites and Divides Us.*

John D. Hannah (B.S., Philadelphia College of Bible; M.A., Southern Methodist Univ.; Th.M., Th.D., Dallas Theological Seminary; Ph.D., Univ. of Texas at Dallas) is department chairman and professor of historical theology at Dallas Theological Seminary. He has been listed in several *Who's Who* publications, was editor of *Inerrancy and the Church*, and has published dozens of articles. He has contributed to many books and resource tools, including *The Bible Knowledge Commentary, The Dictionary of Christianity in America, More Than Conquerors, American National Biography, Handbook of Evangelical Theologians, Vital Theological Issues,* and *Handbook of Biblical Scholars.*

Michael S. Horton (B.A., Biola Univ.; M.A.R., Westminster Theological Seminary; Ph.D. candidate, Wycliffe Hall, Oxford Univ.) is founder and president of Christians United for Reformation (CURE) in Anaheim,

California. He is editor of *The Agony of Deceit*, *Power Religion*, and *Christ the Lord: Discord, Dialogue and Concord* and the author of *Made in America*, *Putting Amazing Back into Grace*, *The Law of Perfect Freedom*, and the 1995 Gold Medallion Award winner *Beyond Culture Wars: Is America a Mission Field or Battlefield?*

R. Kent Hughes (M.Div., Talbot Theological Seminary; D.Min., Trinity Evangelical Divinity School; D.D., Biola Univ.) is pastor of College Church in Wheaton, Illinois. He has written numerous books, including *Disciplines of a Godly Man*, *Are Evangelicals Born Again?*, *The Gift*, *Liberating Ministry from the Success Syndrome*, and nine volumes in the highly regarded Preaching the Word commentary series.

Gary L. W. Johnson (B.A., Univ. of Oklahoma City; Th.M., Ph.D. candidate, Westminster Theological Seminary) is senior pastor of Church of the Redeemer in Mesa, Arizona.

S. Lewis Johnson, Jr. (Th.M., Th.D., Dallas Theological Seminary), has held professorships at Trinity Evangelical Divinity School and Dallas Theological Seminary. He was involved in the Scripture translation of the *New International Version* and the *Berkeley Bible* and is author of *The Old Testament in the New*. He also contributed to *Roman Catholicism: Evangelical Protestants Analyze What Unites and Divides Us*.

John F. MacArthur, Jr. (B.A., Pacific College; M.Div., D.D., Talbot Theological Seminary), pastors Grace Community Church of the Valley in Panorama City, California. His Bible teaching and tape ministries reach millions across the globe. He is the author of many popular books, including *The Ultimate Priority*, *The Family*, *The Master's Plan for the Church*, *The Gospel According to Jesus*, the MacArthur New Testament Commentary series, and the MacArthur Bible Study series.

R. Albert Mohler, Jr. (B.A., Samford Univ.; M.Div., Ph.D., Southern Baptist Theological Seminary) serves as ninth president of Southern Baptist Theological Seminary. Formerly the editor of *The Christian Index*, he has written the forthcoming *Karl Barth and Evangelical Theology* and served as general editor for *Gods of the Age or God of the Ages?* Dr. Mohler was named one of *Time* magazine's most promising leaders age forty and under in the December 5, 1994, issue.

Leonard Payton (B.A., Univ. of Southern California; M.A., Ph.D., Univ. of California, San Diego) did advanced study in Germany and currently serves on ministry staff as chief musician at Redeemer Presbyterian Church in Austin, Texas.

David Powlison (A.B., Harvard Univ.; M.Div., Westminster Theological Seminary; M.A., Ph.D. candidate, Univ. of Pennsylvania) lectures in practical theology at Westminster Theological Seminary, counsels at the Christian Counseling and Educational Foundation, and edits the *Journal of Biblical Counseling*. He is the author of *Power Encounters: Reclaiming Spiritual Warfare* and contributed to *Power Religion: The Selling Out of the Evangelical Church?*

R. C. Sproul (B.A., Westminster College; M.Div., Pittsburgh Theological Seminary; Th.D., Free University of Amsterdam) is chairman of Ligonier Ministries in Orlando, Florida, and is a popular author, theologian, and communicator. Some of his recent books include *Chosen by God*, *Reason to Believe*, *One Holy Passion*, *The Holiness of God*, and *Classical Apologetics*. He teaches at Reformed Theological Seminary in Orlando and Knox Seminary in Ft. Lauderdale.

Robert B. Strimple (B.A., Univ. of Delaware; B.D., Th.M., Westminster Theological Seminary; Th.D., Univ. of Toronto) is professor of systematic theology at Westminster Theological Seminary in California, having served as the school's first president. He is author of *The Modern Search for the Real Jesus* and has contributed to *Christ the Lord*, *Studying the New Testament Today*, and *Roman Catholicism: Evangelical Protestants Analyze What Unites and Divides Us*.

R. Fowler White (B.A., M.A., Vanderbilt Univ.; Th.M., Dallas Theological Seminary; Ph.D., Westminster Theological Seminary) is associate professor of New Testament and Biblical Languages at Knox Theological Seminary in Ft. Lauderdale, Florida. Formerly he was a lecturer at Westminster Theological Seminary for several years and is the author of *Victory and House Building in Revelation 20:1–21:8: A Thematic Study*. He also has served as a freelance editor for Baker Book House and other publishers.

ACKNOWLEDGMENTS

The editor would like to thank the board of Reformation & Revival Ministries, Inc., for their support and genuine friendship in laboring with me for reformation in this generation. Each one of these eight brothers—Don Anderson, Wendell Hawley, Kent Hughes, Richard Johnson, Bob Mulder, John Sale, Tom Shaw, and Don Whitney—is a special blessing to me.

Thanks also to Stacy, to whom this book is dedicated. Without her day-to-day help in my office, much less would be accomplished for the kingdom. She keeps me on track and is a delight to my heart. I find great joy in being a father to Stacy and her brother, Matthew, two wonderful adult children.

Thanks to my wife, Anita, who helped in so many ways, especially by reading and providing encouragement. This book was finished while our household was being moved, and she helped me stick to the project during stressful times. I am, as always, grateful and still deeply in love with her.

This book would not have been possible without Moody Press Editorial Director Jim Bell's support. Gratitude is also appropriate for Joe O'Day, a good editor to work with day to day. I thank him for his professional courtesy and solid help.

Roz Shaw, who served me as a secretary faithfully for several years, is to be thanked for her volunteer secretarial labor and for being a dear friend.

The original idea for this project came from Pastor Gary Johnson of Mesa, Arizona. Thanks for calling with the idea and for urging me to put together this book. Your words of encouragement helped.

Book projects such as this one often have major snags because editors and writers have trouble working together. I have been blessed with the joy of working with some very special contributors to this project. Thanks to all fourteen who made it possible.

This book has been shaped through my own reading and continual exposure to the church across North America over the past four years. I have been especially helped in my perspective through friendship with a number of special people, but none more than the thirteen other members of the Alliance of Confessing Evangelicals, a group that I pray shall offer to the evangelical movement a way of return to the heritage from which it has strayed. I am honored to be a part of this team.

INTRODUCTION:
TWO VITAL TRUTHS

John H. Armstrong

The sixteenth-century Protestant Reformation began as a movement to purify the church of corrupt practices. Within a short time, it directly addressed some of the most basic and foundational doctrines of the Christian faith. The changes that resulted have forever altered the visible Christian community.

Evangelical Christianity, variously defined by historians and social critics, is clearly an heir of this sixteenth-century Reformation. Whether or not American evangelicalism will continue to look anything like historic evangelical Protestantism is another matter. The shape that modern evangelicalism has taken over the last few decades makes it increasingly less Protestant. This is certainly true theologically. It is increasingly true practically in how the church conducts ministry. As the church acts upon its theology, or lack of theology, trends follow. Some are inclined to regard this as a positive turn of events. The contributors to this present volume of essays believe that this new direction presents the church with a crisis that looms with serious consequences upon the ecclesiastical horizon.

The late Francis Schaeffer wrote more than ten years ago of *The Great Evangelical Disaster*.[1] He warned that watershed issues had arisen that demonstrated that evangelicalism was in serious trouble. He decried, in particular, the adoption of a method that no longer maintained concern for truth. Critics replied, as they often do to impassioned fellow evangelicals, that Schaeffer had gone too far. "He was reaching the end of an illustrious career and was disappointed," some said to me. But the trends he cited then, and the issues he raised in particular, are not only still with us, but by all indications the importance of addressing them more directly has not gone away.

Many evangelicals assumed that if we won the struggle to define the inerrancy of Scripture more clearly and if more and more of our evangelical pastors understood this doctrinal issue, we would recover the authoritative role of Scripture in the life of the church. The thesis of this book is that we accomplished much in the inerrancy discussion, but we need to go further. We need to deal more directly with the whole issue of *sola Scriptura* in a fuller and deeper manner. One could say that once we have defended the truth of an inspired text, we still must handle it properly. We must use the Word of God in a way that treats it as fully authoritative in the life of the church. We believe that the crisis that flows out of our understanding of *the authority of Scripture and of the Gospel of Christ* looms with even larger importance for evangelicalism at the end of this millennium.

What will evangelicalism look like if it continues on the course it has followed for the last twenty-five years or so? Will the term *evangelical* even have significance, especially when the name has virtually become an adjective that is used to describe sociologically oriented, contemporary religious persons or movements (e.g., "evangelical" radical/activist, homosexual/lesbian, antifeminist/feminist, Democrat/Republican, businessman/entrepreneur)?

This coming crisis may not yet seem so apparent to many. But the thesis of this book is that disturbing theological emphases are shaping the present direction of evangelical Christianity. These are resulting in the formation of some dark clouds. These clouds look more and more like an emerging storm system on a Midwestern summer afternoon. An early-warning detection system needs to be employed so that church leaders and faithful believers might "discern the times." Pastors need to know what they are up against if they will not go with the flow. Men and women who faithfully serve on church boards, who teach Sunday school classes and children's clubs, and who give countless hours to the service of Christ in the local church need to understand just what is happening. Their historically conservative denominations, mission agencies, and burgeoning parachurch ministries are changing as postmodern influences shape them more and more.

It is the central thesis of this volume that these current challenges to the authority of the biblical gospel are not all that subtle. They are open, plain, and potentially lethal. Both the sufficiency of Scripture (2 Tim. 3:14–17) and the authoritative finality of Christ's gospel as the "power of God for salvation" (Rom. 1:16) are being undermined. What will we do?

TWO VITAL TRUTHS OF EVANGELICALISM

At the time of the Reformation, Luther and the Protestant evangelicals believed that two truths stood at the very center of their reforming effort. These two truths have faithfully stood at the center of evangelicalism, to a greater or lesser degree, for centuries. This has been particularly true of those traditions confessionally related to Reformation theology. (Even in churches linked with the Wesleyan tradition, there has been a concern for these same truths historically.) In this book we will develop an application of these truths in the light of contemporary theology and practice. Our concern is to equip evangelicals to better understand a crisis that is clearly at our doorstep, if not already comfortably present inside our large household.

SOLA SCRIPTURA

What was called the *formal principle* of the Reformation—*sola Scriptura*, or Scripture only—formed the direction of the emerging reform movement. What this truth meant, simply, was that the church should not preach, teach, command, or practice anything contrary to the written Scriptures of the biblical canon. This truth is well stated in an often quoted section of a famous confession:

> The whole counsel of God concerning all things necessary for His own glory, man's salvation, faith and life, is either expressly set down in Scripture, or by good and necessary consequence may be deduced from Scripture: unto which nothing at any time is to be added, whether by new revelations of the Spirit or traditions of men. Nevertheless, we acknowledge the inward illumination of the Spirit of God to be necessary for the saving understanding of such things as are revealed in the Word and that there are some circumstances concerning the worship of God, and government of the Church, common to human actions and societies, which are to be ordered by the light of nature, and Christian prudence, according to the general rules of the Word, which are always to be observed.[2]

The point of all of this is to affirm that Scripture is the *only* source and norm for all *distinctly* Christian knowledge. We learn much from sources other than the Bible. But in matters of faith and practice, Scripture has *unique* authority. Traditions are binding upon us only insofar as they conform to the written Word. Another historic Reformation confession puts this clearly:

> We affirm that we desire to follow Scripture *alone* as a rule of faith and religion, without *mixing with it any other things which might be devised by the opinion of men apart from the Word of God*, and without wishing to accept

for our spiritual government any other doctrine than what is conveyed to us by the same Word without addition or diminution, according to the command of our Lord.3 (Italics added)

Another Protestant confessional statement speaks almost as if it had in mind the present evangelical confusion regarding *sola Scriptura*:

We believe that the Word contained in these books [of Scripture] has proceeded from God, and receives its authority from Him alone, and not from men. And inasmuch as it is the rule of all truth, containing *all that is necessary for the service of God and for our salvation*, it is not lawful for men, nor even for angels, to add to it, to take away from it, to change it. Whence it follows that *no authority, whether of antiquity, or custom, or numbers, or human wisdom, or judgments, or proclamations, or edicts, or decrees, or councils, or visions, or miracles, should be opposed to these Holy Scriptures, but on the contrary, all things should be examined, regulated, and reformed according to them.*4 (Italics added)

It is the opinion of the contributors to this volume that a number of new authorities threaten modern evangelicalism directly. These authorities are often grounded in what the above confession calls "custom, or numbers, or human wisdom, or judgments . . . or visions, or miracles," and they must be challenged when they stand against the authority of the Word and Gospel of Christ.

Historically, evangelical Protestant Reformers believed that Scripture was *canon et regula fidei* (*the* canon and rule of faith). François Turretin, arguably the greatest Reformed theologian after John Calvin, said that the real question is not, Is Scripture *a* rule of faith? The real question is, Is it the *full, sufficient, clear, authoritative, and adequate rule* of faith? Modern evangelicals will agree that it is *a* rule and even defend its inerrancy and authority at a certain level. What has been missed is that they do not generally treat Scripture, at least practically, as if it is *the sole, authoritative rule of faith and practice.*

From Tertullian and Augustine through Luther and Calvin, to Edwards and Warfield, Christianity has built both its theology and practice upon this bedrock principle—the written Scriptures are to be our guide for message and method. We go to the Scriptures to understand the gospel, but we also go to the Scriptures to understand how we evangelize, how we preach, how we help the souls of distressed people, and how we worship the living and true God acceptably. Today we go to many sources to address these and related issues. Thus, Scripture has become for many evangelicals only one of many sources of authority.

Historically, Scripture alone has meant at least four things for evangelicals who remained faithful to the above principles.

First, it meant that *Scripture is fundamentally necessary.* Why? Because God is holy and people are exceedingly sinful. The blindness and corruption of the human mind makes objective revelation essential. This is necessary because, without a self-attesting, objective, final, written revelation, sinful people would pervert the Word of God time and again.

This insight has an important denial contained in it. Humanity is unable to know God apart from the revelation of Holy Scripture. Only here is clear knowledge of the Almighty to be discerned. People have no innate ability to understand grace or redemption. Only in the written Word is this knowledge revealed to them by the Holy Spirit. Scripture is necessary because *only here,* as Calvin observed, does God speak to the church with authority.

Second, *Scripture is authoritative.* This point is implicit in the previous one. Roman Catholicism admitted the first point and even granted this one until Luther insisted that the Bible was *absolute* authority. The offensive word was *sola,* alone. Sinful people would set up their own authority in the church. Only the Word of God can bring it down and exalt Christ to His proper place in the life and practice of the church.

How does Christ rule and govern His church today? We answer, with the Reformers, by and through the Word alone. The Spirit does not lead men and women apart from the Word. The Word and the Spirit are inseparably joined. That is why preaching took on such an important dimension in the Reformation. And that is why, in every great evangelical awakening since the Reformation, the Word preached was fundamentally central. That is why the revivalism of our day should be seriously questioned in light of its continual downplaying of this vital link between Word and Spirit.

Third, *Scripture is sufficient.* This point challenged the supplements that medieval theologians sought to bring to the Word. It also challenged the supplements the church brought to the Word as well (indulgences, for example). Because the Holy Spirit is present in the revelation of the Word, any teaching that goes beyond this Word must be rejected—period. Luther once said that this was true "even if it snowed miracles every day."

The Reformers gladly studied the theologians, read the sources of their time, and listened to the opinions of church leaders. They did not live outside the visible community of the church. They had their numerous claimants to additional revelation, as we do today. Modern charismatics claim revelation, philosophical postulates demand allegiance, and psychological theories clamor for us to maximize human potential. Nothing much has changed, except that modern evangelicals are seemingly giving up the sufficiency of Scripture in larger and larger numbers.

Finally, the Reformers believed that *Scripture is perspicuous.* By this they meant that the Word was essentially clear and plain. Ecclesiastical experts were not needed for one to know God and to read His Word. That did not mean they saw no place for the true scholar or the pastor-theologian. Quite the opposite. They valued the office of teacher and pastor even more highly, precisely because they valued the Word so highly.

Contemporary evangelicalism faces a serious crisis precisely because it has lost its way in this matter of *sola Scriptura.* The major difference now is that the crisis over Scripture is within those groups historically associated with Protestantism, not simply within the Roman Catholic Church.

Practically, we give relative authority to the Scripture. To give it absolute authority would be to question a good deal of what is presently happening in a significant number of areas. We have grown accustomed to things as they are, and as long as they seem to work we plan to stay the course. The Word truly unleashed would judge us. We would be forced to begin a reforming process that would be painful and costly. We are not sure yet if we want to do this, especially as long as the "good times roll."

Further, today's evangelicalism treats experience as final authority. Have you been born again? Have you been led by God? Has God spoken to your heart? Did you feel good about the worship (praise, celebration, or seeker) service? Does the music move you personally? Are your kids excited about the programs? Rarely do we examine matters of religious faith and practice by the Scripture-alone principle. But a miracle, a changed life, a profound testimony—none of these establish the authoritative basis of saving faith. If we do not soon recover the proven truth of *sola Scriptura,* the crisis we face may be seismic in proportions.

SOLA FIDE

The second vital truth historic evangelicalism grasped was centered in the gospel itself. This stemmed from the Reformers' commitment to what was called the *material principle* of the Reformation—*sola fide*. If anything guided evangelical religion, it was its firm grasp of the related truths of *sola fide* (faith alone), *sola gratia* (grace alone) and *solus Christus* (Christ alone). Here the heart of the movement was laid open in its fullest sense. Here a people who loved the gospel and believed that everything must be submitted to its essential truth found strength and power.

The Protestant Reformers referred to this doctrine of *sola fide* as "the article by which the church stands or falls." They insisted that, to be made right with God, a sinner must trust Christ alone, through grace alone. This grace of Christ was accepted solely on the basis of faith, or else salvation was not solely God's work. Evangelicalism always had a mixture of responses to these matters, ranging from the Wesleyan to the Reformed, but when it rose to its high-water marks it openly stressed these great truths with renewed vigor.

In this emphasis on the authority of the gospel message itself, stress is properly placed upon grace. Simply put, God's saving of the sinner is outside the individual. Its focus is on the person and work of Jesus Christ alone, not on what is going on inside a person or on what the sinner does. Grace plus nothing saves the sinner, and this solely because of the merit of Christ. There is nothing I can bring that makes me savable. There is nothing I can contribute that will increase God's mercy, absolutely nothing!

In this true evangelical emphasis, Christ's doing and dying are alone my basis for acceptance with God. This is also the basis for fellowship with Him in the Holy Spirit. And all fellowship with God must be Christ-centered. The Holy Spirit's primary ministry is to glorify Christ and to exalt His work.

In this older evangelicalism, the Holy Spirit gave the gift of faith and repentance to sinners solely through the hearing of the gospel as it is revealed in the Scriptures. This includes the message of substitutionary atonement, a profound truth that evangelicals have uniquely embraced. The justified sinner receives the Spirit through faith in the gospel alone, not through any other means. In the cross, God glorifies Himself in the death of His Son. To preach evangelically is, by definition, to preach the doctrine of the Cross in its full theological sense. This means that preaching on marriage, family, or finance without the word of the Cross at the center is a new form of legalism. It is a modern moralism without Christ and the Cross. It is not, *fundamentally*, evangelical.

Modern evangelicals have drifted far from this understanding and practice. The result is an ever-growing crisis that threatens to drown the evangelical movement in a sea of subjectivism. The sea is filled with the water of relativism and pragmatism. Yes, we have lost our way. We have lost confidence that the preaching of Christ crucified should be our only message (cf. 1 Cor. 1:17–2:5; see esp. 2:2). We are afraid, so it seems, to alienate "boomers" and "busters" with a message of such calculated offense. Has our view of God become so people-centered that we are afraid we may lose our opportunity to reach them without a market-based strategy?

Historically, evangelicals were those who had great confidence in the gospel message. In fact, they believed that their only power was in the message itself—the gospel. It was the gospel that brought life, power, and true growth. The gospel saved families, corrected abusive patterns of behavior, and showed people how to handle money and wealth appropriately. The gospel was everything. It had real authority in every way. Today we seem to have a sad case of theological amnesia. We grope about from seminar to seminar looking for something to help us recover our lost keys. Why?

This book will suggest, in various ways, that one significant reason is found in our loss of confidence in the full and complete authority of the trusted, proven message of the Cross. When evangelicals were at their best, they did not need the endless surveys and strategies of our frenzied era. They trusted the gospel to do its work. They believed that, when it was understood, loved, and preached by the whole church, the Spirit of God was powerfully at work.

REVIVAL?

There is much talk among evangelicals today concerning revival. Claims to the next widespread general awakening abound. Recent campus meetings for repentance and prayer have added excitement to this interest. What are we to make of this?

First, an increase in general piety, at one level, is desirable. But increased piety is *not* real revival. Confession of sin is generally good, but more is needed. The significant danger here is that we may well be getting more of the latent narcissism of our culture than we realize. Even if confession is based on the work of the law bringing true conviction, we still need the gospel of grace that alone brings true life in the Spirit. Present movements are often characterized by repeated references that downplay preaching. This trend is anything but healthy when the church desperately needs preaching full of confidence in the twin truths of *sola Scriptura* and *sola fide*.

Second, could it be that more revivalism, or excitement about what we are doing with God's help, in the end will be the path back to mystical religion *without* the gospel? The nineteenth-century Roman Catholic convert Louis Bouyer once said that he welcomed evangelical revivalism precisely because it would bring us back to Rome. Why? Because revivalism stresses inner feelings and subjective experience, the stuff of Roman Catholicism, not Protestantism.

Biblical religion stresses the objective Gospel of Christ and Him crucified. Until evangelicals get this right, all that the movements of revival will most likely bring is more revivalism. The results of this may bring us even closer to the very crisis this book addresses. Perhaps that is why the late A. W. Tozer once commented that, if revival is more of what we are already doing, then evangelicalism most definitely does not need a revival!

Finally, whenever the Holy Spirit is poured out you will always find a people preoccupied with two concerns—the Scriptures and the gospel. The desire will be to bring all things into submission to the Word of God. This will be the sole authority for all matters of faith and practice. And the gospel will bring real joy. Christ as substitute, Christ as high-priestly Intercessor, Christ as Sovereign over all will be at the center of conversation, labor, and worship. When God's people are preoccupied with Christ, the Christ of the New Testament, then and then only can we rejoice in the evidence that a great work of the Holy Spirit is under way.

Until God is pleased to "rend the heavens" (Isa. 64:1) we must labor to recover these two great truths. If we do not, the challenge to the sufficiency of Scripture and to the authority of the gospel brings us closer to a crisis of immense practical and historical proportions.

NOTES

1. Francis Schaeffer, *The Great Evangelical Disaster* (Wheaton, Ill.: Crossway, 1984).
2. *Westminster Confession of Faith*, Chapter One, Section VI.
3. *Geneva Confession of Faith*, Article V (1536).
4. *French Confession of Faith*, Article V (1559).

PART
1
THE PRESENT
CRISIS OBSERVED

CHAPTER

1

"EVANGELICAL": WHAT'S IN A NAME?

R. Albert Mohler, Jr.

I know what constituted an Evangelical in former times. . . . I have no clear notion what constitutes one now.

Lord Shaftesbury[1]

It is mere cant to cry, "We are evangelical; we are all evangelical" and yet decline to say what evangelical means.

Charles H. Spurgeon[2]

Forty-some years ago, when *Time* publisher Henry Luce declared his era "The American Century," he appeared to be stating the obvious. At the end of World War II, the United States was poised to dominate the world scene in every respect—politically, militarily, scientifically, technologically, economically, and culturally. The former imperial powers of Europe seemed distant memories, and America stood ready to lead and to put its defining stamp upon world culture.

And yet, standing decades after Luce's declaration, we can see both the promise and the peril of his bold assertion. By all accounts, America was the dominant superpower, with the Soviet Union even less a threat than was thought to be at the time. But seeds of inner turmoil and confusion were already sown at midcentury. Though America would remain militarily strong, it would end the "American Century" a very different nation.

Perhaps the same should be said of American evangelicalism. Developing out of the postwar era, what became known as the "evangelical movement" was certainly more clearly defined than what has come to carry the label at century's end. *Newsweek* magazine declared 1976 the "Year of the Evangelical," recognizing the emergence of evangelicalism as a culturally significant force.[3] The movement had grown from a group of young leaders dissatisfied with the insularity and negativism of midcentury fundamentalism into a massive network of colleges, publishing houses, seminaries, periodicals, parachurch agencies, and churches. Millions of Americans identified themselves as evangelical

Christians and testified to a "born-again" experience. Billy Graham was firmly established as one of the most recognized and respected figures on the world scene, and numerous television ministries were carried into American homes via the airwaves and the developing cable television lines.

"After a long period of painful eclipse, evangelicals have emerged as a powerful force in the nation's religious and political life,"[4] stated evangelical historians David Wells and John Woodbridge.

> That all this should be happening in the full blaze of secularism when, only a few years ago, the demise of evangelicalism seemed complete, is all the more remarkable. Indeed, progressive interpretations of our history had assumed that once the decline of evangelical Christianity had been established, it could not be substantially reversed. The modern world would simply pass it by. But here is a movement that is slowly awakening to a new role in American life, vigorously and often creatively speaking to the needs of contemporary society and simply refusing to retire to its assigned oblivion. What are we to make of it?[5]

That closing question remains unanswered, for just as evangelicals were granted recognized standing in the nation's cultural, religious, and political spheres, the internal cohesiveness of the movement began to dissipate.

Theological accommodation to secular ideologies and the demands of the dominant academy became evident in evangelical literature and institutions. The absence of a comprehensive biblical worldview was demonstrated in the lack of linkage between formal convictions and evangelical lifestyles. Scandals and controversies surrounding major evangelical ministries became items of cultural fascination.

By the 1990s serious and unavoidable questions were being asked. In 1992, *Christianity Today*, founded as the flagship evangelical periodical in the 1950s, ran a cover story entitled "Can Evangelicalism Survive Its Success?"[6] The article chronicled the rise of American evangelicalism from simple roots to the vast empire of evangelical publishing houses, schools, and organizations that emerged by the 1970s. The world created by this evangelical empire was a complete subculture. As the authors noted, "It is now possible to proceed from kindergarten to a Ph.D. within evangelical confines, to listen to evangelical media from morning to night, and to consume a steady diet of evangelical books and magazines."[7]

By secular and cultural measures, evangelicalism is a success story

.worthy of the Horatio Alger Award. Though the influence of evangelicalism on the larger culture may be questioned, the institutional and commercial success of the movement is well established. What is not so well established is the spiritual and theological integrity of the movement. As the twentieth century draws to a close, we must now ask whether evangelicalism is in danger of losing its soul.

THE CRISIS OF EVANGELICAL IDENTITY

The "new evangelicals" who appeared on the scene at midcentury possessed a clear sense of theological identity. Standing apart from fundamentalism in spirit and apart from liberal theology in substance, the young leadership sought to identify itself with the recovery of Christian orthodoxy in the tradition of the Reformers and their heirs. As Vernon Grounds explained, evangelicalism is simply Protestant orthodoxy, emphasizing substitutionary atonement, justification through faith, biblical authority ("the indefectible Word of God"), human depravity, and evangelicalism. "This, then, is the nature of Protestant orthodoxy, a twentieth century continuation of the historic faith which springs from a bloody cross and an empty tomb, a Protestant against religious deviants from the Gospel of redemption, a witness to the truth and grace of God in Jesus Christ."[8]

Identifying with the continuation of Protestant orthodoxy provided the evangelicals with a middle way between the increasing heterodoxy accepted by the mainline denominations and the obscurantism, cultural isolation, and separatism of the fundamentalists. Although early evangelicalism was never monolithic, its essential core identity was well established.

The core theological identity of the newly assertive evangelicals was in continuity with the older evangelical traditions that had emerged in the eighteenth and nineteenth centuries. Looking at the evangelical movement as a whole, D. W. Bebbington, a British evangelical, identified the core evangelical convictions as conversionism, activism, biblicalism, and crucicentrism.[9] The self-conscious embrace of such theological convictions was understood to be essential to evangelical identity. As John H. Gerstner explained,

> To the evangelical, theological precision at least on essential matters is vital. Others may imagine that anyone who shows religious earnestness, regardless of his views, or who engages in evangelism, regardless of the

31

evangel which he preaches, can be called an evangelical. Those who have self-consciously assumed this title, however, insist that they have done so on account of their theology.[10]

But evangelicalism in the 1990s is an amalgam of diverse and often theologically ill-defined groups, institutions, and traditions. The older evangelical concern for individual religious experience has often been asserted at the expense of theological clarity. As David Wells laments, "What now defines an evangelical is more often than not merely a private, interior quality that he or she has, rather than very specific doctrinal beliefs. Who is and is not an evangelical therefore becomes a slippery and awkward question."[11]

The issue of evangelical definition is now debated by two opposing parties, each with an agenda for the evangelical future, as well as a reading of the evangelical past.[12] The "Doctrine Party" seeks to define evangelicalism in terms of theological conviction, centered on core doctrinal essentials, whereas the "Experience Party" would establish a rather amorphous notion of religious experience as the evangelical essential.

The collision of the two parties is taking place at virtually every level of evangelical life. The Doctrine Party claims the mantle of the apostolic Fathers, the Reformers, and the Puritans to define and limit evangelical identity to those who hold to the core doctrines of Protestant orthodoxy. Though the battles fought on theological ground were centered on the inerrancy and authority of Scripture through the 1980s, the ground has now grown to include doctrines such as justification by faith alone and the eternal punishment of the impenitent.

The Experience Party has vigorously resisted such doctrinal preoccupation and has attempted to broaden the definition of evangelicalism to include a pluralistic notion of doctrine.[13] This party includes the progressivist evangelicals, who advocate liberal positions on issues such as abortion and homosexuality, and those explicitly calling for a program of theological revisionism to recast evangelicalism in a mode more attractive to late-twentieth-century secular culture and the dominant academic elites. If experience, variously defined, is the norm and theological essentials are negotiable, evangelicalism becomes a loose confederation of groups, individuals, and movements lacking any coherent witness or theology.

The strains and stresses put on the issue of evangelical identity have been evident in the contested efforts to establish a core definition. The 1989 conference on Evangelical Affirmations organized by Carl F. H. Henry and Kenneth Kantzer produced three "marks" of evangelical authenticity: (1) belief in the gospel as set forth in Scripture, (2) commitment to the basic doctrines of the Bible as set forth in the Apostle's Creed and other historic confessions, and (3) an acknowledgment of the Bible as the authoritative and final source of all doctrines.[14] The statement continues: "Without constant fidelity to all three marks, evangelicals will be unable to meet the demands of the future and interact effectively with the internal and external challenges noted in these affirmations."[15] But these affirmations, and similar approaches taken by others, have failed to bring unity and theological consensus across the evangelical landscape. Now, calls to abandon the term come from both the left and right.[16]

I believe that evangelicalism has come to an impasse on this issue, with the two parties unlikely to come to an agreement. Furthermore, the continuing theological revisionism on the evangelical left is making the divide ever more difficult to breach. Though evangelicalism has never been reducible to theological conviction alone, it cannot remain evangelical and be satisfied with anything less than theological fidelity.

THE CRISIS OF EVANGELICAL THEOLOGY

The twentieth-century evangelical movement in America grew out of a sincere and urgent desire to identify with the faithful tradition of the church and the faith "once for all handed down to the saints" (Jude 3). Negatively, the movement understood itself in contrast to modernist and liberal compromise among Protestants and to Roman Catholicism. At the same time, the newly forming evangelical leadership was determined to engage the larger world of thought and culture and to confront those worlds with the gospel.

Nevertheless, the theological unity that once marked the movement has given way to a theological pluralism that was precisely what many of the founders of modern evangelicalism had rejected in mainline Protestantism. Indeed, by the late 1970s it was clear that basic theological fissures were forming. The presenting issue of the 1970s was the authority and inerrancy of Scripture. The so-called "Battle for the Bible" formed lines of opposition and coalition that have grown ever more distant in recent years. Though the division originated in debates over the formal principle of Scripture, it soon spread to material doctrines, including Christology, the Atonement, justification, and virtually every other major doctrine.

Beyond this, it has been extended to the very nature of biblical faith and the discipline of theology. In 1990, a major article in *Christianity Today* celebrated the "Evangelical Megashift," which, its author admits, "is dividing evangelicals on a deep level."[17] In this stunningly candid article, Robert Brow delivers a manifesto for evangelical revision, suggesting that many evangelicals have already come to his way of thinking.

The megashift Brow envisions is a total transformation of evangelical faith away from the Augustinian and Reformation bases upon which it was established and onto a new foundation complete with a wrathless deity and an unnecessary cross. Gone are substitutionary atonement and forensic understandings of justification. God's wrath, newly defined, "never means sending people to an eternal hell."[18] The church is not the assembly of the redeemed but a fellowship poised to declare all sins forgiven. "A whole generation of young people has breathed this air," celebrates Brow, and evangelicalism will never be the same.

In both these assertions Brow may be correct, for the influence of such a transformation is already to be felt:

> Many readers of *Christianity Today* will recognize that they have moved in some of these directions without being conscious of a model shift. And the old model can be modified and given qualifications for a time. But once three or four of the changes have occurred, our thinking is already organized around the new model. We may still use old-model language and assume we believe as before, but our hearts are changing our minds.[19]

Four years later Brow collaborated with Clark H. Pinnock in their work *Unbounded Love: A Good News Theology for the 21st Century*, a volume that greatly expanded the arguments set forth in Brow's "Megashift" article.[20] Brow and Pinnock proposed a new rendering of God and a theology they labeled "creative love theism." Such a "composite model" of theism, they argue, would include a new understanding of God as open and relational, and an affirmation of "a wideness in God's mercy," which denies the Reformed doctrine of election, and a reconceptualization of God as "a mutual and interrelating Trinity, not as an all-determining and manipulative transcendent (male) ego."[21] Their "creative love theism" is indeed somewhat creative, but this is not theism as measured by historic Christian theism.

As several other contributors to this present volume will demonstrate, this model is not as original as some might suspect. Its heritage actually lies in the human-centered focus of the Arminian tradition, as Pinnock acknowledges. The Arminian God ultimately lacks omniscience, omnipotence, and transcendent sovereignty. The Atonement, in this scheme, is not about the Son of God assuming human flesh and taking our place on the cross, paying the penalty for our sins. "We must realize that Jesus did not die in order to change God's attitude toward God."[22] The theological reconceptualization proposed and championed by Pinnock and Brow is not just an updated evangelicalism; it is a rejection of everything the Reformers taught and believed. More urgently, it is a rejection of the sovereign God revealed in Scripture.

Pinnock's concept of "a wideness in God's mercy" also reveals the extent to which some evangelicals have responded to the contemporary challenge of religious pluralism by abdicating evangelical understandings of salvation. These individuals argue that the non-Christian religions of the world can be revelatory and even redemptive (though most would insist that Christ remains Savior for all). They reject the traditional exclusivist posture in favor of various inclusivist and pluralist schemes.[23]

Some now argue against hell as eternal torment in favor of annihilationism.[24] Some also argue for a postmortem opportunity to confess Christ. Several revisionist theologians claiming evangelical credentials collaborated in what they proposed as a "biblical" challenge to traditional theism. In this project Pinnock was joined by Richard Rice, John Sanders, William Hasker, and David Basinger. The dimensions of the theological megashift are here apparent: "We need a theology," the authors argue, "that is biblically faithful and intellectually consistent, and that reinforces, rather than makes problematic, our relational experience with God."[25] Though the authors would doubtless resist the characterization, they have decided to make revelation come to terms with experience, rather than subjecting experience to the priority and authority of revelation.

In their rendering, God's purposes are not always accomplished but may be thwarted. Sovereignty is relative and relational. Omniscience is limited and omnipotence is redefined. The authors resist the "biblical-classical synthesis," which centers on divine transcendence, and thus reject the understanding of the divine attributes offered by such theologians as Stephen Charnock, Louis Berkhof, A. W. Tozer, J. I. Packer, William G. T. Shedd, and Carl F. H. Henry. Jacob Arminius, they suggest, corrected some dimensions of the Augustinianism of Luther and Calvin but left it for his heirs to make the decisive break with the older theism. As Pinnock elsewhere acknowledges, these new constructions are not so new at all. The megashift is actually "the old Arminian or non-Augustinian thinking."[26]

Arminius's self-declared heirs are now ready to finish his project—to break with the traditional theism that was shared by the Fathers and the Reformers and to replace it with a more relational theology. Thus, some evangelicals now embrace the notion of a more user-friendly deity who waits passionately but impotently to see what His creatures will do.

Will evangelicals embrace this megashift in large numbers? Pinnock, who decades ago had been known as a young evangelical committed to traditional orthodoxy and biblical inerrancy, sets the issue straightforwardly:

> This struggle for control will coalesce around the definition of evangelical. With the growing prominence of non-Augustinian interpretations within the evangelical camp, how will the "powers that be" respond? Politically, evangelicals prefer democratic pluralism, but it remains to be seen if they will exhibit tolerance toward this new diversity in the forefront of their ranks.[27]

Pinnock has correctly identified the issue. Evangelical integrity is essentially tied to evangelical conviction. The issue is not, in the final analysis, the theological authority of Augustine or the Reformers but the true nature of biblical theism. As D. A. Carson asserts, evangelicals should ask "not what evangelicalism can tolerate, but what Scripture authorizes and forbids."[28]

Evangelicalism is not healthy in conviction or spiritual discipline. Our theological defenses have been let down, and the infusion of revisionist theologies has affected large segments of evangelicalism. Much damage has already been done, but a greater crisis yet threatens.

THE CRISIS OF EVANGELICAL TRUTH

The growing confusion in evangelical theology points to a new and even more dangerous development—the evangelical embrace of postmodern ideologies.[29] Lured by the siren call of the postmodern theorists, several evangelical theologians have forsaken any claim to objective truth. Roger E. Olson, professor of theology at Bethel College and Seminary, celebrates that "several evangelical theologians are calling for and laying the groundwork for a radical 'revisioning' of evangelical theology that can be called 'post-conservative' in that it sets aside the intense reaction against modernity that has characterized so much conservative Protestant theology in this century."[30]

The reaction against modernity that Olson wishes to eliminate entails a rejection of established evangelical notions of truth itself. Traditional evangelicals, assert the evangelical postmodernists, are hopelessly mired in epistemological realism, the correspondence theory of truth, and notions of absolute truth. The scope and scale of the "radical revisioning" these postmodern evangelicals promote is staggering.

Stanley J. Grenz, among the most visible proponents of an evangelical postmodern approach, criticizes the evangelical preoccupation with propositions and reformulates the authority of Scripture. The Bible is not objectively and universally authoritative (or true?) but should be assumed as authoritative by the Christian community because it "functions as the central norm for the systematic articulation of the faith of that community."[31] Thus, the authority of Scripture appears to be culturally relative, as is the truth of its doctrines, however expressed.

Behind all this are the postmodern theorists who have shaped the elite academic discourse of the last decade. Figures such as Jacques Derrida, Jean-François Lyotard, Richard Rorty, Stanley Fish, and Michel Foucault have established the postmodern world of the academy, and their influence has at last reached the halls of evangelical thought.

One of the most remarkable manifestations of the evangelical embrace of postmodernist ideologies is *Truth Is Stranger Than It Used to Be,* by J. Richard Middleton and Brian J. Walsh of Toronto's Institute for Christian Study. Middleton and Walsh reject the notion of absolute truth outright: "Since all worldviews in a postmodern reading are merely human inventions, decisively conditioned by the social context in which they occur, and certainly not given to us by either nature or revelation, any 'truth' we claim for our cherished positions must be kept strictly in quotation marks."[32]

Thus, truth is not an absolute, objective category. Such concepts of truth are dismissed as hopelessly modern underpinnings of a totalizing and oppressive metanarrative, with which the postmodernists will have nothing to do. What the postmodern theorists will do is inundate the evangelical reader with convoluted and distorted reasoning—all predicated on what may charitably be described as an eccentric conception of modernity.[33]

How, then, according to the postmodernists, shall we understand the nature and authority of the Bible? It appears that Scripture holds sway, not because it is objectively revealed or even objectively true, but because it is the "antitotalizing narrative." It is the canon of the Christian community and, thus, is the narrative of the community and the vessel of the Christian story, not the depository of propositional or objective truth. Is this consistent with the evangelical doctrine of Scripture? Middleton and Walsh suggest that Scripture is marked by an "odd angularity."[34] They say, "The trouble is that, if we were honest, we would have to admit that there are many biblical texts that we find difficult to take as normative. Indeed, there are passages in Scripture that we find downright offensive."[35]

Lest we miss the full extent of their argument, Middleton and Walsh go on to make clear their willingness to employ a form of the "internal prophetic critique" used by liberationist and feminist theologians to reject the authority and truthfulness of troublesome texts. "There is a sense, then," they argue, "in which genuine faithfulness to the authority of Scripture means that we must go not only beyond the biblical text but sometimes even *against* the text."[36] Further, "Faithfulness improvisation thus does not mean blind submission to every text of Scripture but the enactment of God's redemptive purposes through discernment of the thrust of the metanarrative."[37]

Thus, the "hermeneutics of suspicion" is now fully in this evangelical tent. The reader decides what is and is not true and authoritative in the biblical text by judging whether a text corresponds with what is taken to be the central thrust of the entire biblical narrative. Of course, behind this view of Scripture is a corresponding view of God, Christ, the Atonement, and the entire theological system:

> God's authority is not that of an implacable tyrant who demands blind obedience. . . . This is the Author of an unfinished drama who invites us to participate in a genuinely open future in which we can indeed make a difference, as we implement in new, even unforeseen circumstances the plot resolution that Jesus initiated through his death and resurrection.[38]

A similarly disastrous approach is taken by Philip D. Kenneson in another recently released volume. The title of his chapter, "There's No Such Thing as Objective Truth, and It's a Good Thing, Too," more or less summarizes his argument.[39] According to Kenneson, the evangelical concern for truth is wrongheaded and irrelevant. The notion of truth as objective, he argues, is rooted in the correspondence theory of truth and metaphysical realism, both of which he discards as the debris of modernity. Truth, explains Kenneson, is "internal to a web of beliefs; there is no standard of truth independent of a set of beliefs and practices."[40] As authorities, Kenneson cites radical relativists such as Richard Rorty. But is Kenneson himself guilty of relativism? His defense against the charge is worthy of *Alice in Wonderland*: "In short, because I have neither a theory of truth nor an epistemology, I cannot have a relativistic one of either."[41] Are we to be relieved?

Postmodernism is, in reality, modernity in its updated costume, a hypermodernity made all the more seductive by its sophisticated dress. But success on postmodernity's terms is surrender for the church. An understanding of objective truth independent of the knower (standing alone or in community) is basic to Christianity and—against the claims of Karl Barth—to the biblical worldview itself.

If Scripture is not objectively true, independent of our acknowledgment, and if God is not objectively real, independent of our knowledge of Him, then we are without hope. If Jesus Christ did not die on the cross as our substitute and if He was not resurrected on the third day, if we have not been justified by faith and if His righteousness has not been imputed to us, then we are dead in our sins. Christianity is predicated upon a claim to absolute, objective *truth*, though we never claim that, in our fallenness, our own *knowledge* is ever absolute. To surrender this ground is to surrender the faith itself.

How is it that evangelicals can so openly and thoroughly embrace postmodern ideologies and theories of truth? Is it not remarkable that the books cited above were published by an evangelical press with a long-standing reputation for biblical faithfulness and a basis of faith that affirms the inherently propositional confession of the unique, divine inspiration, entire trustworthiness and authority of the Bible?[42] Postmodernism is attractive to many evangelicals because it is seen as a way to slice through the difficult issues of revelation and authority while still claiming evangelical identity. But, as Roger Lundin warns,

> The language of postmodernism is anything but a morally neutral tool that people of any persuasion might pick up and use to some appointed end. Instead, that vocabulary commits its user to a very specific vision of the self, truth, and the ethical life—a vision fundamentally at odds with the most basic affirmations of the Christian creeds.[43]

THE CRISIS OF EVANGELICAL ECCLESIOLOGY

The theological and philosophical issues discussed above are part and parcel of the discourse of the evangelical elites. At the popular level, a different assault on truth threatens. Those in the pews of evangelical churches, warns David F. Wells, "have now turned in on themselves and substituted for the knowledge of God a search for the knowledge of self."[44]

The massive cultural shifts that have so altered the American land-scape have changed the most fundamental assumptions embodied in our culture and—to borrow a phrase from Peter Berger—the "plausibili-ty structures" that shape the way Americans think.[45] Americans are now fanatic devotees of the cult of self-fulfillment and personal autonomy. The language of theology has been replaced by the vocabulary of the therapeutic. All issues of meaning are reduced, where possible, to ques-tions of personal significance. Truth is marginalized where it is not rejected outright. Relativism masquerades as pluralism, and the idols of television, "infotainment," and consumerism portray a world of uncon-ditional and unlimited choices.

Where, in all this, is the church? Pundits have often asserted that "evangelical ecclesiology" is an oxymoron—an inherent contradiction in terms. In an earlier day, this referred to the lack of evangelical con-sensus on contested issues related to the church. Since evangelicalism spans several denominational families, an intentional effort was made to keep ecclesial distinctives beyond contentious debate. In the present, however, "evangelical ecclesiology" is an oxymoron for a far more dan-gerous reason. Given the cultural transformations and the absence of biblical knowledge and sustained theological reflection, many evangeli-cals seem to have virtually no ecclesiology at all.

As John MacArthur and Leonard Payton will display more fully in later essays, this problem is particularly evident in the theological vacu-ity of much evangelical worship, where the culture of entertainment has supplanted biblical conceptions of worship and the character of the church. Evangelical consultants urge churches to conduct user-friendly worship intended to be nonoffensive to the secular attender. The emer-gence of "praise worship" has combined a much-needed return to sim-ple biblical praise with the repetition of mantra-like phrases of questionable theological content.

Although worship may be contemporary and remain authentic, it cannot be "seeker-oriented" and remain true to the biblical concept of genuine worship. True worship focuses on God—our gracious, loving, holy Lord—the Trinitarian God who delights in the praises of His peo-ple. The marks of true worship include the singing of hymns, the read-ing of Scripture, the prayers of the people, the observance of the Lord's Supper and baptism, and the preaching of the Word.

By this measure, much of what takes place in evangelical churches is anything but worship. The issue here is not style but content. Encouraging signs of renewed interest in worship are apparent, but these are mixed with unsettling signs of "theotainment" in the guise of evangelical worship. But worship is not the only issue of concern. The absence of biblical church discipline is a clear and present danger to the integrity of evangelical churches. In far too many cases, the church increasingly looks like the world—and the world takes immediate notice.

CONCLUSION

The gathering clouds that threaten the integrity and vitality of the evangelical movement include other issues of concern. These include the ethical revisionism of some evangelicals who are growing increasingly open to homosexuality and abortion. If we evangelicals compromise the sanctity of human life—born and unborn, young and aged, healthy and infirm—we will forfeit our moral integrity as well. We will betray our conviction and join the secular chorus of self-determination and "rights talk." Some evangelicals have embraced revisionist biblical exegesis in an effort to legitimate homosexual behavior and relationships. Thus, we voice an uncertain sound on one of the most critical ethical issues of the day—an issue that holds a far greater significance than sexual behavior.

Nevertheless, signs of promise also appear. Anglican theologian Alister McGrath suggests that "the Christian vision of the future now seems increasingly to belong to evangelicalism."[46] This may be so, and McGrath has marshaled considerable argument to make his persuasive case. But if it is so, an even greater burden is upon us. The stewardship of such an opportunity must call for our most faithful biblical and theological witness. We must call the church to fidelity—to true worship, authentic discipleship, and the preaching of the gospel to all peoples. But we must first get our houses in order, or we shall indeed face a coming evangelical crisis. If we evangelicals are not faithful to our calling, our opportunity, and our commission, God will raise up others to accomplish His sovereign purpose.

NOTES

1. E. Hodder, *The Life and Work of the Seventh Earl of Shaftesbury, K.G.,* cited in D. W. Bebbington, *Evangelicalism in Modern Britain: A History from the 1730s to the 1980s* (London: Unwin Hyman, n.d.), 1.
2. Cited in Iain Murray, *The Forgotten Spurgeon* (Edinburgh: Banner of Truth, 1966), 25.

3. This had much to do with the presidential campaign of Jimmy Carter and the issue of "born-again" Christianity, which seemed to be a new concept for the mainstream media.

4. David F. Wells and John D. Woodbridge, eds., *The Evangelicals: What They Believe, Who They Are, Where They Are Changing,* rev. ed. (Grand Rapids: Baker, 1977), 9.

5. Ibid.

6. Nathan O. Hatch and Michael S. Hamilton, "Can Evangelicalism Survive Its Success?" *Christianity Today,* 5 October 1992, 21–31.

7. Ibid., 28.

8. Vernon Grounds, "The Nature of Evangelicalism," *Eternity* (February 1956), 43. The editor's subtitle of the article is telling: "A scholar points out that [evangelicalism] is not an 'ism' but mainstream Christianity."

9. Bebbington, *Evangelicalism in Modern Britain,* 3.

10. John H. Gerstner, "Theological Boundaries: The Reformed Perspective," in Wells and Woodbridge, *The Evangelicals,* 33.

11. David F. Wells, "No Offense: I Am an Evangelical," in *A Time to Speak: The Evangelical-Jewish Encounter* (Grand Rapids: Eerdmans, 1987), 37–38.

12. For further reference, see R. Albert Mohler, Jr., "Southern Baptists and American Evangelicals: A Common Quest for Identity," in *Southern Baptists and American Evangelicals,* ed. David S. Dockery (Nashville: Broadman & Holman, 1993), 224–39.

13. At the academic level, these issues have erupted with a focus on evangelical historiography, with Donald W. Dayton carrying on a personal crusade to revise evangelical histories to make way for the Arminian/Wesleyan/Pentecostal traditions as major shaping forces. See "What Is Evangelicalism?" in the special issue of *Christian Scholar's Review* 23, no. 1 (1992), which features an extended argument between Dayton and other historians.

14. Carl F. H. Henry and Kenneth Kantzer, eds., *Evangelical Affirmations* (Grand Rapids: Zondervan, 1990), 37.

15. Ibid.

16. Some, such as Donald W. Dayton and William Abraham, have relegated the term to the philosophical category of an "essentially contested concept"—that is, a concept that involves continuous debates about its own meaning. Tellingly, both continue to press for their own rendering of evangelical definition.

17. Robert Brow, "The Evangelical Megashift," *Christianity Today,* 19 February 1990, 12–14. Replies from D. A. Carson, Clark H. Pinnock, Robert E. Weber, and Donald G. Bloesch follow on pp. 14–17.

18. Ibid., 13.

19. Ibid., 14.

20. Clark H. Pinnock and Robert C. Brow, *Unbounded Love: A Good News Theology for the 21st Century* (Downers Grove, Ill.: InterVarsity Press, 1994).

21. Ibid., 8.

22. Ibid., 103.

23. This literature is vast, and growing ever larger—an indication of activity and interest in these new proposals. See, for example, Gabriel Fackre, Ronald H. Nash, and John Sanders, *What About Those Who Have Never Heard?: Three Views on the Destiny of the Unevangelized* (Downers Grove, Ill.: InterVarsity Press, 1995); and

William V. Crockett and James A. Sigountos, eds., *Through No Fault of Their Own?: The Fate of Those Who Never Heard* (Grand Rapids: Baker, 1991).

24. See David L. Edwards and John R. W. Stott, *Evangelical Essentials: A Liberal-Evangelical Dialogue* (Downers Grove, Ill.: InterVarsity Press, 1988).

25. Clark H. Pinnock, Richard Rice, John Sanders, William Hasker, and David Basinger, eds., *The Openness of God* (Downers Grove, Ill.: InterVarsity Press, 1994), 7–8.

26. Clark H. Pinnock, "The Arminian Option," *Christianity Today*, 19 February 1990, 15.

27. Ibid.

28. D. A. Carson, "Is Sacrifice Passé?" *Christianity Today*, 19 February 1990, 15.

29. For a detailed consideration of these issues, see R. Albert Mohler, Jr., "The Integrity of the Evangelical Tradition and the Challenges of the Postmodern Paradigm," in *The Challenge of Postmodernism*, ed. David S. Dockery (Wheaton, Ill.: BridgePoint/Victor, 1995), 67–88.

30. Roger E. Olson, "Whales and Elephants: Both God's Creatures but Can They Meet? Evangelicals and Liberals in Dialogue," *Pro Ecclesia* 4 (Spring 1995): 169–70.

31. Stanley J. Grenz, *Revisioning Evangelical Theology: A Fresh Agenda for the 21st Century* (Downers Grove, Ill.: InterVarsity Press, 1993), 94.

32. J. Richard Middleton and Brian J. Walsh, *Truth Is Stranger Than It Used to Be: Biblical Faith in a Postmodern Age* (Downers Grove, Ill.: InterVarsity Press, 1995), 4–5.

33. For example, Middleton and Walsh (*Truth Is Stranger Than It Used to Be*) say,

    Modern ideals have served to legitimate patriarchal, European (and later American) violence against native peoples, blacks, and other people of color, women and nature itself. That is, under modernity, and under present postmodern conditions, humanity is pulled in two contrary directions, offered two contradictory alternatives for being human, which we may characterize as tyrant and victim, or centered and decentered, or imperial and impotent. This difference is that in postmodern times, the imperial self is stripped of its ideological pretensions (though its violence is not abated) and the decentered and victimized self has come to be valorized. (p. 110)

    The statement is pretentious, but the authors never explain why modernity is to blame for these ills. Tyrants, violence, victims, and oppression existed before modernity and where modernity has never extended its reach. Are we to believe that these evils are to be abated in the sway of moral relativism? Modernity has indeed presented Christianity with grave challenges, but it is disingenuous to root the correspondence theory of truth and realistic metaphysics in the modern age.

34. Ibid., 176.

35. Ibid. Middleton and Walsh further comment on the same page, "Indeed, in our experience, those who assert most forcefully an unquestioning submission to biblical authority are precisely those who avoid the odd angularity of the actual text of Scripture and refuse to struggle with our postmodern disorientation." The authors seem not to understand that evangelicals who assert biblical inerrancy acknowledge the "angularity" of the biblical text but recognize in this the sovereign purpose of God, whose word it is.

36. Ibid., 184.

37. Ibid., 185.

38. Ibid.

39. Philip D. Kenneson, "There's No Such Thing as Objective Truth, and It's a Good Thing, Too," in *Christian Apologetics in the Postmodern World*, ed. Timothy R. Phillips and Dennis L. Okholm (Downers Grove, Ill.: InterVarsity Press, 1995), 155–70.

40. Ibid., 163.

41. Ibid., 161.

42. See Keith and Gladys Hunt, *For Christ and the University: The Story of InterVarsity Christian Fellowship of the U.S.A., 1940–1990* (Downers Grove, Ill.: InterVarsity Press, 1991), 381.

43. Roger Lundin, "The Ultimately Liberal Condition," *First Things* 52 (April 1995): 23. See also his very fine volume *The Culture of Interpretation: Christian Faith in the Postmodern World* (Grand Rapids: Eerdmans, 1993).

44. David F. Wells, *No Place For Truth; Or, Whatever Happened to Evangelical Theology?* (Grand Rapids: Eerdmans, 1993), 7. See also his second volume in this project, *God in the Wasteland* (Grand Rapids: Eerdmans, 1994).

45. These shifts are not unique to the United States, of course, but are generalized throughout postindustrial Western society. My present concern, however, is with American evangelicalism.

46. Alister McGrath, "Why Evangelicalism Is the Future of Protestantism," *Christianity Today,* 19 June 1995, 18. See also his expanded argument in *Evangelicalism and the Future of Christianity* (Downers Grove, Ill.: InterVarsity Press, 1995).

2

MARTIN LUTHER: AN EVANGELICAL ORIGINAL

W. Robert Godfrey

The Protestant Reformation of the sixteenth century focused on two of the most important elements of Christianity. These two elements constitute the very core of what it has meant historically to be evangelical. One element was the doctrine of justification—sometimes called the *material principle* of the Reformation. Justification addressed the crucial issue of how the sinner is reconciled to God. The other element was the doctrine of Scripture—sometimes called the *formal principle* of the Reformation. The doctrine of Scripture concerned not only the truthfulness of the Bible but also its sufficiency and clarity to function as the ultimate authority in the life of the church.

Both elements were carefully forged in the context of a crisis regarding the truth. If they are lost to the present generation, a new crisis of truth will result. Both are vital to the health of the church. In this chapter we shall consider how one aspect of this historical crisis has direct bearing on the present crisis in evangelical Christianity.

THE BACKGROUND

Before the Reformation, the medieval Western church had certainly recognized the Bible as the utterly true and reliable revelation of God. But in practice the authority of the Bible had become limited by ideas about the authority of tradition and the authority of ecumenical councils and of the pope. The dominant assumption in the medieval church was that the Bible, tradition, and the pope were authorities that always agreed and complemented one another. Yet even in the Middle Ages tensions existed about the relations of these authorities to one another. Experts in canon law had questioned the infallibility of the pope. Some conciliarists had argued the superiority of councils to popes. Some theologians, like John Wyclif and Jan Hus, had claimed contradictions between the Bible and tradition.

The Reformation brought a new and sharper focus to the issue of religious authority in the church. The Reformers became convinced that the authority of the Scriptures to reform the church had been fatally compromised by false notions about the authority of tradition and the papacy. They believed that only by recapturing the teaching of the Bible itself on its own supreme authority could the well-being of the church be restored. This conviction about the Bible came to be known by the slogan *sola Scriptura*, "Scripture alone."

In this matter, as in so many others during this time, Martin Luther was the pioneer. Luther came to articulate powerfully and clearly the doctrine of the sole authority of Scripture. But, as with other doctrines, he came to that conclusion through a process of reflection and experience. In this chapter my specific purpose will be to look at that process with the intention of gaining a better understanding of Luther and of the doctrine of *sola Scriptura* in the sixteenth century. My wider purpose will be to add a necessary historical perspective to the discussion of the present issues regarding the doctrine of Scripture and the authority of the Gospel of Christ.

THE PROGRESS OF LUTHER'S THOUGHT

Luther's entire theology developed slowly from the time he entered the monastery in 1505 until he became a public figure in 1517 by nailing the Ninety-five Theses on indulgences to the church door in Wittenberg. The development of his theology, especially after he first began teaching the Scriptures as a professor at Wittenberg in 1512, centered in a growing criticism of Aristotle in philosophy and a growing appreciation of Augustine on grace. His theology continued to develop significantly after 1517.

Many scholars date his "evangelical breakthrough" on the doctrine of justification as occurring in 1518. Certainly between 1517 and 1521, when Luther was outlawed at the Diet of Worms, his theological insight sharpened dramatically. Historians often look to the great treatises of 1520—"The Babylonian Captivity of the Church," "An Appeal to the Ruling Class of German Nationality," and "The Freedom of the Christian"—as the defining moments of Luther's theology. But the year 1519 is also crucial. In that year Luther was forced to face clearly the formal principle of the Reformation.

In July 1519 Martin Luther participated in a debate that is known to history as the Leipzig Disputation. This disputation proved to be a key factor in the development of Luther's theology of Scripture and a turning point in the history of the Reformation. In retrospect, its importance is of the first order. E. G. Schweibert called it "one of the greatest debates in European history."[1] At the time it seemed unlikely that this debate should become so significant. This unusual development is only one of many ironies that attended this event.

After 1517 Luther became an increasingly famous man. The attack that he and his colleagues at the University of Wittenberg launched on aspects of medieval theology aroused the ire of many defenders of Rome. One of those defenders was Johann Eck, a traditionalist who taught theology at Ingolstadt. In writing he attacked Luther's teaching on the indulgences and the teaching of Luther's senior associate at Wittenberg, Andreas Karlstadt, on grace. Luther was eager to defend himself but believed that Eck had attacked primarily to make a name for himself. He said that Eck was more motivated by *chrysos* (gold) than by *Christus*.

The conflict between Eck and the Wittenberg men led to a decision to organize a face-to-face debate in the city of Leipzig. The location was not a sympathetic one for the Wittenberg theologians. Leipzig was the capital of ducal Saxony, which was ruled by a staunch Roman Catholic. The university in Leipzig was a rival to Wittenberg (located in electoral Saxony) and had been founded by Roman Catholic opponents of Jan Hus, the Czech reformer, one hundred years earlier.

Ironically, the invitation to the disputation at first was sent not to Luther but only to Karlstadt, inviting him to debate Eck on the issue of grace. Luther was annoyed that he was not invited (which may have been Eck's intention), and in time a further invitation was extended to Luther also to participate and to debate Eck on the subject of indulgences.

In preparation for the debate, Luther prepared a series of theses for debate on the points at issue and, almost as an afterthought, added a thirteenth thesis on the church: "The very callous decrees of the Roman pontiffs which have appeared in the last four hundred years prove that the Roman church is superior to all others. Against them stand the history of eleven hundred years, the test of divine Scripture, and the decree of the Council of Nicaea, the most sacred of all councils."[2] By this thesis Luther challenged the claims of supremacy of the pope over the whole church and suggested that history, Scripture, and the Council of Nicaea stood against Rome.

The Wittenbergers arrived in Leipzig on June 24, 1519. Luther and Karlstadt were accompanied by supporters, including two hundred armed students. The entrance into the city was not auspicious. A wheel fell off one wagon, throwing Karlstadt and his wagonload of books into the mud.

A humanist scholar from Leipzig, Petrus Mosellanus, has left us a remarkable description of the debaters from his own observations of the debate.[3] First, he wrote of Luther, who clearly impressed him:

> Martin is of medium height with a gaunt body that has been so exhausted by studies and worries that one can almost count the bones under his skin; yet he is manly and vigorous, with a high, clear voice. He is full of learning and has an excellent knowledge of the Scriptures, so that he can refer to facts as if they were at his fingers' tips. He knows enough Greek and Hebrew to enable him to pass judgments on interpretations. He is also not lacking in subject material and has a large store of words and ideas. In his life and behavior he is very courteous and friendly, and there is nothing of the stern stoic or grumpy fellow about him. He can adjust to all occasions. In a social gathering he is gay, witty, lively, ever full of joy, always has a bright and happy face, no matter how seriously his adversaries threaten him. One can see in him that God's strength is with him in his difficult undertaking. The only fault everyone criticizes in him is that he is somewhat too violent and cutting in his reprimands, in fact more than is proper for one seeking to find new trails in theology, and certainly also for a divine; this is probably a weakness of all those who have gained their learning somewhat late.

Mosellanus went on to write briefly of Karlstadt, who had his strengths but was not as effective as Luther:

> All this is true of Karlstadt as well, only in somewhat lesser degree, except that he is of shorter stature, with a face dark brown and suntanned, a voice indistinct and unpleasant, and a memory that is weaker, and he is more rapidly roused to anger.

The last description is of Eck, for whom Mosellanus had much less sympathy:

> Eck, in contrast, is a great, tall fellow, solidly and robustly built. The full, genuinely German voice that resounds from his powerful chest sounds like that of a towncrier or a tragic actor. But it is more harsh than distinct. The euphony of the Latin language . . . is never heard in his mode of speech. His mouth and eyes, or rather his whole physiognomy, are such that one would sooner think him a butcher or common soldier than a theologian. As far as his mind is concerned, he has a phenomenal memory. If he had an equally acute understanding, he would be the image of a perfect man. He

lacks quickness of comprehension and acuteness of judgment, qualities without which all the other talents are vain. And this is the reason that, in debating, he throws everything together promiscuously and without selection—arguments from reason, Scripture texts, citations from the fathers—without considering how inept, meaningless and sophistical is most of what he says. He is concerned only with showing off as much knowledge as possible, so as to throw dust in the eyes of the audience, most of whom are incapable of judging, and make them believe that he is superior.

The debate between Karlstadt and Eck on grace took place from June 27 to July 3. The debate between Luther and Eck lasted from July 4 to July 13 (with the exception of Sunday, July 10). Initially Luther and Eck focused on the matter of indulgences, but then they turned to five days of debate on the primacy of the pope.

Luther preached on Sunday, July 10, at a church in Leipzig. Ironically the lectionary text of the day was Matthew 16:13–19. Luther was required to address in his sermon the subject of the rock on which Christ built his church.

An even profounder irony was that just a few blocks from where the debate was held, John Tetzel lay dying. Tetzel was the Dominican friar whose sale of indulgences had provoked Luther into writing the Ninety-five Theses in 1517. Luther, with pastoral concern that was typical of him, wrote Tetzel a letter of spiritual comfort.

The debate that developed between Luther and Eck on the authority of the pope was remarkable. Martin Brecht has observed, "The Leipzig debate's epochal significance lies in the conflict over the primacy of the pope, which never before in the history of Christianity had occurred in this magnitude."[4] Luther denied that the papacy was a divine institution, but he was willing to recognize a legitimate role for the papacy as a human institution. At least this was Luther's public position. Privately he was beginning to believe—as some did in the Middle Ages—that the office of the papacy was the historical manifestation of the Antichrist.

As Luther's Thesis 13 indicated, Luther initially based his arguments about the papacy on tradition and on Scripture. He argued that the Greek church had known nothing of papal primacy and that the Council of Nicaea had considered the Roman see as equal to some other sees. He also argued from 1 Corinthians 3:22f., 15:24f., and Ephesians 4 that Christ was the only head of the church.

Eck's response presented historic claims for papal supremacy that were more than four hundred years old. He also argued that Luther's position was the same as that of the Hussites. The identification of

Luther with Hus was an effective debating tactic. Hus was a condemned heretic who had been executed for his heresy at an ecumenical council of the church. If Luther agreed with Hus, then he too must be a heretic.

Luther amazed the audience by boldly defending aspects of Hus's thought. He insisted again that Christ is the head of the church. He argued this point again from Scripture. It seems that at this point he really began to see the doctrine of *sola Scriptura*. He realized that the appeals to history and tradition were uncertain. Popes and councils had made mistakes. He was beginning to see that the church needed an authority from God that is absolutely true, clear, and sufficient. As a professor of the Scriptures Luther had for some time operated with confidence in the Word of God, but he had never faced the idea that Scripture and tradition might be fundamentally at odds with one another. At Leipzig he did see that contradiction and realized that only Scripture could be the ultimate authority in the church.

Luther said of scholastic theology, "There I lost Christ, but now I have found him in Paul."[5] He knew that in all his studies of traditional medieval theology he had not found the Gospel of Christ. But in his studies of the Bible he did find Christ. That discovery was the first step to *sola Scriptura*. The next step was at Leipzig, where the need for an authority that could judge the history and development of the church came powerfully to him.

LUTHER'S EXPRESSION OF THE AUTHORITY OF SCRIPTURE

Several years later in 1521, Luther would give classic expression to his commitment to the authority of the Scriptures in his most famous statement: the "Here I stand" speech before the emperor at the Diet of Worms. There he articulated clearly the truth that he had first seen at Leipzig:

> Since then Your Majesty and your lordships desire a simple reply, I will answer without horns and without teeth. Unless I am convicted by Scripture and plain reason—I do not accept the authority of popes and councils, for they have contradicted each other—my conscience is captive to the Word of God. I cannot and I will not recant anything, for to go against conscience is neither right nor safe. God help me. Amen.[6]

After the debate at Leipzig, Luther and Eck each aptly summed up the position of his opponent. Luther said of Eck, "I grieve that the Holy

Doctor penetrates the Scriptures as profoundly as a water spider the water; in fact, he flees from them as the devil from the Cross. Therefore, with all reverence for the Fathers, I prefer the authority of the Scriptures, which I commend to the future judges." Eck in response said of Luther, "The impatient monk is more scurrilous than becomes the gravity of a theologian. He prefers the authority of Scripture to the Fathers and sets himself up as a second Delphic oracle who alone has an understanding of the Scriptures superior to that of any Father."[7]

THE BASIC CONFLICT

These brief summary statements present the basic conflict between the Roman and Protestant positions. Luther says that the Bible is our authority and that all human understanding, even that of the venerated Fathers of the church, must be evaluated by and reformed by the Bible. Eck complains of Luther's arrogance in assuming that only he understands the Bible and is superior to the Fathers. Luther complains that Eck does not even try to understand the Bible, while Eck sees Luther as undermining the authority of the church.

A careful record of the debate was kept and, as had been agreed by the parties, this record was sent to the University of Erfurt and the University of Paris for evaluation and judgment. Erfurt never did render a judgment and Paris delayed until 1521. Ironically the Paris theologians handed down their decision while Luther was at Worms awaiting another verdict on his teaching. Word of their decision did not reach him until he was safely hidden from the world at the Wartburg.

The judgment of Paris, which went against Luther, concluded with a statement of some basic principles by which theologians ought to operate in order to understand the Scriptures:

1. The Scriptures are obscure.
2. The Scriptures cannot be used by themselves.
3. The Scriptures must be interpreted by Masters, especially by the Masters of Paris.
4. The Fathers are obscure.
5. The Fathers cannot be interpreted by themselves.
6. The Fathers must be interpreted by Masters, especially by the Masters of Paris.

7. The Sentences [of Peter Lombard—the foundational medieval textbook in systematic theology] are obscure.

8. The Sentences cannot be used by themselves.

9. The Sentences must only be interpreted by Masters, especially by the Masters of Paris.

10. Therefore, the University of Paris is the chief guide in matters of Scriptural interpretation, for its decrees against Luther and Melanchthon are clear and can be understood by everyone.[8]

Luther must have smiled as he read this judgment of the Paris theologians. The Scriptures, the Fathers, and Peter Lombard are all obscure, but the contemporary theologians are clear, especially those of Paris. The pride of such a statement was stunning. But Luther must also have been amused that the Paris statement made no mention of the pope as interpreter of the truth. The theologians of Paris and various bishops of the French church had long argued a measure of independence for their church from Rome. Some of the theologians had also argued that the pope was the administrative and judicial head of the church but that he had to learn the truth that he was to enforce from the theologians.

For Luther, this judgment reinforced his conviction that the church needed—and had in the Scriptures—a single, clear authority from which it knew the gospel. It confirmed the legacy of Leipzig: the Protestant doctrine of *sola Scriptura*.

CONCLUSION: THE DOCTRINE TODAY

Many voices in the church today question whether *sola Scriptura* is a doctrine that is credible or helpful. Not only Roman Catholics, but many Protestants, wonder whether one can claim that the Scriptures are in fact clear and sufficient when Protestantism is so divided. Did *sola Scriptura* unleash a subjectivism and individualism upon the church that was more harmful than the authoritarianism of the medieval church? Is the final irony of Leipzig that Luther's discovery there has been more destructive of Christian truth than the papal claims that he rejected? Luther would surely be appalled at the current state of Protestantism. But he would insist that the problems of Protestantism cannot be laid to the doctrine of *sola Scriptura* any more than human sins can be blamed on God.

Roman apologists frequently argue against Protestantism that the only alternative to an authoritative church is radical individualism.

Many Protestants have accepted this dichotomy and claimed that the rights of individual conscience are supreme. Such a dichotomy misses the whole point that Luther argued in his view of the authority of Scripture.

Luther sought in the Bible an authority that was beyond the errors and frailties of human wisdom and insight. He believed that as sinful humans the Fathers, the doctors, the popes, and the members of ecumenical councils could and did fall into doctrinal errors. He certainly believed that individual Christians would do the same. He did not seek to replace the authority of the pope with the authority of the individual believer, a commonly accepted evangelical view of our time. (Neither would he approve the liberal Protestant tendency to accept the professor as the authoritative interpreter of the Bible.) Luther believed that the Bible was clear enough to interpret itself. No other authority was necessary.

Luther was not naive in this belief. He recognized that Christians would differ in their reading of the Bible and that each would have to follow his conscience in this matter and face the judgment of God for his reading and understanding of the Bible. He believed that the Bible was clear enough that a careful reader could and should find the truth of salvation there. (We must remember that Protestants who accept the Bible as their authority and are heirs of the Reformation do agree with one another on the basics of salvation even if they are divided into various denominations. We should also remember that the Roman Catholic Church is deeply divided theologically, with great confusion as to what the Bible, tradition, and even the popes actually teach in a binding manner.)

Indeed, Luther in his own day faced the individualism and subjectivism that some see as the fruit of the Reformation. He faced it first in the spirit of fanaticism that he saw in some Anabaptists. For example, Thomas Münzer proclaimed himself a prophet so filled with the Holy Spirit that he did not need the Bible. To this rash self-confidence Luther replied that he feared Münzer believed that "he had swallowed the Holy Ghost, feathers and all."[9] Luther saw that such arrogance would create a thousand popes and that human authority would continue to supplant the authority of the Bible.

Luther also faced the problem of individualism in the divisions between himself and the Swiss reformers, Zwingli and Oecolampadius. Mark Edwards has shown that Luther did sometimes oppose the claims of Zwingli and others with his own personal authority as the pioneer in recovering the gospel.[10] He saw himself as parallel to Paul, not in terms of being an apostle but in terms of being a faithful teacher attacked by the wolves. Luther believed strongly that the Evil One always attacked the church from without by persecution and from within by false teachers. Of the false teachers' use of the Bible, he wrote, "Others tear it to pieces, scourge and crucify it, and subject it to all manner of torture until they stretch it sufficiently to apply to their heresy, meaning, and whim."[11] But the fault lies not in the Bible or the doctrine of *sola Scriptura* but rather in the sinful misuse of the Bible.

Luther recognized that the interpretation of the Bible was not a matter for individuals alone. Tradition and the church, both as an institution and as the fellowship of the faithful, were useful and important in interpreting the Bible. But they were not ultimate authorities in that process of interpretation.

Luther did not compromise his insistence that only the Bible is the authority for the church. The authority of any teacher must be judged by his faithfulness to the Scriptures. The Bible is true, sufficient, and clear, and can therefore lead us to Christ. "In a word, if Scripture is obscure or ambiguous, what need was there for its having been divinely delivered to us? Were we not obscure and ambiguous enough by ourselves without having the situation made worse for us by obscurity, ambiguity, and darkness coming to us from heaven?"[12]

Luther's confidence was not in himself and his wisdom as an interpreter of the Bible. When confronted at Worms with the question "Are you alone wise?" he was deeply troubled. He resolved the question by insisting that the issue was not his wisdom but the wisdom of God. Was God able to reveal Himself in a way that is comprehensible? Luther was convinced that He was. Luther was driven to his conclusions, not by his own wisdom, but by the Word of God itself. His conviction about *sola Scriptura* is well summarized in this statement: "I am not concerned about myself, but I shall defend Christ's word with a joyful heart and renewed courage, without regard to anyone. To this end God has given me a joyful and fearless spirit, which I trust they shall not harm in all eternity."[13]

NOTES

1. E. G. Schweibert, *Luther and His Times* (St. Louis: Concordia, 1950), 413.
2. Martin Luther, *Luther's Works* (Philadelphia: Fortress, 1957), 31:318.

3. Cited in Martin Brecht, *Martin Luther, His Road to Reformation 1483–1521* (Philadelphia: Fortress, 1985), 313–15.
4. Ibid., 317.
5. Ibid., 325.
6. Roland Bainton, *Here I Stand* (New York: Abingdon, 1950), 185.
7. Schweibert, *Luther and His Times*, 412.
8. Ibid., 436.
9. Cited in Bainton, *Here I Stand,* 261.
10. Mark Edwards, *Luther and the False Brethren* (Stanford, Calif.: Stanford Univ. Press, 1975), 112ff.
11. E. M. Plass, comp., *What Luther Says* (St. Louis: Concordia, 1959), 1:72.
12. Ibid., 1:74.
13. Brecht, *Martin Luther*, 346.

CHAPTER
3
DOES THEOLOGY
STILL MATTER?

Gary L. W. Johnson

Theology truly mattered for a sixteenth-century monk named Martin Luther. It mattered significantly for all the Reformers. And it mattered for the early Puritans who founded this nation. It also mattered in the struggles with liberalism that our more immediate forefathers engaged in during the earlier decades of our century. But does it matter today? Really? Significantly? Especially among evangelicals who have increasingly become absorbed with the agenda of the popular culture?

Theology does matter; indeed, I wish to show that it matters supremely. A healthy Christianity cannot survive without theology, and theology must matter today, especially in our mindless and irrational culture. It should especially matter among evangelicals who confess saving attachment to Jesus Christ. But current challenges to the authority of the biblical gospel often come from within our churches, from practitioners who are increasingly disinterested in serious theology. Efforts to repackage Christian truth into an acceptable "popular theology" aside, the problem is acute.

Yes, theology matters! Whether we are speaking of *how* theology is done according to its various disciplines—exegetical, biblical, systematic, historical, or practical—or how theology speaks to popular culture directly, theology matters! It matters, as a typical Puritan theologian argued, because it is that which enables us to live well unto God.[1]

This was once a given in evangelical thought and practice—theology mattered to every true worshiper of the Lord Jesus Christ. William Ames, in a time when theology profoundly mattered, was typical of his era when he contended that theology was for everyone. It was not simply the domain of a small group of academic experts. It was the personal concern of the most humble merchant or homemaker. That was because theology, by its very nature and function, was believed to speak not only to the intellect but also to the common *sensus*, to human feelings and emotions.[2] So important is this last aspect of theology that John Owen, a Puritan who often is accused of being overly scholastic in the worst sense of the word, could write, "Let us proclaim it boldly—the man who is not inflamed with divine love is an outsider to all theology!"[3]

Yes, theology still matters, or at least it should. And evangelicals who increasingly show little regard for theology or who demonstrate a willingness to accept what one person refers to as "tacky theology" need to take to heart the words of contemporary Lutheran scholar Martin Marty: "There will inevitably be theology: will it be good or bad, conscious or unconscious, disciplined or diffuse?"[4]

AN APPRAISAL OF PRESENT-DAY EVANGELICALISM
"I do not want you to be unaware." (1 Cor. 10:1)

David Wells, in his two groundbreaking books *No Place for Truth* and *God in the Wasteland*, echoes the same concern as the Puritan William Ames when he states that theology is fundamentally the knowledge that belongs first and foremost to the people of God; therefore, the proper and primary audience for theology should be the church. Its purpose is to nurture the people of God.[5] Wells is not alone in his alarm about the crisis of our time—and rightfully so, as many developments demonstrate. The astounding degree of theological illiteracy within the evangelical church and the growing bias against theology in wider evangelical circles are both marks of the problem I propose to address in this chapter.

Response to David Wells and his work has been wide-ranging. Some evangelicals have dismissed him as a gadfly, whose only concern is the restoration of a particular kind of theology.[6] Tragically, most seem to simply ignore him. But Wells is by no means alone in his bleak assessment of the evangelical scene. Three decades ago the noted sociologist Peter Berger predicted our situation with remarkable accuracy:

> When churches abandon or de-emphasize theology, they give up the intellectual tools by which the Christian message can be articulated and defended. In the resulting chaos of religious ideas the principal criterion left to the community as it seems to find its way is, quite naturally, that of expediency.[7]

Although most of today's professing evangelicals would acknowledge that theology, in *some* sense of the word, does matter, a recent survey in *Christianity Today* revealed that this is more lip service than anything else.[8] According to this survey (which, by the way, was attached to the lead story of the issue), theology, in *any* sense of the word, is really *not* all that important to the very people to whom it should matter most: those in the pew and in the pulpit. Both groups listed theological knowledge as *last* in terms of pastoral priorities.

It was interesting, and at the same time very disturbing, to note what each surveyed group considered more important than theology when it came to pastoral priorities. For the people in the pew, *spirituality* was of first importance, followed by relational skills, character, and then communication skills. It is difficult to decipher what is really meant by *spirituality* in this survey, since the respondents so distantly removed it from theological knowledge.[9] The nineteenth-century Scottish theologian James Orr wrote of those who would exalt spirituality at the expense of theology:

> Christianity, it is sometimes said by those who represent this view, is a life, not a creed; it is a spiritual system, and has nothing to do with dogmatic affirmations. But this is to confuse two things essentially different—Christianity as an inward principle of conduct, a subjective religious experience, on the one hand, and Christianity as an objective fact, or an historic magnitude, on the other. But can even the life be produced, or can it be sustained and nourished, without knowledge?[10]

How can true spirituality be divorced from the knowledge of God (theology)? "There can be no vital spirituality," writes Donald Bloesch, "without a sound theology."[11]

The same lack of reflection evident in the pew also appeared in the priorities of pastors. They considered relational skills the top priority, followed by management abilities, communication skills, and then spirituality. Wells's assertion that the Christian ministry is being redefined in terms of the CEO and the psychologist, whose task it is to engineer good relations and warm feelings, is manifestly ratified by this survey.[12] It is difficult to imagine patients or surgeons listing medical knowledge as the least important item in that respective field—or, for that matter, those involved and affected by *any* particular vocational endeavor—without massive repercussions.

The thing that most disturbed me about the accompanying *Christianity Today* article, however, was the way it interpreted the data gleaned from this survey. Because seminary professors put a high priority on theological knowledge, they were considered out of touch with reality and did not have "a good understanding of the needs of local churches or the culture." The article concludes with this ominous remark: "Something's got to happen. The church is not going to wait. If the seminaries don't wake up and come along, they will be left in the dust." Wake up to what? The survey does reveal the pressing need for seminaries to change, but the not-so-subtle conclusion that the article draws from the survey is the wrong one. The article implied that *less* theology (or maybe *no* theology) in the seminary curriculum is the direction needed. The problem, however, as diagnosed by post-Reformation scholar Richard A. Muller, is just the opposite:

> Seminaries have been guilty of creating several generations of clergy and teachers who are fundamentally ignorant of the materials of the theological task and prepared to argue (in their own defense) the irrelevance of classical study to the practical operation of ministry. The sad result has been the loss, in many places, of the central, cultural function of the church in the West and the replacement of a culturally and intellectually rich clergy with a group of practitioners and operations-directors who can do almost anything except make sense of the church's theological message in the contemporary context.[13]

During the last phase of my own graduate studies, I taught church history as an adjunct professor in a well-known Christian college. Over a period of three years, about three hundred students passed through my classes. One of the things I asked them to do from time to time was to keep track of the sermon topics they were hearing in their home churches. The disproportionate share of these were topical "how to" sermons that focused on relationships and the like and had more in common with John Bradshaw than with the text of Scripture. (During the U.S. military operation "Desert Storm," I did notice an increase in speculative prophetic themes among those my students listed.)

Distinctively doctrinal sermons that would have at one time been essential to an understanding of the evangelical faith were conspicuous by their absence. Very few could remember hearing a sermon on the deity of Christ. An even smaller number could recall *ever* hearing a sermon on the doctrine of justification by faith, the article of faith by which Luther said "the church stands or falls." For most of the students, the Protestant Reformation was simply a historical event with no more personal significance for them than the coronation of Charlemagne.

Concurrent with my duties at this particular institution, I taught part-time at another small college that was not evangelical. Here the students were, for the most part, completely secular in their orientation (some of them would occasionally miss my Monday morning class because of hangovers). A reading of Jonathan Edwards's sermon "Sinners in the Hands of an Angry God" to students from both colleges produced surprising results. Most of the students from the evangelical institution responded to Edwards like their secular counterparts from the other school. Edwards left them in a state of irritation and bewilderment. Neither group could imagine anyone in his right mind actually believing that God could be anything like that. My standard retort was to quote John Donne's remark: "You must have a very mean and unworthy estimate of God if you stipulate that He ought to behave as you yourself would behave if you were God!"[14]

My findings appear to be a microcosm of what is occurring on a much larger scale in the evangelical church. The research efforts of Gallup, Barna, and Hunter all indicate that evangelicals are, for the most part, as secular in their orientation as non-Christians.[15] The data reveals, among other things, an astounding degree of theological illiteracy: 84 percent of those who claim the evangelical label embrace the notion that in salvation God helps those who help themselves, 77 percent believe that human beings are basically good and that good people go to heaven regardless of their relationship to Christ, while more than half of those surveyed affirmed self-fulfillment as their first priority. An equal number had a difficult time accepting the concept of absolute truth. I fear that this may be only the tip of a massive iceberg.

It should not come as a big surprise that when theology is obviated, churches become preoccupied with other things. Entertainment in the form of drama and comedy skits replaces preaching, which, unless it is entertaining, is often described as boring.[16] More and more stress is placed on music style that attempts to evoke an emotional response simply for its own sake.[17] Most of what passes for preaching on "Christian" television, especially among the so-called Word of faith teachers, is either sub-Christian or just out-and-out heresy, blasphemy, and weirdness. "Paganism," laments Os Guinness, "is growing up in our churches. Speculative gnosticism is resurgent in our own circles. A horror of great darkness is welling up in our own house."[18] Theologian Donald Bloesch soberly warns that "a church that does not take theology seriously is unwittingly encouraging understandings of the faith that are warped or unbalanced."[19]

Despite the fact that evangelicals are more than willing to pay lip service to the importance of theology, the evangelical church at large belies that claim. "While evangelical theology is still professed, it is losing its power to define what being an evangelical means and how evangelicalism is practiced."[20]

OUR HUNGER-BITTEN EVANGELICALISM
"Who has bewitched you?" (Gal. 3:1)

David Wells makes à cogent case that one of the reasons for this present aversion to theology within evangelicalism is due, in large measure, to the forces of modernity. This is especially true when we turn our attention to the evangelical pulpit, which has in large measure succumbed to the triumph of the therapeutic.[21] (David Powlison offers some needed correctives in chapter 12.) This is painfully obvious in the way psychology has captured the evangelical mind. Evangelicals by their vocabulary betray the fact that they have forgotten the language of biblical and systematic theology, while learning instead the balderdash of pop psychology. Across the board, evangelicals virtually revel in terms such as *dysfunctional, codependent, victimization, self-affirming*, and the like, but most haven't a clue about the meaning of God-given words such as *propitiation* and *justification*.[22] "Psychologists," writes David Powlison, "not pastors or theologians, maintain cultural authority in the evangelical church with respect to people and their problems. They are the experts, with the authority to define what is right and wrong, true and false, good and bad, constructive and destructive."[23]

In addition to the forces of modernity, Mark Noll and Os Guinness have pointed the guilty finger at another culprit: Pietism. The intellectual problem of Pietism, as Noll chronicles it, lies in its excesses:

> Pietists had rediscovered the truth that Christianity is a life as well as a set of beliefs. The difficulty arose when some Pietists began to view Christian faith as only a life, without a concern for beliefs at all. This led to fascination with practice, deep involvement in spiritual experience, and absorption in the psychological dimensions of the faith. Objective realities of revelation were sometimes almost totally eclipsed.[24]

This same anti-intellectual strain of Pietism, Guinness contends, is still with us: "Whenever evangelicals have an experience of direct, personal access to God, we are tempted to think or act as if we can dispense with doctrine, sacraments, history and all the other superfluous paraphernalia of the church—and make our experience the sum and soul of our faith."[25]

This particular weakness was not unique to Pietism. One of the lesser-known, but critical, debates that occurred between the Remonstrants and their Calvinist opponents at the Synod of Dort centered on this same issue.[26] Is theology, as such, theoretical (*theoria*) or practical (*praxis*), or both? *Theoria* (lit., "to look at") was defined as doctrine known in and for itself. *Praxis* (lit., "to do") was understood as teaching known for the sake of the end toward which it directs the knower. The Reformed argued that theology must be understood as both. The Remonstrants, on the other hand, argued that theology is *strictly* practical, consisting in nothing but assent and obedience to precepts and faith in promises. Theology was understood to be purely practical and utilitarian. This perspective, if consistently maintained, will eventually remove all fundamental articles of the Christian faith, including the Trinity and the Incarnation—simply because these cardinal doctrines are not rooted in *praxis* per se but are in fact grounded in *theoria*.

The subsequent history of the Remonstrants shows that very few of them could resist the slide into Socinianism, Unitarianism, and Deism. If this view of theology had been accepted, the Reformed insistence on doctrinal norms would have collapsed—indeed, as Richard A. Muller has noted, "the theocentric character of Reformed theology would have to give way to an essentially anthropocentric drive toward *praxis*."[27] When theology becomes anthropology, it becomes simply a form of worldliness. [28]

The problem that presently plagues evangelicalism in our day bears more than a passing resemblance to that which characterized the Pietists and Remonstrants. And the resulting crisis we now face, like theirs, is in the words of Muller, "the result of severance of theory from practice and practice from theory that has made many theological theoreticians question the intellectual and spiritual future of the church at large and the academic future of their disciplines—and that has led many ministerial practitioners to doubt the value of all things theological."[29]

The problem doesn't end there. How are we to understand what is *practical*? Ken Myers has alerted us to the all-too-common notion that, when people ask for *practical* advice on what to do about living in an increasingly decadent culture, they usually want *easily followed* advice.[30] *Practical* has lost its meaning. It no longer means "in practice" but "readily achievable." Furthermore, this nontheological approach to practicality, coupled with the mad pursuit of relevance for its own sake, ends up serving as a cortege for ethics. True and false, right and wrong give way to likes and dislikes. Personal preferences serve to validate individual behavior. Personalized eclecticism has become epidemic among evangelicals; as a result ethics have become more complex than ever. "Rather than people simply siding with the good against forces of evil, they now juxtapose multiple concepts of the good and situationalize these concepts in a way that makes all of them relativistic."[31] Evangelicals are going to be forced to learn the bitter lesson that the arbiters of secular morality in our day cannot be kept at bay once the theological underpinnings of ethics are removed. A fog has settled in upon the evangelical church, and that will make tracking the maze all the more difficult.

WISDOM FROM AN EARLIER ERA

The name B. B. Warfield does not elicit the kind of respect it once did in evangelical circles. Donald Dayton, who writes from a Wesleyan perspective, has said that the Reformed tradition to which Warfield belonged should now be viewed as being peripheral to the evangelical world.[32] Progressive evangelicals dislike his formulation of biblical inerrancy. Evangelical Arminians, and especially the new breed of radical Arminians as represented by Clark Pinnock, find his unbending Calvinism extremely distasteful, whereas Pentecostals and Charismatics resent his seminal contribution to the issue of the cessation of apostolic charismata. I, nonetheless, concur with Mark Noll in holding up Warfield as one of the voices from the past that evangelicals would do well to heed.[33]

Like John Owen before him (with whom he is often compared as being excessively scholastic),[34] Warfield said that theology does not exist when only the intellect is busied with the apprehension of logical propositions about God but can come into existence only in beings that possess religious nature and through the actions of the religious faculty. The knowledge of God, accordingly, which it is the end of theology to produce, is that vital knowledge of God that engages the whole person.[35] As long as we remain in the region of the pure intellect, we remain out of the proper region of theology, since it is the product of, appeals to, and impinges on the religious elements in human nature, and nothing is "theology" that does not move in this sphere.[36] No single Christian doctrine has been revealed to people merely as a tenet in philosophy to make them wise; each and every one is sent to them as a piece of glad tidings that they may be made wise unto salvation.[37]

For this reason it is important that we should pause to remind ourselves that intellectual training alone will never make a true minister, that the heart has rights the head must respect, and that it behooves us above everything to remember that the ministry is a spiritual office.[38] This touches our feelings as well, and no one should ever doubt that religion is, among other things, a feeling; nor need we doubt that the implications of this feeling, if fully drawn out and stated, would give us a theology—and a theology, let us say it frankly at once, that would be true and would enter into Christianity as the fundamental element of its doctrinal system.[39] But the pressing question is, What produces the specific form of religious feeling that is distinctive of Christianity as opposed to other religions? What is it that distinguishes Christianity? It has to be Christianity's distinctive doctrines, and, therefore, to be indifferent to doctrine, as if it were only an index of the life flowing on steadily beneath it and independently of it, is to be indifferent to Christianity itself.[40] It cannot be a matter of indifference what doctrines we preach or whether we preach any doctrine at all. We cannot preach at all without preaching some sort of doctrine; and the type of religious life that grows up under our preaching will be determined by the nature of the doctrines we preach.[41]

The world around us will gladly tolerate a nondoctrinal Christianity. It will gladly allow for a gospel emptied of theological content and meaning, but why would the church want a gospel like that? Such a gospel would be devoid of the biblical emphasis on sin, judgment, and satisfaction for sin. No doubt such a gospel would be welcomed by many who now stand aloof from the church. But this would be not because the world had been brought into the church but because the church had been merged into the world.[42] There are few phenomena in the theological world more striking than the impatience that is exhibited on every hand with the effort to define truth and to state with precision the doctrinal presuppositions and contents of Christianity. This indifference is at root dislike; and the easy affirmation that doctrines are useless passes very readily into the heated assertion that they are noxious. Dead indifference is frequently more difficult to deal with than the most lively assault. It is not hard to show the folly of theological indifferentism; but just because it is indifferent, indifferentism is apt to pay little attention to our exhibition of its folly. If we could only get it to care![43]

We are often confronted with the line that, since good Christians arise under every form of faith on practically every point of doctrine, it cannot be of much importance what people believe.[44] So why argue over such things? It is certain that many in our midst take such a stance. They fear controversy more than error.[45] We agree that there are limits to be set for the controversial spirit, but these limits are not to be sought in motives of convenience or prudence. An anemic Christianity that is not virile enough to strive for the truth can never possess the nerve to die for it.[46] A truth not worth defending very soon comes to be seen as a truth not worth professing.[47]

We do well to be concerned over doctrinal apathy within evangelicalism. This general indefiniteness in doctrinal construction is coming upon us like a flood. The outlines of doctrinal statements are becoming more and more blurred in the hands of our more recent guides. We are hearing more and more frequently sharp complaints of the "intellectualism" that is assumed to be inherent in any clear conception of doctrinal truth.[48] But if we read our Bibles thoughtfully, we will come to the same opinion as Paul in Galatians: that it is not a matter of small importance whether we preserve the purity of the gospel.[49] If the history of the church teaches us anything, it is that a corrupt form of Christianity itself menaces, from time to time, the life of healthy Christianity.

Why make much over what appear to be minor points of difference among those who serve the one Christ? Because a pure gospel is worth preserving.[50] A mutilated gospel produces mutilated lives, and mutilated lives are positive evils. Whatever the preacher may do, the hearers will not do the same without a system of belief; and in their attempt to frame one for the governing of their lives out of the fragments of truth that such a preacher will grant to them, is it any wonder that they should go fatally astray? At best, people will be driven to a kind of empirical theologizing, attempting with necessarily imperfect knowledge to coordinate for themselves the truths of religion and those that follow as consequences from them; and so will build up an erroneous system of belief that will mar their lives. At worst, they will be led to discard the neglected or discredited truths—and with them the whole system of Christianity—which they see, even though the preacher does not see, to be necessarily correlated with them; and so they will lapse into unbelief. In either case, they may rightly lay their marred or ruined lives at the preacher's door.[51]

We are sadly experiencing, on a rather large scale, a subjectivism that betrays its weakened hold on the objective truth and reality of Christianity by its neglect or even renunciation of its distinctive objective character.[52] Nowadays men cheerfully abandon the whole substance of Christianity, but they will hardly be persuaded to surrender the name.[53] They really wish to have a creedless Christianity. "Creeds," they shout, "are divisive things; away with them!" If there must be such things, at least let us prune all their distinctive features away and give ourselves a genial and unpolemic Christianity, one in which all the stress is laid on life, not dogma.

Where does this leave us? An *undogmatic* Christianity is no Christianity at all.[54] We are often told that "Christianity is a person, not a doctrine." How true! Christianity is a person; but on pain of reducing it to magic, which would no longer possess any ethical and, consequently, any religious quality, we must grant that Christianity, precisely because it is *essentially* a person, is also a body of facts and ideas. When the apostle Paul declared, "I determined to know nothing among you except Jesus Christ, and *Him crucified*" (1 Cor. 2:2; italics added), he was defining a special doctrine of Jesus as the essence of Christianity.[55]

It has become customary to distinguish between what is called the *fact* and what is called the *theory* when dealing with special doctrines and to profess belief in the fact of sin, the Incarnation, the Atonement, and the like, while despairing of discovering any tenable explanation of them. But we must realize that Christianity cannot exist as facts separated from doctrines. *Christianity consists in facts that are doctrines and in doctrines that are facts.*[56] The preacher of the gospel, therefore, must be prepared to know Christianity theologically. He must know the gospel thoroughly—know it in all its details and in all its power—and it is the primary business of the seminary to give him this knowledge of the gospel.[57]

It is sometimes said that some people love theology more than they love God. Do not let it be possible to say that of you. Love theology of course; but love theology for no other reason than this: Theology is the knowledge of God—and it is your meat and drink to know God, to know Him truly, and, as far as it is given to mortals, to know Him wholly.[58]

We will have theology, of that you can be sure. People differ only as they make sound or unsound theological distinctions and, through these distinctions, embrace and live by truth or error. Whatever may be said of a so-called Christianity that is nothing but *opinions*, there is no Christianity that does not begin with opinions, that is not formed by opinions, and that is not the outworkings of those opinions in life. Only we would do better to call them *convictions*.

Convictions are the root on which the tree of vital Christianity grows. No convictions, no Christianity. Scanty convictions, hunger-bitten Christianity. Profound convictions, solid and substantial religion. Let no one fancy that it can be otherwise. Ignorance is not the mother of religions but of irreligion. The knowledge of God is eternal life, and to know God means that we know Him aright.[59]

CONCLUSION

Theology really does matter! If we neglect theology, especially in the pulpit, we are committing a crime against Christ's little ones. The present state of the evangelical church (which I think is accurately represented by the previously cited survey in *Christianity Today*) is plainly traceable to the absence of doctrinal teaching and preaching in our pulpits.[60] Harry Blamires rightly said that

> the Christian Gospel is addressed to men and women whose lives present them with emergencies—with dangers, temptations, demands, threats, and risk. That is only another way of saying that we are fallen creatures living in a fallen world. You can test the validity of any sermon, any theological book, by asking: How far is it addressed to men and women in a state of emergency?[61]

Likewise, John Owen has somewhere in his voluminous writings said that, if our preaching does not prepare people to face eternity, we are very poor preachers. His one-time assistant David Clarkson picked up on this refrain when he wrote,

> You declare your design to be for a kingdom, an everlasting kingdom; you must strive, and wrestle, and combat to compass it. Here lies your business, here should your care be employed. If, instead of this, you turn your cares upon the things of this life, you fall a-gathering cockles or picking straws, instead of seeking that kingdom; the things of time are of no more value than straws in comparison of it.[62]

NOTES

1. William Ames, *The Marrow of Theology*, trans. and introduced by John Dykstra Eusden (Boston: Pilgrim, 1968), 78.

2. Ibid., 2.

3. John Owen, *Biblical Theology*, an English interpretation from the Latin text of William Gould, by Stephen P. Westcott (Pittsburgh: Soli Deo Gloria, 1994), xlvi.

4. Martin E. Marty, "Foreword," in Helmut Thielicke, *A Little Exercise for Young Theologians*, trans. Charles L. Taylor (Grand Rapids: Eerdmans, 1963), xiv. "Tacky theology" is an expression coined by Richard J. Mouw in *Consulting the Faithful: What Christian Intellectuals Can Learn from Popular Religion* (Grand Rapids: Eerdmans, 1994), 10. Mouw declares that he is not willing to settle for tacky theology but is willing to live with a little tackiness for starters as a pedagogical strategy (p. 11). The trouble with tacky theology, however, is that it begets tacky worship and tacky spirituality, things that are all too common in evangelicalism today.

5. David F. Wells, *No Place for Truth; Or, Whatever Happened to Evangelical Theology?* (Grand Rapids: Eerdmans, 1993); and *God in the Wasteland: The Reality of Truth in a World of Fading Dreams* (Grand Rapids: Eerdmans, 1994), 29ff.

6. Roger E. Olson, who reviewed *No Place for Truth* in the July 19, 1993, issue of *Christianity Today*, says, "I suspect what Wells wants is not just a return to theology but a restoration of the reign of an old-style Puritan, Calvinist theology among evangelicals" (p. 58). Reviews often reveal more about the reviewer than the book under review. Olson assesses the book *The Openness of God* (ed. Clark Pinnock [Downers Grove, Ill.: InterVarsity Press, 1994]) in *Christianity Today* (9 January 1995, 30–32) as "a powerful and persuasive book. It is creative, bold, and Bible based." The individual chapters in this book are lauded with expressions such as "a powerful case," "demonstrates convincingly," "argues persuasively," "powerfully portrays," "the most challenging," and "it makes a strong case" (p. 31). This is in reference to a book that, by any generous historical definition of the word, cannot be called *evangelical*, as Robert Strimple shows clearly in chapter 8.

7. Peter Berger, *Noise of a Solemn Assembly* (New York: Doubleday, 1961), 121.

8. *Christianity Today*, 24 October 1994, 74–78.

9. The word *spirituality* has become terribly vague due to its widespread use by New Age mystics such as Shirley MacLaine and Matthew Fox. Wells (*God in the Wasteland*, 222) cautions his fellow evangelicals about the danger of an evangelical spirituality becoming indistinguishable from New Age spirituality as a result of losing its biblical and theological center. Note, for example, how Virginia Ramey Mollenkott, who at one time served as an associate editor for *Christianity Today*, uses the words *evangelical* and *spirituality*. She now calls herself "an evangelical lesbian feminist" (cf. her 1992 book *Sensuous Spirituality: Out from Fundamentalism* and its review by Peter Jones in *Tabletalk* 17, no. 8 [August 1993]: 11–13).

10. James Orr, *The Christian View of God and the World* (reprint, Grand Rapids: Eerdmans, 1948), 21.

11. Donald G. Bloesch, *Crumbling Foundations: Death & Rebirth in an Age of Upheaval* (Grand Rapids: Academic Books, 1984), 111.

12. Wells, *No Place for Truth*, 177.

13. Richard A. Muller, *The Study of Theology: From Biblical Interpretation to Contemporary Formulation* (Grand Rapids: Zondervan, 1991), xiii.

14. Cited by Harry Blamires, *Recovering the Christian Mind: Meeting the Challenge of Secularism* (Downers Grove, Ill.: InterVarsity Press, 1988), 118.

15. Cf. George Gallup and Jim Castelli, *The People's Religion* (New York: Macmillan, 1989); George Gallup, *Religion in America, 1990* (Princeton: Princeton Religion Research Center, 1990); George Barna, *What Americans Believe* (Glendale, Calif.: Regal, 1991); James Davison Hunter, *Evangelicalism: The Coming Generation* (Chicago: Univ. of Chicago Press, 1987).

16. The ABC television program with Peter Jennings "In the Name of God" (March 16, 1995) highlighted this aspect in one of the large user-friendly churches that had adopted in its services an approach à la David Letterman. One prominent church marketeer (*The Baby Boomerang* [Ventura, Calif.: Regal, 1990], as cited in Douglas D. Webster, *Selling Jesus: What's Wrong with Marketing the Church* [Downers Grove, Ill.: InterVarsity Press, 1992], 82ff.) demonstrates how this mentality affects preaching:

   > "When I preach," Doug Murren explains, "I figure I have about one or two minutes for people to decide if they want to listen to me or not." He compensates for this pressure by selecting his sermon topics from the self-help sec-

tion in the local bookstore and surveying people in his church for pressing needs. . . . Besides "how-to" sermons with practical "take-away" points, Murren advises pastors, "Limit your preaching to roughly 20 minutes, because boomers don't have too much time to spare. And don't forget to keep your messages light and informal, liberally sprinkling them with humor and personal anecdotes."

17. "Music style," says megachurch pastor Rick Warren, "is the single greatest positioning factor in a local church, even more than preaching style" (*Leadership* 14, no. 2 [Spring 1993]: 24). Note the emphasis here on *style*, whether it has to do with music or preaching. "The contemporary demand for 'powerful preaching' is usually understood as referring not to the preaching of powerful *doctrines* but to powerful and authoritative styles of preaching" (Alister McGrath, *Evangelicalism & the Future of Christianity* [Downers Grove, Ill.: InterVarsity Press, 1995], 152).

18. Os Guinness, *Fit Bodies Fat Minds: Why Evangelicals Don't Think and What to Do About It* (Grand Rapids: Baker, 1994), 131. He later adds, "As evangelical churches grow careless about orthodoxy, instances of heresy, blasphemy and nonsense are mounting" (p. 150).

19. Bloesch, *Crumbling Foundations*, 107.

20. Wells, *God in the Wasteland*, 206. "It is evangelical *practice* rather than evangelical profession that reveals the change" (Wells, *No Place for Truth*, 108).

21. Wells, *No Place for Truth*, 72–76. Elsewhere Wells writes,

> We are constantly employing "the vocabulary of human deficit.". . . Our lexicon of terms describing inward deficits has greatly expanded in this century, and most especially during the past three decades. Words and phrases such as "low self-esteem," "depressed," "stressed out," "obsessive compulsive," "identity crisis," "mid-life crisis," "self-alienated," "authoritarian," "repressed," "burned out," "anxious," and "bulimic" have come to be used in connection with matters of self-identity only quite recently, and they all point to losses, to things that are inwardly awry or malfunctioning. (*God in the Wasteland*, 98)

22. "No one will doubt," wrote B. B. Warfield, "that Christians of today must state their Christian beliefs in terms of modern thought. Every age has a language of its own and can speak no other. Mischief comes only when, instead of stating Christian belief in terms of modern thought, an effort is made, rather, to state modern thought in terms of Christian belief" (*The Works of Benjamin B. Warfield, X: Critical Reviews* [reprint, Grand Rapids: Baker, 1981], 322).

23. David Powlison, "Integration or Inundation?" in *Power Religion: The Selling Out of the Evangelical Church?* ed. Michael Scott Horton (Chicago: Moody, 1992), 199.

24. Mark A. Noll, *The Scandal of the Evangelical Mind* (Grand Rapids: Eerdmans, 1994), 48.

25. Guinness, *Fit Bodies Fat Minds*, 38. This same point was made by J. Gresham Machen (*What Is Faith?* [reprint, Grand Rapids: Eerdmans, 1962], 36) in the 1930s: "Those who discard theology in the interest of experience are inclined to make use of a personal way of talking and thinking about God to which they have no right."

26. The Remonstrants were, at their core, pure rationalists, and as Warfield (*Selected Shorter Writings of Benjamin B. Warfield*, ed. John E. Meeter [Nutley, N.J.: Presb. & Ref., 1970], 1:371) has noted, "Pietist and Rationalist have ever hunted in couples and dragged down their quarry together. They may differ as to why they deem theology mere lumber, and would not have the prospective minister waste his time in acquiring it."

27. Richard A. Muller, *Post-Reformation Reformed Dogmatics: Volume I Prolegomena to Theology* (Grand Rapids: Baker, 1987), 221. We are witnessing within the ranks of the evangelical Arminians a resurgence of a similar type of Arminianism. The so-called *new model* evangelicalism that was highlighted in *Christianity Today* ("Evangelical Megashift: Why You May Not Have Heard About Wrath, Sin, and Hell Recently," 19 February 1990) was correctly identified by Clark Pinnock as not being new at all. It "is really the old Arminian or non-Augustinian thinking" (p. 15). This type of Arminianism, it should be noted, was not the kind embraced by John Wesley.

28. R. Kent Hughes (*Are Evangelicals Born Again? The Character Traits of True Faith*, [Wheaton, Ill.: Crossway, 1995]) observes, "Contemporary evangelicalism's assimilation of modernity's self-focus has had a telling effect on its theology because when the emphasis switches from God to self, theology becomes anthropology; man becomes the beginning point of theology rather than God" (p. 13).

29. Muller, *The Study of Theology*, x.

30. Ken Myers, "Deliberate Life Together," *Tabletalk* 19, no. 2 (February 1994): 58.

31. Robert Wuthnow, *Christianity in the Twenty-first Century: Reflection on the Challenge Ahead* (New York: Oxford Univ. Press, 1993), 105.

32. As cited in Wells, *No Place for Truth*, 133. Warfield (*Selected Shorter Writings*, 2:315), on the other hand, made this observation: "It is just as well that the world should realize with increased clearness that Evangelicalism stands or falls with Calvinism and that every proof of Evangelicalism is a proof of Calvinism." This remark, by the way, was made in light of John Miley's Arminianism, especially as it pertained to the doctrines of sin and the atonement.

33. Mark Noll, "Evangelicals and the Study of the Bible," in *Evangelicalism and Modern America*, ed. George Marsden (Grand Rapids: Eerdmans, 1984), 119.

34. Donald Bloesch, in his very helpful *Christian Foundations: A Theology of Word & Spirit* ([Downers Grove, Ill.: InterVarsity Press, 1994] 80), mistakenly contends that Warfield was committed to a thoroughgoing rationalism as expressed by either *intelligo ut credam* ("I understand in order to believe") or *credo quia intelligo* ("I believe because I understand"). Warfield did indeed put a premium on a well-reasoned faith. But note how he nuanced this:

> We not only have no desire to deny, we rather wish to proclaim, the great truth involved in the watchword of the greatest of the fathers and schoolmen, *Credo ut intelligam* ["I believe in order to understand"], and adopted by the Reformers in the maxim of *Fides praecedit rationem* and before the Reformers or schoolmen or fathers, proclaimed by Paul in the immortal words that "the natural man receiveth not the things of the Spirit of God, for they are foolishness unto him; and he cannot know them because they are spiritually judged" (1 Cor. 2:14). None but the Christian man can understand Christian truth; none but the Christian man is competent to state Christian doctrine. (*Selected Shorter Writings*, 2:273ff.)

Elsewhere he says:

> The revelations of the Scriptures do not terminate upon the intellect. They were not given merely to enlighten the mind. They were given through the intellect to beautify the life. They terminate on the heart. Again, they do not, in affecting the heart, leave the intellect untouched. They cannot be fully understood by the intellect, acting alone. The natural man cannot receive the things of the Spirit of God. They must first convert the soul before they are fully comprehended by the intellect. Only as they are lived are they under-

stood. Hence the phrase, "Believe that you may understand," has its fullest validity. No man can intellectually grasp the full meaning of the revelations of authority, save as the result of an experience of their power in life. (Ibid., 2:671)

35. Warfield, *Selected Shorter Writings*, 2:210.

36. Ibid., 2:12.

37. Ibid., 2:258.

38. Ibid., 2:468.

39. Ibid., 2:272.

40. Ibid., 2:273. "There is no creative power in doctrines, however true; and they will pass over dead souls leaving them as inert as they found them: it is the *Creator Spiritus* alone who is competent to quicken dead souls into life; and without him there has never been and never will be one spark of life produced by all the doctrines in the world" (ibid., 2:274).

41. Warfield, *Selected Shorter Writings*, 2:286.

42. Ibid., 1:47.

43. Ibid., 2:221.

44. Ibid., 2:224.

45. Ibid., 2:216.

46. Ibid.

47. Ibid., 2:678.

48. Ibid., 2:294. This is still with us. "There has been a tendency to associate theology with elitist interests, and a subsequent drive to rid the evangelical faith of them both. Popular evangelical faith has developed a bias against theology (not to mention the intellect), and what is more, it has elevated the bias to the level of a virtue" (Wells, *No Place for Truth*, 188).

49. Warfield, *Selected Shorter Writings*, 2:665.

50. Ibid., 2:666.

51. Ibid., 2:287.

52. Ibid., 2:145. Wells (*God in the Wasteland*, 99) sees an identical problem: "There is in present day evangelicalism a hunger for God but an aversion to theological definition of that experience. There is a hunger for God but a disenchantment with dogma or doctrine." This very thing was actually celebrated in the cover story of *Christianity Today*: "Reaching the First Post-Christian Generation" (12 September 1994, 18–23), especially page 22, where we read "an emotional experience of God is more important than its theological content." The danger inherent in such a position, as C. S. Lewis pointed out (*God in the Dock: Essays on Theology and Ethics* [Grand Rapids: Eerdmans, 1970], 141), is that "religious experience can be made to yield almost any sort of God."

53. Warfield, *Selected Shorter Writings*, 1:48.

54. Samuel G. Craig, ed., *Biblical and Theological Studies* (Philadelphia: Presb. & Ref., 1968), 578.

55. Warfield, *Selected Shorter Writings*, 2:255.

56. Ibid., 2:232–34. Along similar lines, the late Gordon Clark (*In Defense of Theology* [Milford, Mich.: Mott Media, 1984], 119) once remarked, "Christianity minus intelligible doctrine is simply unintelligible doctrine minus Christianity."

57. Warfield, *Selected Shorter Writings*, 1:376.

58. Ibid., 2:480.

59. Ibid., 1:368.

60. Church growth guru C. Peter Wagner, in his book *Your Spiritual Gifts Can Help Your Church Grow* (Ventura, Calif.: Regal, 1979), lists twenty-seven spiritual gifts, but preaching is not one of them (p. 129). Indeed, as far as Wagner is concerned, there is no correlation between preaching and church growth (p. 229). The same position is stated with even greater clarity in his book *Leading Your Church to Growth* (Ventura, Calif: Regal, 1984), 170.

61. Blamires, *Recovering the Christian Mind*, 14.

62. *The Works of David Clarkson* (reprint, Edinburgh: Banner of Truth, 1988), 2:171.

PART
2
THE CRISIS OF
REVELATION

CHAPTER
4

DOES GOD SPEAK TODAY APART FROM THE BIBLE?

R. Fowler White

Evangelical Protestant faith has always affirmed, as a central tenet of its understanding of divine revelation, that the Word of God must have supreme authority in religion. Evangelicalism has historically held this view in close conjunction with the work of the Holy Spirit. The truth can be stated this way:

> The living and true God, the Father of our Lord Jesus Christ, who is supreme head of a living church, is not mute. He speaks—and He speaks clearly—by His Spirit and through His written word, the Bible.[1]

Therefore, as the author of Hebrews aptly puts it, we must see to it that we do not disregard "Him who *is* speaking" (Heb. 12:25).[2]

These statements are among the claims that define those who have traditionally identified themselves as evangelicals. They are my own affirmations as an evangelical theologian. They are, further, the affirmations of the contributors to this present volume of essays. Certain evangelicals, however, have begun to add an additional proposition. It is extremely important that we understand this additional proposition and the effect it is having on present evangelical thought and practice. A crisis is on the horizon, and those who are unaware may well be caught off guard.

This new proposition states that God also speaks to His people today *apart* from the Bible, though He never speaks in contradiction to it. As qualified as this statement seems to be, few evangelicals today would question whether it is true. After all, if nothing that God may say today apart from the Scriptures actually *contradicts* what He has already said in the Scriptures, what is the big deal? Simply put, the big deal is whether or not it is actually true that God speaks to His people apart from the Bible. Is this new affirmation itself a contradiction of the Scriptures? Has God, in fact, told His people in the Bible that they should hear His voice in both spoken and written words? Does not this new view threaten to set aside the historic doctrine of the sufficiency and finality of Scripture?

Lest anyone be prematurely self-assured of having the right answers to these questions, consider the issue from another point of view. If we deny that God speaks today apart from the Scriptures, are we quenching His Spirit (1 Thess. 5:19)? Some, such as William DeArteaga, have said exactly that.[3] Others state the matter in an even more serious way. Jack Deere, a former Dallas Theological Seminary professor, now conference speaker, author, and Presbyterian (PCUSA) pastor, has made the following assertions:

> In order to fulfill God's highest purposes for our lives we must be able to hear his voice both in the written word and in the word freshly spoken from heaven. . . . Satan understands the strategic importance of Christians hearing God's voice so he has launched various attacks against us in this area. One of his most successful attacks has been to develop a doctrine that teaches God no longer speaks to us except through the written word. Ultimately, this doctrine is demonic even [though] Christian theologians have been used to perfect it.[4]

Shocking words for sure, but arresting, aren't they? We need a good deal of candor if we are to fully appreciate what is being said here. If DeArteaga, Deere, and others of similar mind are right, if the Bible does indeed teach the church to hear God's voice both through its pages and apart from them in words "freshly spoken from heaven," then the contributors to this present volume and those who agree with them are at least guilty of quenching the Spirit, if not of outright refusal to hear the very voice of God. We, of all people, are especially in need of fanning into flame those gifts of the Spirit through which God would speak to His church today (cf. 2 Tim. 1:6).

With this fuller appreciation for what is at stake, I will evaluate certain key arguments that have led others to affirm that God still speaks today apart from the Bible. In the past we might have turned to Pentecostal and charismatic teachers for such argumentation, since this affirmation has been a defining trait and *modus operandi* of their circles. But in recent years a whole new wave of evangelicalism has arisen among teachers from historically non-Pentecostal and noncharismatic circles. These teachers and authors have been at the forefront of the whole discussion regarding the hearing of God's voice. Because of this new group of influential teachers, we will focus our particular attention on the arguments advanced by them, principally Wayne Grudem and Jack

Deere. Though this may mean that I must entertain some views unique to Grudem and Deere, it is nevertheless my aim to take into account what is distinctive to *all* who affirm the doctrine that God speaks today apart from the Bible.[5]

DEFINING OUR TERMS

We need to ask ourselves, first, what does it mean to say that "God speaks today"? Keeping in mind the traditional meaning that "God speaks today through the Bible," the phrase has come to be used in two other senses. For some, the words "God speaks today" are simply a popular, if misleading, way of describing the fact that God guides and directs His people by His Spirit in the application of His written word through promptings, impressions, insights, and the like. Most non-Pentecostals and noncharismatics have explained these (more or less) intuitive experiences in terms of the Spirit's works of illumination, leading, and conviction. A few would even acknowledge that, among those who fit a given psycho-spiritual profile, these experiences might be accompanied by things seen or heard. All of these experiences are, however, carefully distinguished from the Spirit's work of revelation.[6] Hence, though the Spirit's illumination and guidance may sometimes focus on phenomena such as promptings or impressions, those phenomena are not specifically interpreted as involving the biblical ministry-gifts of revelation, such as prophecy and tongues or their correlates (e.g., visions, dreams, auditions).

Others, of course, use the words "God speaks today" to mean that He guides and directs His people by giving them words of direction through all the same media that the Bible portrays Him as using in the past (e.g., visions and auditions, prophets and angels). As Deere says, "God can and does give personal words of direction to believers today that cannot be found in the Bible. I do not believe that he gives direction that contradicts the Bible, but direction that cannot be found in the Bible."[7] We find the evidence for this claim, Deere argues, in the various methods God has used in the past to speak to His people.

For example, during the age of the Old Testament, Deere observes, "God spoke to his children . . . in an audible voice, in dreams and visions, through circumstances and fleeces, through inner impressions, through prophets, through angels and through Scripture."[8] Turning to the Gospels, Deere notes that "one of the basic keys to the ministry of Jesus was that he only did what he saw his Father doing and he only spoke the words that his Father gave him to speak."[9] According to Deere, the same pattern can be seen in Acts: "Special guidance [was] given to the apostles and others by visions, angelic voices, the Holy Spirit, etc."[10]

Finally, in the New Testament epistles, Paul instructs the churches concerning their use of the revelatory gifts of "prophecy, tongues, words of wisdom, words of knowledge, and discernment of Spirits [sic]."[11] Moreover, as Deere understands it, the author of Hebrews expresses his belief that angelic visitations were possible in his day when he reminded his readers that "some have entertained angels unawares" (13:2 KJV).[12]

By contrast, then, with the previous definition of the phrase "God speaks today," Deere concludes that "on a prima facie reading of the Scriptures, one would expect God to continue communicating to his children throughout the church age with the same variety of methods he has always used."[13]

WORDS SO BROADLY DEFINED

Let's admit it: the idea that God continues to communicate with us using exactly the same methods that He has always used is not only provocative but has a certain attraction. Making it all the more interesting, Deere's contention that the issue of whether God speaks today apart from the Bible is basically a matter of recognizing that God uses the same means to communicate today as He used in the past.[14]

As we ponder this claim, let us not make the mistake of saying that God has never spoken apart from Scripture, for indeed He has done just that. For example, though Moses had committed to writing the words God spoke to him, God continued to speak apart from those Scriptures through the prophets who came after Moses. Having elicited this acknowledgment from us, however, Deere wants us to take an additional step: he urges that, as God has done in the past, so we should expect Him to do in the present.

As noble as Deere's conclusion may sound, it is a seriously deficient theological view precisely because it does not respect the biblical link between the means through which God spoke and the content He conveyed through those means, namely, *His very words*. In this light we must observe that, despite his intentions to the contrary, Deere actually depreciates the means through which God has communicated in the past. He insists that those means are always connected with "words of direction" from God without defining those words in other than personal and ministerial terms. But, by defining these words so broadly, he leaves the impression that the words God spoke long ago are on a par with the words He speaks today. That parity is actually crucial to Deere's whole agenda. The simple problem is this: It is not true. To see this fact, we need only reconsider Deere's examples.

As the Old Testament portrays it, whenever God spoke apart from Scripture in the past, He never spoke, or had others speak, anything other than His very own words. Just how radically true this was in Old Testament days is emphasized in Deuteronomy 18, arguably the fundamental biblical text on the role of the Old Testament prophet. Speaking of the prophets to and through whom He would speak after Moses, God Himself says, "I will put My words in his mouth, and he shall speak to them all that I command him. . . . Whoever will not listen to My words which he shall speak in My name, I Myself will require it of him" (vv. 18–19).[15] Therefore, during the Old Testament period, the words of direction that God spoke "apart from the Scriptures" (i.e., apart from, say, the writings of Moses) were His own words, always expressing accurately what He intended to communicate and invariably invested with absolute authority.

What was true of God's speech alongside the Scriptures during the Old Testament period was also true of his speech alongside the Old Testament Scriptures during the ministries of Jesus and the apostles. The words that the Father spoke to Jesus, and that Jesus spoke in turn to His hearers, were not less than the Father's very own words. Deere is right to call our attention here especially to John's gospel, which has a particular interest in the Father's communication with and through His Son (see John 3:34; 7:16; 8:28; 12:49–50; 14:10, 24, 31).

Similarly, the words of direction that God communicated to and through the apostles were His very words. This is the import of Jesus' remarks to the apostles during His Farewell Discourse: "But the Helper, the Holy Spirit, whom the Father will send in My name, He will teach you all things, and bring to your remembrance all that I said to you" (John 14:26). Again Jesus said to them:

> When He, the Spirit of truth, comes, He will guide you into all the truth; for He will not speak on His own initiative, but whatever He hears, He will speak; and He will disclose to you what is to come. He will glorify Me, for He will take of Mine and will disclose it to you. (16:13–14)

Thus, Paul, whom Christ added to His apostolate, says of himself and his fellow apostles, (1) the Holy Spirit made known to them the things freely given to us believers by God (1 Cor. 2:10, 12), and (2) they spoke of those things, "not in words taught by human wisdom, but in those [words] taught by the Spirit" (2:13)—words invariably accurate and fully authoritative.[16]

The same is evident in Acts: the words of direction that God communicated to and through the apostles and others were always His very own words. Deere and those who agree with him are fond of citing Acts 16:9–10 (Paul's vision of the Macedonian call) as an example of the personal-ministerial and extrabiblical revelation that does not contradict God's revelation in Scripture.[17] Certainly, the revelation in this passage is "personal-ministerial and extrabiblical," that is, apart from Scripture as it existed at that point. But, just as certainly, it is nothing less than one of those always accurate, invariably authoritative words from God.

Consistent with this portrayal of the apostles in Acts, the New Testament prophets are, at least ostensibly, depicted in Acts as following in the footsteps of their Old Testament forebears—that is, they too receive words from God through the Spirit that are His very own words. There are only three occasions in the New Testament where the actual contents of a specific post-Pentecost prophecy are recorded: the two prophecies of Agabus (Acts 11:27–28; 21:10–11) and the prophecy of John in the book of Revelation.[18] We may leave aside the example of the book of Revelation, since no one discussing the issue before us questions that the visions in that book communicated God's own words.

As for Agabus, Luke portrays this New Testament prophet as one who spoke whatever words the Holy Spirit had to say. In fact, in Acts 21:10–11, "Agabus' use of dramatic symbol and quotation formula [tying his own hands and feet with Paul's belt and introducing his oracle with the words 'This is what the Holy Spirit says'] would have signaled to his audience that [his] prophecy was the same in kind as oracles delivered by OT prophets."[19] Indeed, though some persist in questioning the accuracy of Agabus's prophecy in Acts 21, "in every respect, Luke expected his readers to view Agabus in continuity with OT prophets."[20]

We cannot discuss them here, but other instances from Acts confirm that the words communicated to the apostles and others through many different media were invariably accurate, fully authoritative words from God (e.g., Acts 8:26, 29; 9:10–12; 10:9–19; 13:1–3; 18:9–10). As for the angelic visitations to which the author of Hebrews refers (Heb. 13:2), the only words the Bible ever represents God's angels as speaking or otherwise communicating were God's very own (Heb. 2:2; Gen. 18–19; Zech. 1:14–16; Rev. 1:1; 22:6).

My aim in all that I have considered so far is to demonstrate that—for all the interest Deere has in teaching us the biblical model of hearing God as practiced by Jesus, the apostles, and others—he fundamentally misrepresents the very model he has chosen. Deere creates the impression that the revelatory words God spoke in biblical times are on a par with the words He speaks today. Even if he is right that the "words of direction" in the Bible are both personal and ministerial words, he has still not produced a single incontrovertible biblical example in which those words are anything other than God's very own words. To the contrary, in every example that has come to my attention, God saw to it that whatever He intended to communicate was always accurately expressed and invariably invested with His authority. This brings me to some important evidence I have not yet considered—namely, Paul's instructions regarding the church's use of the revelatory gifts.

NO LONGER SPEAKING AS BEFORE

Deere's aim is to persuade that just as God used revelatory gifts to give words of direction to His children in biblical days, so He still does today. But this is simply not the whole picture. For Deere, the words God speaks today through those gifts are simply not on a par with the inerrant, fully authoritative words that He spoke in the past.[21] To find the basis of Deere's affirmations here, we must turn to Professor Wayne Grudem's influential writings on New Testament prophecy.[22]

Grudem's position can be summarized this way: In the New Testament gift of prophecy (and its correlates—visions, dreams, auditions, words of knowledge, and wisdom) the church should find a source of practical, though fallible, guidance. To adequately consider this proposition, we must notice that Grudem says very plainly that God now speaks as He has never previously spoken. Though the means through which God speaks are purportedly the same, the words He speaks are different from everything He has said before—to the Old Testament saints, to Jesus, to the apostles. In short, the words God speaks have been redefined, for they are no longer His very words, inerrant and authoritative.

If the Bible actually says that this is the case, then so be it. But we need to consider Grudem's evidence from the Bible. Aside from his treatment of Agabus the prophet, Grudem's chief support for prophecy as a source of *fallible practical guidance* comes from two texts: 1 Corinthians 14:29 and 1 Thessalonians 5:20–22.

In 1 Corinthians 14:29, Paul writes, "Let two or three prophets speak, and let the others pass judgment." The issue relevant to our concerns is the unidentified object on which "the others pass judgment." Is it the true and false elements in each oracle,[23] or is it the true and false oracles (of true and false prophets, respectively) among the many oracles the church heard? As others have done, Grudem takes the former view, primarily because the Greek verb (*diakrinō*) translated "pass judgment" involves a sorting or sifting activity.[24] In favor of the latter view, note that Paul refers to "prophets" (plural) speaking their revelations in 14:29–30, not to mention "prophecies" (plural) in 1 Thessalonians 5:20. In other words, the apostle presupposes that the churches would be hearing multiple prophecies from multiple prophets. In this light, Grudem's interpretation is clearly not in keeping with Paul's exact words. The apostle does *not* instruct the churches to sort out the true and false *elements in any particular prophecy*. Rather, he instructs them to sort out the true and false *prophecies among the many they would hear.*[25]

When we compare this view of 1 Corinthians 14:29 with the use of the verb *diakrinō* within and outside the New Testament, we find that it is perfectly consistent with that usage: The verb is applied to sifting wheat from chaff (Philo), distinguishing the clean from the unclean (Josephus), separating the guilty from others (Josephus), discerning good from evil (*Testament of Asher*), sorting true from false (Philo), distinguishing Jews from Gentiles (Acts 15:9; cf. 11:2), distinguishing certain people from others (1 Cor. 4:7), and forming a right (instead of a wrong) judgment of oneself (11:31).[26] This evidence falsifies Grudem's claim that the New Testament prefers—and Paul would have preferred—the verb *krinō* over *diakrinō* "when speaking of judgments where there are only two possibilities, such as 'guilty' or 'not guilty', 'right' or 'wrong', or 'true' or 'false'."[27] But we look in vain for *any* examples where *diakrinō* implies judgments involving more than two possibilities.

To round out our discussion of *diakrinō*, notice its use in 1 Corinthians 6:5: "Is it so, that there is not among you one wise man who will be able to decide between his brethren?"[28] Contrary to Grudem's argument, in the context immediately following 6:5, Paul shows his awareness of only two possible outcomes when a believer has a grievance against his neighbor: one will be wronged or defrauded (v. 7), the other guilty of wrongdoing or defrauding (v. 8). The pertinent point, however, is that the wise man's duty, as implied by *diakrinō*, is to sort out the wrongdoer from his victim on the basis of the evidence. By analogy, in 1 Corinthians 14:29, the duty of "the others" is to sort out the true prophet from the false prophet on the basis of their oracles (see, e.g., 1 Cor. 12:3; 14:37; cf. Eph. 4:14–15 with 4:4–6, 11).

My conclusions are virtually the same when I consider 1 Thessalonians 5:20–22. In 5:20 Paul warns the Thessalonians not to despise prophecies. Clearly, the Thessalonians' esteem for prophecy was not what it should have been. But why? As 2 Thessalonians 2:1–3, 15 suggests, they had overreacted to an influx of false prophecies that were confusing them and threatening to lead them astray.[29] Consequently, in 1 Thessalonians 5:21–22, Paul corrects the Thessalonians' overreaction by directing them to test everything and, having done so, to adhere to what is good and to avoid what is evil. Paul's exact wording in 5:20 ("prophecies" [plural]), coupled with the testing for good and evil in verses 21–22, implies that he was expecting the church to test multiple prophecies among which they would find false prophecies as well as true ones.[30] Thus, the instructions to the Thessalonians mirror Paul's command in 1 Corinthians 14:29: The testing of prophecies presupposes that the prophecies heard in the churches might well have included both true and false prophecies (from both true and false prophets, respectively) among them.

In light of these factors, we have to say that Grudem fundamentally misunderstands Paul's directives in 1 Corinthians 14:29 and 1 Thessalonians 5:20–22. The accuracy of the interpretation presented here, however, is confirmed by its consistency with the broader teaching of the Bible. According to that teaching, the church, like Israel, judged prophecies in order to separate the true prophets from the false (Deut. 13:1–5; 1 Kings 13; Matt. 7:15–20 with 12:32–37 and 24:23–26; 1 John 4:1–6; cf. Rom. 16:17–19). In carrying out this responsibility, the church exercised discernment based on the explicit, absolute standards of good and evil (1 Thess. 5:21–22), truth and error (1 John 4:1–6), and thus determined the source of the prophecies they heard, whether they were from the Holy Spirit or from some other source.[31]

We may say, therefore, that for Paul and the rest of the New Testament authors, the judging of New Testament prophecies was a process of evaluating the prophets' oracles in order to pass judgment on the prophets themselves and thus discern the source of their oracles. This interpretation, we submit, is alone able to account for the admonitions that Christ and His apostles gave to the church regarding false prophecies and false prophets. The church was told in no uncertain terms not to tolerate prophets whose words were false or evil and were thus a threat to lead them astray (Matt. 7:15–20 with 12:32–37 and 24:23–26; 1 John 4:1–6; 1 Thess. 5:22; 2 Thess. 2:3, 15; Rev. 2:20–23; cf. Rom. 16:17–19).

CONCLUSION

Some present-day evangelicals, Jack Deere and Wayne Grudem among them, believe and teach that God speaks today apart from the Bible. According to these teachers, God gives words of personal or ministry direction to His people using all the same means that He used in the past. Yet, when we consider the evidence for these views, we find that their resemblance to what the Bible actually depicts is more apparent than real. Whatever else Deere is teaching, he is not teaching the model of hearing God's voice as practiced in the Bible itself. Similarly, Grudem has transformed Paul into an eccentric who is patently out of step with other New Testament authors, indeed with all other biblical authors, when it comes to the crucial matter of judging prophecies.

In my judgment,[32] what these teachers and their disciples fail to appreciate is that, in the Bible, God's activity of speaking apart from the Scriptures occurred at a time when those documents were still being written. Interestingly, during that long history of Scripture writing, God's people did live by a "Scripture plus" principle of authority, and, in keeping with that principle, God employed various means to speak His extrascriptural words to them. But today the church is faced with a new situation: now, with centuries of Christian orthodoxy, we confess that the writing of Scripture is finished, that the canon is actually closed.

But *why* does the church affirm that the canon is closed? The only demonstrable basis for this affirmation is that God's giving of revelation, spoken and written, is always historically joined to and qualified by God's work of redemption.[33] Now that God has accomplished salvation, once-for-all, in Christ, He has also spoken His word, once-for-all, in Christ and in those whom Christ authorized and empowered by His Spirit (Heb. 1:1–2; 2:3–4; Matt. 16:15–19; John 14:26; Eph. 2:19–20). With the completion of salvation in Christ comes the cessation of revelation. Consequently, the church now lives by a "Scripture only" principle of authority. To tamper with this principle invites a host of theological and pastoral problems. The proof of this observation can be seen in the effect of these "prophecies" upon many who are being led far afield from the sufficiency of the gospel itself. Its finality and complete sufficiency is, in reality, subtly assaulted by these claims to modern prophecies.

Finally, the Bible gives us no reason to expect that God will speak to His children today apart from the Scriptures.[34] Those who teach otherwise need to explain to God's children how these words "freshly spoken from heaven" can be so necessary and strategic to God's highest purposes for their lives when their Father does nothing to ensure that they will ever actually hear those words. Indeed, they must explain why this is not quenching the Spirit. Moreover, the promise of such guidance inevitably diverts attention from the Scriptures, particularly in the practical and pressing concerns of life. Let us never underestimate just how serious this diversion really is. In the Bible the church hears God's true voice; in the Scriptures, we know that He is speaking His very words to us. Advocates of words "freshly spoken from heaven" should beware: By diverting attention from the Scriptures, they quench the Spirit who is speaking therein.

NOTES

1. Throughout this chapter, the terms the *Bible*, the *Scriptures*, and *Scripture* will refer to the Scriptures of the Old and New Testaments, excluding those books commonly called the Apocrypha.

2. The *New American Standard Bible* rightly brings out the ongoing nature of God's action of speaking by translating the present participle (*ton lalounta*) in Heb. 12:25 as "Him who is speaking." The accuracy of this insight is confirmed by the fact that His speaking is contrasted with God's past warnings in the same verse.

3. William DeArteaga, *Quenching the Spirit: Examining the Centuries of Opposition to the Moving of the Holy Spirit* (Altamonte Springs, Fla.: Creation House, 1992).

4. Mark Thompson, "Spiritual Warfare: What Happens When I Contradict Myself," *The Briefing* no. 45/46 (24 April 1990): 11. This quotation, originally taken from a 1990 conference talk by Jack Deere, is cited without denial, qualification, or retraction by Deere in his essay "Vineyard Position Paper #2: The Vineyard's Response to *The Briefing*" (Anaheim, Calif.: Association of Vineyard Churches, 1992), 22–23.

5. For an informative, detailed, and (virtually) nonevaluative survey of charismatic views of prophecy, see Mark J. Cartledge, "Charismatic Prophecy: A Definition and Description," *Journal of Pentecostal Theology* 5 (1994): 79–120.

6. Illustrative of this viewpoint are the following words from John Murray ("The Guidance of the Holy Spirit," in *Collected Writings of John Murray, Volume 1: The Claims of Truth* [Edinburgh: Banner of Truth, 1976]):

> We must rely upon the Holy Spirit to direct and guide us in the understanding and application of God's will as revealed in Scripture, and we must be constantly conscious of our need of the Holy Spirit to apply the Word effectively to us in each situation. The function of the Holy Spirit in such matters is that of illumination as to what the will of the Lord is, and of imparting to us the willingness and strength to do that will. . . . As we are the subjects of this illumination and are responsive to it, and as the Holy Spirit is operative

in us to the doing of God's will, we shall have feelings, impressions, convictions, urges, inhibitions, impulses, burdens, resolutions. Illumination and direction by the Spirit through the Word of God will focus themselves in our consciousness in these ways. . . . It is here, however, that careful distinction is necessary. The moment we desire or expect or think that a state of our consciousness is the effect of a direct intimation to us of the Holy Spirit's will, or consists in such an intimation and is therefore in the category of special direction from him, then we have given way to the notion of special, direct, detached communication from the Holy Spirit. And this, in respect of its nature, belongs to the same category as belief in special revelation. The only way whereby we can avoid this error is to maintain that the direction and guidance of the Holy Spirit is through the means which he has provided, and that his work is to enable us rightly to interpret and apply the Scripture in the various situations of life, and to enable us to interpret all the factors which enter into each situation in the light of Scripture. (pp. 188–89)

7. Deere, "Vineyard Position Paper #2," 15. The similarity between Deere's teaching and that of Pentecostal theologian J. Rodman Williams (*Renewal Theology* [Grand Rapids: Zondervan, 1988–92], 1:43–44 and 2:382) is worth noting.

8. Deere, "Vineyard Position Paper #2," 23.

9. Ibid.

10. Ibid.

11. Ibid.

12. Ibid.

13. Ibid. Deere's description of hearing God's voice is profoundly similar to the (more or less) typical charismatic description. See Cartledge, "Charismatic Prophecy," 82–99.

14. See not only Deere's "Vineyard Position Paper #2," 22–24, but also his *Surprised by the Power of the Spirit: A Former Dallas Seminary Professor Discovers That God Speaks and Heals Today* (Grand Rapids: Zondervan, 1993), 213–15.

15. In Numbers 12:6–8 and Deuteronomy 13:1–5, God links the activity of the prophet with the dreams and visions of the seer. Notice that, even when God employed different media to speak with the prophets after Moses, that distinction did not change the nature of what they spoke: they, like Moses, spoke the very words of God.

16. Wayne Grudem, *Systematic Theology: An Introduction to Biblical Doctrine* (Grand Rapids: Zondervan, 1994), 60–61.

17. I first heard Deere cite this passage in a paper presentation at the annual meeting of the Evangelical Theological Society, November 1991. See also his "Appendix 7: The Sufficiency of Scripture and Distortion of What Scripture Teaches About Itself," in *The Kingdom and the Power: Are Healing and the Spiritual Gifts Used by Jesus and the Early Church Meant for the Church Today?* ed. Gary S. Greig and Kevin N. Springer (Ventura, Calif.: Regal, 1993), 440.

18. Richard B. Gaffin, "A Friend's Response to Wayne Grudem" (paper presented at the annual meeting of the Evangelical Theological Society, 21 November 1992), 2.

19. John W. Hilber, "Diversity of OT Prophetic Phenomena and NT Prophecy," *Westminster Theological Journal* 56 (1994): 255. Also, the introductory phrase Agabus uses (*tade legei*) is identical to the phrase John uses to introduce his direct quotation of Christ's messages to the seven churches of Asia Minor in Revelation 2:1, 8, 12, 18; 3:1, 7, 14 (Robert L. Thomas, "Prophecy Rediscovered? A Review of the

Gift of Prophecy in the New Testament and Today," *Bibliotheca Sacra* 149 [1992]: 91). Moreover, the words are equivalent to the phrase "what the Spirit says to the churches," which closes each of Christ's messages (Rev. 2:7, 11, 17, 29; 3:6, 13, 22). Furthermore, as Hilber (p. 255 n. 47) points out, Grudem fails to take into account that Agabus's introductory words are the quotation formula in the Greek Old Testament for "Thus says the Lord." Clearly, this is the most relevant background for our interpretation of Acts 21:11. In fact, Hilber (ibid.) points out that Agabus's "substitution of 'Holy Spirit' for 'Yahweh' [the LORD] is consistent with the theological tendency in Acts to attribute divine work to the Holy Spirit."

20. Hilber, "Diversity of OT Prophetic Phenomena," 256. Hilber notes that Grudem concedes the accuracy of Agabus's prophecy in Acts 11:28. On the accuracy, if imprecision, of Agabus in Acts 21, see Hilber (pp. 250 n. 31, 255–56) and the literature he cites, as well as David B. McWilliams, "Something New Under the Sun?" *Westminster Theological Journal* 54 (1992): 325–26.

21. Deere has intimated his agreement with Grudem's position on New Testament prophecy, which denies the infallibility of present-day prophetic utterances (see n. 22 below). Nevertheless, in his published comments on God's "fresh words from heaven," Deere has not explicitly ruled out the possibility that those words may be God's own words unmixed with words from other sources. All he has said is that they do not contradict the Bible. The latter affirmation does not preclude the infallibility of these "fresh" words of direction, provided Deere believes that God reveals His will on two tracks, one public and one private. On this latter point, see the conclusion to this chapter.

22. See Wayne Grudem, *The Gift of Prophecy in the New Testament and Today* (Westchester, Ill.: Crossway, 1988); and Grudem, *Systematic Theology*, 1049–61. Though not explicitly stated in his writings to date, Deere's indebtedness to and general agreement with Grudem are discernible and otherwise well known among those who have heard him comment on the subject of New Testament prophecy. In a planned forthcoming book, tentatively entitled *Surprised by the Voice of God*, Deere's own thoughts on the New Testament revelatory gifts will be published. For the present essay, the broad outline of his teaching and its compatibility with Grudem's views have been gleaned from "Vineyard Position Paper #2," 14–15, 22–24; and from *Surprised by the Power of the Spirit*, chap. 10 ("Why God Gives Miraculous Gifts") and Epilogue ("Hearing God Speak Today").

23. Grudem, *The Gift of Prophecy*, 74–79; cf. 104–5.

24. Ibid., 76–79. Of 1 Corinthians 14:29, M. M. B. Turner ("Spiritual Gifts Then and Now," *Vox Evangelica* 15 [1985]) has written, "The presupposition is that any one New Testament prophetic oracle is expected to be *mixed* in quality, and the wheat must be separated from the chaff" (p. 16).

25. For a similar conclusion, see Hilber, "Diversity of OT Prophetic Phenomena," 256–58.

26. Grudem, *The Gift of Prophecy*, 76.

27. Ibid., 77.

28. Ibid.

29. According to 2 Thessalonians 2:2, a false prophet or an oracle of a false prophet ("spirit" NASB; "prophecy" NIV; Gk. *pneuma*) had disturbed and was threatening to deceive the Thessalonians. Contrary to Grudem's analysis (*The Gift of Prophecy*, 104–5), we have no indication that they had overreacted to Paul's teaching that true prophecies were less authoritative than Scripture.

30. Contrary to Grudem's inference (*The Gift of Prophecy*, 104–5), Paul's words do not

imply that there were many things that were not good in the true prophecies the Thessalonians were hearing.

31. In line with this picture we find Paul citing standards by which the congregations should judge prophecies (1 Cor. 12:3; 14:37; 1 Thess. 5:21–22; 2 Thess. 2:15; and perhaps Eph. 4:4–15 with 4:4–6, 11). These standards are in stark contrast to Grudem's graded scale of value and truth in New Testament prophecies. See Grudem, *The Gift of Prophecy*, 76–77. Strikingly, Pentecostal theologian Williams (*Renewal Theology*, 2:382 n. 164, 2:386 n. 187) emphatically rejects Grudem's interpretation of New Testament prophetic oracles as a mixture of true and false and of the judging activity applied thereto.

32. For a more complete exposition of the concerns broached in this conclusion, see Gaffin, "A Friend's Response to Wayne Grudem," 6–12. See also Richard B. Gaffin, *Perspectives on Pentecost: New Testament Teaching on the Gifts of the Holy Spirit* (Phillipsburg, N.J.: Presb. & Ref., 1979), 97–99, and his "The New Testament as Canon," in *Inerrancy and Hermeneutic: A Tradition, A Challenge, A Debate*, ed. H. M. Conn (Grand Rapids: Baker, 1988), 172–81.

33. See Herman N. Ridderbos, *Redemptive History and the New Testament Scriptures*, 2d rev. ed., trans. H. De Jongste and rev. R. B. Gaffin, Jr. (Phillipsburg, N.J.: Presb. & Ref., 1988), passim, esp. p. 31. Of special note, though Deere teaches that the canon is closed, he fails to grasp the relationship between revelation and redemption and can therefore provide no rationale or basis for his teaching.

34. It remains for those who differ with this conclusion to produce the evidence that shifts the burden of proof from themselves to others.

CHAPTER
5
PREACHING:
GOD'S WORD TO
THE CHURCH TODAY

R. Kent Hughes

There have been times when preaching that I have felt as though I were standing apart from myself observing someone else speak. It sometimes happens when I become aware of an unnatural silence. The ever-present coughing ceases, bringing an almost physical silence to the building through which my words sail like arrows. I am surprised at the intensity and focus of what I am saying. Sometimes it lasts for a few moments; once in a while, I experience it for a whole sermon. I am describing, of course, the preaching of the Word in the power of the Holy Spirit. It is a humbling experience. It is totally of God. And it makes me even more eager to preach the Word.

Given my enthusiasm, you might suppose that all Bible-carrying preachers share my eagerness. But such is not the case. Over the years, I have encountered ministers, some of whom were fellow students, who have despaired of study and of preaching.

Less and less of their time is devoted to prayer and preparation. Some spend no more than two or three hours in preparation for Sunday. One such pastor makes a habit of preparing his sermon on Saturday night while watching television! Such preaching inevitably makes spare use of Scripture and becomes a series of stories linked around a devotional thought. Some have given up preaching altogether and have shifted to what they call more "hands-on" ministries.

Some have been very candid. "Preaching doesn't work like they told me in seminary." "People don't want to hear it." "Exposition is for a bygone age." "Exposition is by definition boring." So with these, and similar dismissals, the preaching of God's Word is shelved, and the centerpiece of the Reformation (the pulpit) is moved, in effect, to the back of Bible-believing churches.

Preaching is clearly under fire today. Evangelical Christianity has historically been anchored to the supreme authority of the Scriptures. Its high-water marks have come when powerful preaching of the gospel was at the center of its life. With the contemporary challenges to the sufficiency of preaching, the authority of the gospel is itself challenged, since the gospel's power and preaching are so vitally linked in the New Testament (1 Cor. 1:17–18).

To be fair, preaching is far more difficult today than in past decades. There was a time across America when Sunday's sermon was the most stimulating event of the week. Then came the wireless and ABC and NBC in megadecibels. With this came the advent of the notorious "shortened attention span." Media-sotted people simply cannot listen as well or as long as their grandparents. And now we have a postliterate culture that does not read and has difficulty following reasoned discourse apart from visual stimulation.

Toss into this mix a loose set of attitudes known as postmodernity, which enthrones subjectivity and self-focus, and today becomes as challenging a time to preach the Word as has ever existed in Western culture. Nevertheless, God has chosen to speak through His written Word and its verbal proclamation.

What is needed is a radical refreshment from the fountainhead —God's Word on God's Word—specifically, the Word in preaching, the Holy Spirit in preaching, Christ in preaching, and the hearer in preaching.

THE WORD IN PREACHING

OLD TESTAMENT

It is no accident that the frontispiece of the Psalms presents the lavish image of a flourishing tree as emblematic of a life nourished by God's Word. The image was monumental to the ancient biblical mind because of the arid landscape. A life rooted in God's Word would stand tall, verdant, fruitful, and unfading in a desolate world.

> He is like a tree planted by streams of water,
> which yields its fruit in season
> and whose leaf does not wither.
> Whatever he does prospers.
> (Ps. 1:3)

Underlying this grand image is the reality of the incredible life-giving power of God's Word, which is so lyrically celebrated in Psalm 19. There the psalmist sings of God's words "reviving the soul . . . making wise the simple . . . giving joy to the heart . . . giving light to the eyes" (vv. 7–8). He says of His precepts,

> They are more precious than gold,
>> than much pure gold;
> they are sweeter than honey,
>> than honey from the comb.
>> (Ps. 19:10)

The Word of God is the apex of nourishment—ultimate sweetness.

God's people were to understand that His Word was sufficient for everything in life. Thus, in the 176 verses of Psalm 119, the psalmist gives a twenty-two-stanza song (one stanza for each letter of the Hebrew alphabet) to say in effect that "God's Word is sufficient for everything from A to Z."

God's Word was everything to a child of the old covenant. Perhaps God's most eloquent statement of its divinely ordained primacy comes through the prophet Isaiah at the climax of his prophecy: "This is the one I esteem: he who is humble and contrite in spirit, and trembles at my word" (Isa. 66:2). Such regard for God's Word was so important that the Lord goes on to say that sacrificial worship becomes a travesty apart from reverent obedience to it:

> But whoever sacrifices a bull
>> is like one who kills a man,
> and whoever offers a lamb,
>> like one who breaks a dog's neck;
> whoever makes a grain offering
>> is like one who presents pig's blood,
> and whoever burns memorial incense,
>> like one who worships an idol.
>> (Isa. 66:3)

The awesome position accorded God's Word under the old covenant was dramatized in the reverential prescriptions given in the *Mishnah* for the handling of the Torah (Law) and the *Haftarah* (prophets) in synagogue worship.

NEW TESTAMENT

When we turn to the New Testament we find that Jesus was the supreme man of the Word. Indeed, He did meditate on it day and night. As a preteen His knowledge of the Scriptures astounded the teachers of the law (cf. Luke 2:47). At the beginning of His ministry, when He was tempted by Satan, His encyclopedic knowledge of the Word enabled Him to defeat His tempter with three deft quotations of Scripture that displayed incredible subtlety of thought (Luke 4:1–13; cf. Deut. 8:3; 6:13, 16). The Word, wielded by Jesus, was a mighty sword.

Those who follow Him are likewise to take up "the sword of the Spirit" (Eph. 6:17). In *The Pilgrim's Progress*, John Bunyan has his warrior heroes Mr. Great-heart and Mr. Valiant-for-truth converse during the respite after a battle. The two spiritual warriors, still sweating and breathing heavily, sit down to catch their breath. After a moment, Mr. Great-heart gestures approvingly to Mr. Valiant-for-truth and says,

> "Thou has worthily behaved thyself. Let me see thy sword." So he showed it to him. When he had taken it into his hand and looked thereon awhile, he said, "Ha! It is a right Jerusalem blade." Then said Mr. Valiant-for-truth, "It is so. Let a man have one of these blades, with a hand to wield it and skill to use it, and he may venture upon an angel with it. . . . Its edges will never blunt; it will cut flesh, and bones, and soul, and spirit, and all."[1]

Some weapon—God's Word!

> For the word of God is living and active. Sharper than any double-edged sword, it penetrates even to dividing soul and spirit, joints and marrow; it judges the thoughts and attitudes of the heart. Nothing in all creation is hidden from God's sight. Everything is uncovered and laid bare before the eyes of him to whom we must give account. (Heb. 4:12–13)

God's Word cleaves through our hard-shelled souls like a hot knife through butter. Certainly we Christians find this to be true in our lives. There are sections of God's Word that cut through all the pretensions and religious facade, leaving us flayed, exposed, and convicted. When God wills it, His Word will pierce *anyone*.

George Whitefield, the great eighteenth-century evangelist, was hounded by a group of detractors who called themselves the "Hell-fire Club." They derided his work and mocked him. On one occasion one of them, a man named Thorpe, was mimicking Whitefield to his cronies, delivering his sermon with brilliant accuracy, perfectly imitating his tone and facial expressions, when he himself was so pierced that he sat down and was converted on the spot![2] Thus, the sword of the Spirit is far more than a defensive weapon, because God's Word does penetrating surgery to effect the salvation and health of human souls.

Those called to shepherd His flock must become master swordsmen, masters of exposition. This is precisely how the apostle Paul regarded his own ministry: "I have become [the church's] servant by the commission God gave me to present to you the word of God in its fullness" (Col. 1:25). Preaching, opening the Word, was at the heart of Paul's ministerial call. Paul's words are a mandate for exposition! His advice to his disciple, Timothy (and by implication to all preachers), makes it doubly clear:

> Until I come, devote yourself to the public reading of Scripture, to preaching and to teaching. (1 Tim. 4:13)

> Do your best to present yourself to God as one approved, a workman who does not need to be ashamed and who correctly handles the word of truth. (2 Tim. 2:15)

> All Scripture is God-breathed and is useful for teaching, rebuking, correcting and training in righteousness, so that the man of God may be thoroughly equipped for every good work. (2 Tim. 3:16–17)

> In the presence of God and of Christ Jesus, who will judge the living and the dead, and in view of his appearing and his kingdom, I give you this charge: Preach the Word; be prepared in season and out of season; correct, rebuke and encourage—with great patience and careful instruction. For the time will come when men will not put up with sound doctrine. Instead, to suit their own desires, they will gather around them a great number of teachers to say what their itching ears want to hear. They will turn their ears away from the truth and turn aside to myths. But you, keep your head in all situations, endure hardship, do the work of an evangelist, discharge all the duties of your ministry. (2 Tim. 4:1–5)

The refreshing force of the flow of the Scriptures is clear—those who would lead the flock of God must be trees that are rooted in and tremble before His Word. They must see Jesus' knowledge of, dependence upon, and use of this Word of God as their example—however exalted it might be. They must become master swordsmen in their skillful use of God's Word for the defense and surgery and cure of souls. They must preach the Word. They must not succumb to the spirit of the age, which would have them believe that exposition is for a bygone era.

Like Martin Luther, they must rest their ministry on the sufficiency of God's Word. His knowledge of it was vast; it seems that he had virtually all the Vulgate memorized, as well as his Greek Testament. But his dependence on God's Word was even greater:

> I simply taught, preached, wrote God's Word: otherwise I did nothing. And when, while I slept or drank Wittenberg beer with my Philip and my Amsdorf, the Word so greatly weakened the papacy that never a Prince or Emperor inflicted such damage upon it. The Word did it all.[3]

THE HOLY SPIRIT IN PREACHING

Having been refreshed as to the call to preach the Word, preachers next need a fresh dependence on the Holy Spirit's enabling power. Ironically, "exposition" so-called can be a cold-blooded, lifeless affair. It is possible for a preacher to follow the expository method and never preach in the power of the Holy Spirit. Many highly educated ministers are this way—able, learned, and powerless.

Here again Jesus is the example because His preaching came after the Holy Spirit's descent upon Him and in full Spirit-dependence. The sequence is unmistakable. The heavens were "torn open" (Mark 1:10; cf. Luke 3:21), and then, with all eyes focused on the sundered sky, the Holy Spirit circled downward, fluttering on the bodily wings of a dove, and lighted on Jesus. A palpable descent for all to see. And then the Father spoke: "You are my Son, whom I love; with you I am well pleased" (Luke 3:22). Following this, Jesus, "full of the Holy Spirit" (4:1), returned from the Jordan and was then led into the wilderness and tempted. Emerging victorious, Jesus returned to Galilee and ultimately stood in the synagogue in Nazareth and began His preaching ministry by announcing "The Spirit of the Lord is on me" (Luke 4:18; cf. Isa. 61:1–2). Jesus preached only in the power of the Holy Spirit!

All apostolic preaching was in the power of the Holy Spirit, as Paul explained to the Corinthians: "My message and my preaching were not with wise and persuasive words, but with a demonstration of the Spirit's power, so that your faith might not rest on men's wisdom, but on God's power" (1 Cor. 2:4–5). The book of Acts—the lyrics of that epic book—ring with these expositions and their great effect.

When it happens today, it is sublime. Dr. Martyn Lloyd-Jones of London's famed Westminster Chapel experienced as much of this as any modern preacher:

> I am looking on. I am speaking, but I am really a spectator. I am amazed at what is happening. I am listening, I am looking on in utter astonishment,

for I am not doing it. . . . In a sense, I am as much a spectator as the people who are listening to me. There is this consciousness that it is outside me, and yet I am involved in it; I am merely the instrument and the vehicle and the channel of all this.[4]

The same thing happens to me on occasions. Sometimes it is fleeting, as I am driving home the truth of the text. Other times, it may happen when I am less passionate and simply explaining God's Word. Other times I have realized it only in retrospect.

Significantly, the two most remarkable times in my recent experience had a common thread, namely, the *corporate prayer of my congregation*. On a memorable December day, I was asked to address a countywide prayer breakfast. The breakfast honored those who serve in county and local government. So many of the more than one thousand in attendance were not churchgoers. I was given nineteen minutes, precisely. Feeling the proper weight of the opportunity, I began to pray fervently months in advance. I met with the breakfast committee for prayer. I wrote numerous personal notes to my friends asking for prayer. My congregation held me high before the throne of grace. The result? During those nineteen minutes I sensed the power of the Holy Spirit as I had few times in my life.

The other time was when I returned to the pulpit after my wife's providential deliverance from death. She had lost two-thirds of her blood due to a surgical hemorrhage. Admittedly the segue of our life situation and the Scripture text for that Lord's day (Luke 8, the healing of the woman with the hemorrhage and the raising of Jairus's daughter) was divinely arranged. But the foundation of it all was the massive prayer that had been offered over those two weeks.

The power of the Holy Spirit is a participatory phenomenon. It comes when the preacher and his people seek God. Lloyd-Jones advises pastors, but his advice has broad application and wisdom for the whole church:

> Seek Him! Seek Him! What can we do without Him? Seek Him! Seek Him always. But go beyond seeking Him; expect Him. Do you expect anything to happen to you when you get up to preach in a pulpit? . . . Seek this power, expect this power, yearn for this power; and when this power comes, yield to Him. Do not resist.[5]

Preaching in the power of the Holy Spirit can never be boring—unless one is bored with God. And it is supremely sufficient, for the Holy Spirit is sufficient.

CHRIST IN PREACHING

So the remedies mount: a refreshment as to what the Scriptures are and our call to preach them; a refreshment to our call to preach in the power of the Holy Spirit, and then a refreshment as to our call to preach Christ.

OLD TESTAMENT

Jesus, of course, gave us the example and rationale on the road to Emmaus, when, "beginning with Moses and all the Prophets, he explained to them what was said in all the Scriptures concerning himself" (Luke 24:27, cf. vv. 44–47). We have it from His lips. It is dominical. The Old Testament is about Jesus—not just the prophecies, not just the sacrificial system, not just the Tabernacle—but the entire Old Testament.

> You diligently study the Scriptures because you think that by them you possess eternal life. These are the Scriptures that testify about me, yet you refuse to come to me to have life. (John 5:39–40)

> But I have had God's help to this very day, and so I stand here and testify to small and great alike. I am saying nothing beyond what the prophets and Moses said would happen—that the Christ would suffer and, as the first to rise from the dead, would proclaim light to his own people and to the Gentiles. (Acts 26:22–23, cf. 8:34–35)

> For no matter how many promises God has made, they are "Yes" in Christ. And so through him the "Amen" is spoken by us to the glory of God. (2 Cor. 1:20)

> Concerning this salvation, the prophets, who spoke of the grace that was to come to you, searched intently and with the greatest care, trying to find out the time and circumstances to which the Spirit of Christ in them was pointing when he predicted the sufferings of Christ and the glories that would follow. It was revealed to them that they were not serving themselves but you, when they spoke of the things that have now been told you by those who have preached the gospel to you by the Holy Spirit sent from heaven. Even angels long to look into these things. (1 Peter 1:10–12)

Christ, of course, is not seen in the specious pietistic typology that sees Rahab's red cord as the blood of Christ but rather in the great salvific events and personages of Israel's history.

Israel's history points to the kingdom and to the coming King. The epic sagas of Genesis repeat the theme. The Exodus foreshadows the great deliverance wrought by Christ, a salvation that is by grace alone.

The stories of the Judges—of people such as Ehud, Gideon, and Samson—are stories of minisalvations that point to the ultimate work of grace through Christ.

The lives of the great leaders, such as David and Moses and Joshua, foreshadow Christ. Listen to Martin Luther on the story of David and Goliath:

> When David overcame the great Goliath, there came among the Jewish people the good report and encouraging news that their terrible enemy had been struck down and that they had been rescued and given joy and peace; and they sang and danced and were glad for it (1 Sam. 18:6). Thus this gospel of God or New Testament is a good story and report, sounded forth into all the world by the apostles, telling of a true David who strove with sin, death, and the devil, and overcame them, and thereby rescued all those who were captive in sin, afflicted with death, and overpowered by the devil.[6]

God would work a sovereign deliverance through the son of David even as He had sovereignly done through young David. David prefigures the true saving event of Christ.

NEW TESTAMENT

So wherever you turn in sacred writ, whether to the Psalms or to the prophets, you come to Christ. And it is doubly so in the New Testament. Is Ephesians 5 about marriage and family? Yes, on one level. But ultimately it is about Christ. Is Matthew 5:17–48 about kingdom ethics? Yes. But it is about Christ.[7] Is the book of Philippians about joy? Yes. But it is about Christ.

Could there be any grander, more scintillating theme in all history than Christ? What joy to search the Scriptures and repeatedly find Christ (cf. John 5:39–40).

E. V. Hill, pastor of Mount Zion Missionary Baptist Church, tells of the ministry of an elderly woman in his church who they all called "1800" because no one knew how old she was. "1800" was hard on unsuspecting preachers because she would sit in the front row, and when the preacher began she would say, "Get Him up!" (she was referring to Christ). After a few minutes, if she didn't think it was happening, she would again shout, "Get Him up!" If a preacher did not "Get Him up!" he was in for a long, hard day. Dear old "1800" was no theologian, but her instincts were sublime. True scriptural preaching exalts Jesus. It cannot fail to "Get Him up!" because both testaments lift Him up.

There is nothing more salutatory or greater than getting Him up.

Then I looked and heard the voice of many angels, numbering thousands upon thousands, and ten thousand times ten thousand. They encircled the throne and the living creatures and the elders. In a loud voice they sang:
"Worthy is the Lamb, who was slain,
to receive power and wealth and wisdom and strength
and honor and glory and praise!" (Rev. 5:11–12)

THE HEARERS AND PREACHING

Jesus was fond of challenging the crowd—"He who has ears, let him hear" (Matt. 11:15; 13:9; cf. Isa. 6:9)—because even the Word preached in the power of the Holy Spirit did not penetrate nonlisteners. Even so, today the Word preached in the power of the Spirit, with all its radical Christocentricity, will prove "insufficient" in the lives of mere listeners. The preaching of the Word is sufficient whether one listens or not, but to the nonhearer it becomes, as it were, insufficient.

Ancient listeners had trouble truly hearing God's Word. And today, this long-standing problem is drastically multiplied. Many church attenders listen to God's Word the way they listen to an airline flight attendant explain an aircraft's safety features—totally "tuned out." The giving of the traditional preflight talks has to be one of the worst jobs on any flight! The moment the flight attendant begins, he or she endures a ritual of "frequent flyer rejection." The "shades go down" in the passengers' eyes, the newspapers go up, the headphones go on. Honestly, do you listen? No, unless there's some turbulence, then you try to recall—"What did she say?" One flight attendant, exasperated by the inattention, altered her talk's wording to "When the mask drops down, place it over your navel and continue to breathe normally"—and no one noticed! Hearing requires several essential disciplines.

LISTENING

Number one is listening, a skill that has been impaired by modern culture's glut of words. Billions of words are spoken every second. And sometimes, it seems, they are all assaulting us through TV, radio, VCRs, and the multiple conversations around us. We are a distracted people. It is also an established scientific fact that the visual media has reduced our average attention spans. Some people are so keyed to visual response that they can't engage unaided audio instruction. In addition, the postmodern mind, which responds so readily to self-directed, subjective, feelings-oriented messages, has difficulty following the reasoned arguments of Scripture.

And then, of course, many people, even though they are in the church, simply do not want to hear God's Word. Paul enlightened Timothy in this regard: "The time will come when men will not put up with sound doctrine. Instead, to suit their own desires, they will gather around them a great number of teachers to say what their itching ears want to hear. They will turn their ears away from the truth and turn aside to myths" (2 Tim. 4:3–4). So, for these various reasons, listening is not in vogue and is, at best, difficult—and congregations may look like the 6:30 A.M. flight to Chicago.

Listening requires discipline. Listening is work! (Should we use such a word?) What can we do? (1) Pray! The way to come for the preaching of the Word is to pray for the preacher and pray for yourself. In fact, this is the recommended procedure throughout the entire service. Imagine what would happen if a thousand people did this every time we worshiped. (2) Come prepared to listen; understanding that listening is work. The will to concentrate one's hearing is fundamental. You cannot listen to God's Word the way you listen to TV—"kicked back" with a bag of chips in hand. (3) Keep your Bible open to the text. Always turn to the other texts that are referenced. Mark key words, list references, draw arrows. Make a mess in the margins. (4) Even better, take notes. One of the curious by-products of the Great Awakening in the American colonies was a sudden interest in shorthand. It was not unusual to see men and women, quill pens in hand, carrying portable inkwells hurrying to a preaching service on the village green. The same thing had happened in Scotland under similar circumstances.[8] Revived hearts make scribbling hands.

APPLICATION

The labor of listening becomes true biblical hearing when it produces reflection and application. This is no easy task either, because ours is a nonreflective age. Perhaps while sitting quietly, thinking, you have had the experience of having someone ask if you were all right. The apex of hearing is reached in application, that is, discerning what it means to me and what I ought to do.

REFRESHING THE WORLD

The preaching enterprise is a grand event when we are refreshed to its essentials.

Word. God's Word is a mighty, life-giving blade. It steels the soul; it penetrates the heart; it cuts; it heals. And those who preach are to be master swordsmen who correctly handle the word of truth (2 Tim. 2:15). "In the presence of God and of Christ Jesus, who will judge the living and the dead, and in view of his appearing and his kingdom," they have this charge: "Preach the Word" (4:1–2).

Spirit. The mighty sword is to be wielded in the power of the Holy Spirit. We are to seek it. We are to long for it. We are to pray for it so that our preaching is "not with wise and persuasive words, but with a demonstration of the Spirit's power" (1 Cor. 2:4).

Jesus. Both Word and Spirit are to coalesce in one great task—the exaltation of Jesus Christ: To "Get Him up!"

Hearers. But the preacher must have hearers—"'He who has ears, let him hear'" (Matt. 13:9).

But, of course, I'm speaking to the choir. What about the postmodern world? What about those who are not interested in the reasonableness of Christianity—who even distrust reason? How can such preaching make a difference?

The answer is twofold. First, when a church sits under the authority of God's Word preached in the power of the Spirit and lives it out in substantive glory to Christ, the only explanation becomes that God is real. Thus, people with entirely different worldviews—subjectivists, anti-rationalists—can be ineluctably drawn to the gospel. Second, God's Word, preached in the power of the Holy Spirit, is invasive. There is no heart beyond its hurt; there is no heart beyond its grace.

May the crisis of contemporary evangelical preaching be met by a grand recovery of full confidence in the authority of the Word and the work of the Spirit.

NOTES

1. John Bunyan, *The Pilgrim's Progress* (New York: Dodd, Mead, 1974), 283.
2. C. H. Spurgeon, *The Metropolitan Tabernacle Pulpit* (Pasadena, Tex.: Pilgrim, 1974), 34:115.
3. John R. W. Stott, *Between Two Worlds* (Grand Rapids: Eerdmans, 1982), 25.
4. Tony Sargent, *The Sacred Anointing* (London: Hodder & Stoughton, 1994), 15.
5. Ibid., 49.
6. Graeme Goldsworthy, *Gospel and Kingdom* (New South Wales, Australia: Lancer/Anzea, 1992), 106.
7. D. A. Carson ("Matthew," in *The Expositor's Bible Commentary*, ed. Frank E. Gaebelein [Grand Rapids: Zondervan, 1984], 8:142–45) convincingly argues that "the best interpretation of those difficult verses says that Jesus fulfills the Law and the Prophets in that they point to him, and he is their fulfillment."

8. F. R. Webber (*A History of Preaching in Britain and America* [Milwaukee: North-western, 1952], 1:329) writes,

> Religion was discussed everywhere. Groups of people engaged in discussions on market day, knots of men and women gathered on the corners of village streets, and lingered long in the churchyards on Sunday. The sermons of the great leaders, and of less prominent men, were reviewed again and again during the week, and every point was discussed carefully by the people. One of the curious by-products of the Awakening was a sudden interest in short-hand. Men and women studied shorthand in order that they might take down the sermons that were stirring the English-speaking countries. This had happened once before in Scotland, and it made its appearance once more in all countries where the influence of the Awakening was felt. It was not at all unusual to see men with a portable inkwell strapped about them, and a quill pen thrust over an ear, hastening to join the throng assembling on the village green. Some of the printed sermons of George Whitefield are the notes taken down in shorthand by these volunteer reporters, and their value depends upon the degree of education of the scribe, and his knowledge of shorthand. Obviously they transcribed them into longhand in their own way, and usually without the benefit of editing on the part of the preacher. All too often they fall short of the actual spoken words.

PART
3
THE CRISIS OF
GOSPEL AUTHORITY

CHAPTER
6
ONLY ONE GOSPEL

R. C. Sproul

Paul's epistle to the Galatians begins with some striking and unusual comments. The writer, normally calm and cautious, becomes very aggressive and brutally direct. The style and manner almost shock us at first, especially if we have read other portions of the correspondence of this man Paul.

What motivates him to say, "But even if we, or an angel from heaven, should preach to you a gospel contrary to what we have preached to you, he is to be accursed [lit. anathema]!" (Gal. 1:8)? And, again, in verse 9 we encounter by way of studied repetition the words "As we have said before, so I say again now, if any man is preaching to you a gospel contrary to what you have received, he is to be accursed!" What motivates this scholar/theologian to adopt such an approach, to engage in such heat?

The language and tone are particularly striking because of the character of the man who writes it. The apostle Paul, a man of unparalleled tenderness, exhibits time and again a profound love for the lambs that belong to Christ. We know, further, that Paul was an uncommonly patient man who had to bear with persistent persecution and affliction for the sake of the gospel and the church of Christ. We also know that the apostle Paul had great concern that people guard their tongue, that people be long-suffering and patient with one another, and that they pursue as much as possible to be at peace with everyone. Paul warned the church against the great danger of a spirit of contentiousness, which causes people to fight, quarrel, and argue over every point of disagreement and every little difference of opinion. Plainly, Paul urges Christians not to be characterized by a bellicose and belligerent spirit.

THE DISTRESSED APOSTLE

Having said this by way of prologue, knowing that the epistle to the Galatians comes from the pen of a man who had such a deep concern for the peace of Christ, it is striking that in contrast to his other epistles we find here perhaps the strongest language Paul ever used in the letters that form part of the canon of the New Testament. In fact, Paul is so distressed with the Galatian situation that his words virtually border on vehemence. He is deeply moved, deeply concerned, and deeply distressed.

Contrary to popular misconception, Jesus often had serious conflict, especially with religious error. In the gospel of Mark we note, for example, that Jesus was angry on several occasions. He spoke out of anger to the Pharisees, who were twisting and distorting the truth of God. Recently, someone commented to me, "You know, listening to the text in Mark and Jesus' interchange with the Pharisees makes me wonder if Jesus would speak this way today, because He's obviously not trying to win friends and influence people. It seems like our Lord's words here were actually designed to antagonize His audience." It is safe to say that it was not Jesus' normal custom to provoke argument just for the sake of argument. Nor was He antagonistic because He was of a particular personality type. But what I do see in the New Testament is that, when an essential truth of God is on the line, Jesus takes off the kid gloves and speaks very directly.

When we come to Galatians we see Paul following the example of our Lord. Notice how he begins this epistle like he begins almost all of his letters—with a warm and tender greeting: "Grace to you and peace from God our Father, and the Lord Jesus Christ" (Gal. 1:3). At the beginning Paul is still speaking about grace and peace, but, after he goes through this initial salutation, he immediately expresses what I would call "apostolic astonishment." The apostle declares to the people in the Galatian community that he is utterly amazed about something. A report has come to him that he hears in stunned disbelief and can't seem to get over it.

The Greek word that is translated "amazed" (*thaumazō*, Gal. 1:6) is very strong. It is used in the Gospels to describe the crowd's reaction whenever they witness a miracle by Jesus—"We can't believe it" or "It's astonishing." It has been variously translated as "astonished, marveled, amazed, and surprised." In Hellenistic letters, the expression "I am astonished that . . ." was a literary device used to express both irritation and irony, as well as outright surprise. But here Paul seems shocked.[1]

So with this strong word—"I am amazed!"—Paul begins the body of the letter to the Galatians: "I am amazed that you are so quickly deserting Him who called you by the grace of Christ, for a different gospel." Paul is beside himself with consternation. How is it possible that the best news that has ever been preached on the face of this earth, which these people in this early Christian church received with great joy, has been given up so quickly? They have heard the Gospel of Jesus Christ that promised to them heaven itself, the forgiveness of all their sin, and they are wandering away from it. They have apparently understood clearly that the gospel calls upon them to receive the promises of Christ and to put their trust in Him and Him alone, yet they are turning away from this saving Good News. And he says they have done this "quickly." Though the Galatians could have immediately lapsed from the gospel, it seems, rather, that only a "short duration of time had elapsed since Paul first preached the gospel in Galatia."[2]

I remember hearing some years ago evangelist John Guest give his testimony relating how he had been converted in Liverpool, England, following an evangelistic meeting. He testified that when he went home that night through the streets of Liverpool he was so elated, so overjoyed, that he literally ran down the streets and leaped over fire hydrants and kicked his heels in the air. That same kind of response had to be the initial reaction of many of these Galatian believers. And yet Paul hears that now they've left the gospel for another gospel, which he tells them is, in actuality, no gospel at all.

What had happened to them? They had been, quite simply, seduced. This was accomplished through the teaching of the sect of the Judaizers. Their error was to mix together faith in Christ with a reliance upon their obedience to the works of the law as the ground of their salvation. Where they made a good beginning, trusting in the merit of Christ and in the work of Christ alone for their redemption, now they had begun to move away from this foundation to trust *partly* in Christ, *partly* in their own efforts, *partly* in their own performance, *partly* in their own achievements, *partly* in their own merit, and *partly* in their own obedience to the law of God. Paul looked at this perversion of grace and faith and said, "Don't you understand that you are leaving not simply a doctrine but that you are actually turning away from Him, from Him who is the gospel, from Jesus Christ, who alone has purchased your salvation?"

It is important to note that in Galatians 1:6–7 Paul corrects himself in midsentence. He's not satisfied with the way he expresses it initially—"I am amazed that you are so quickly deserting Him who called you by the grace of Christ, for a different gospel"—because in the next breath he says that this gospel, "which is really not another," is no longer gospel, because another gospel is not really *the* gospel. Paul is saying to them, very plainly, that there really is not *another* gospel, because there's only one gospel.

This phrase "a different gospel; which is really not another" has bothered some scholars. But what Paul seems to be saying, quite plainly, is this: The gospel to which you are now turning is a *substitute* gospel; thus, it really is not a gospel at all. So we could translate it, "a different gospel, which (in reality) is not (even) another."[3]

Paul says in the plainest way possible that there are some who are troubling the Galatians and want to pervert the Gospel of Christ. They want to change it. They want to alter it a little bit. Perhaps they want to attempt improvement upon it.

As a result, apostolic astonishment gives way to what I believe to be the most serious and strong rebuke the apostle Paul ever makes in the New Testament canon: if anybody (and he doesn't spell out who anybody might be) should alter this message of the gospel, let him be under God's curse for it. You may recall that Paul had to withstand Peter himself on this issue. But Paul did not shrink from debating, even with Saint Peter himself, when it came to the question of the gospel. He said, in effect, "I don't care who it is. I don't care if it's Apollos! I don't care if it's Peter! I don't care if it's Gabriel, the highest archangel of all! I don't care if it is an emissary from heaven, an angel, who comes down into your church and teaches you a different gospel—if anyone teaches any other gospel than that which you have received from Jesus Christ, let him be accursed."

This is not mild language. The Greek for "accursed" is *anathema*. This word is most interesting, though it is infrequently used today. The late New Testament scholar J. Gresham Machen helpfully wrote of it:

The derivation of it is very simple: ana means "up"; the is a root meaning "to place" or "to put"; ma is a noun ending with a passive significance. Hence an anathema is "a thing that is placed up." The word came to refer especially to what is "placed up" in a temple as a votive offering to a god. So the word is used in Lk. 20:5.

How can a word that means "votive offering" possibly come to have the negative sense of "accursed"? The answer seems fairly clear. The fundamental idea, when a thing is called anathema, is that the thing has been taken from ordinary use and has been handed over to God. If it is a good thing, it has been handed over to Him for His use; if it is a bad thing, it has been handed over to Him for destruction; in either case, people have no more to say about it—it has been taken out of ordinary relationships and is "devoted" to God.

So here Paul says—if the original sense of the word is to be regarded as still in view—that the punishment of the man who attempts to lay violent hands upon the gospel of Christ should be in God's hands; that man should be regarded as beyond human power to help; he should be regarded as having fallen into that state about which the Epistle to the Hebrews says: "It is a fearful thing to fall into the hands of the living God."[4]

This isn't a Luther or a Calvin ranting and railing against some heretic in the dim past. This is the apostle Paul, under the inspiration of God the Holy Spirit, saying that if anybody teaches any gospel other than what was received from God through Paul, let him come under the very condemnation of God—literally, "let him be damned."

But notice that immediately following this strong word he repeats himself. He seems to fear that some might miss his point, and as a master communicator he can't allow that to happen. Maybe you don't get this either. That is always a very real danger in every age. So let me say it again, just as Paul says it again, for strong emphasis: I say to you, again, if anybody preaches any other gospel than that which you have received through the revelation of Christ, *let him be damned.*

NO TRIFLING NEEDED

In Martin Luther's great theological classic *The Bondage of the Will*, which was his reply to the *Diatribe* of Erasmus of Rotterdam, Luther thanked Erasmus for not raising petty theological issues. He wrote to this careful humanist scholar, "I thank you Erasmus that you haven't bothered me with trifles." On another occasion Luther wrote of the centrality of the gospel:

> This is also the only article that had to suffer a constant persecution by the devil and the world. . . . Other articles were also assailed, but not one of them has occasioned as much bloodshed and martyrdom as this one. . . . When this article arises, the devil is mad and furious, and the world is full of flaming anger and burning madness. All histories show that all heresies and errors arose when this article fell. . . . For everything depends and rests on this one, and it brings all the others in its train. This is the article of supreme importance, so that whatever errs in the other surely does not have this one right either; and even if he holds to the others, but does not have this one, all is in vain anyway.[5]

That says it very well. No trifles are needed when we are dealing with the central issues related to the gospel itself. Yet so often today, when I hear Christians arguing about religious practices, or fighting and debating over doctrine, they're often discussing trivial matters. Luther said, in effect, "Hey, I'm not gonna fight about Mary or about the pope or about relics or even about these other differences we have with respect to the sacraments and all the rest, but *I will fight over justification*, over the very article upon which the church stands or falls. There is no negotiation here—none."

I've often wondered in my own soul how it was possible for one man to stand against the whole world in the sixteenth century. He stood so openly, and this regarding perhaps the most volatile, theological issue in the history of the church. But every century has witnessed serious debates and divisions within the body of Christ. In the fourth century, as we can see in the Nicene Creed, it was the Arian heresy that denied the deity of Christ as an absolutely essential portion of the gospel message. In the fifth century, it was the Monophysites and Eutycians. At the Council of Chalcedon in 451 the church once more condemned major heresies—heresies that denied either the human nature of Christ or the divine nature. And through all of these debates there were people who split off from the historic body of Christ.

The schism of 1054 between the Western and Eastern churches was another tragic moment in church history. But all these debates, as serious as they were, pale to insignificance when they are compared with the seriousness of the rupture that came to the body of Christ in the sixteenth century. In one limited sense, the Protestant Reformation was the greatest tragedy ever to happen. The visible body of Christ disintegrated and broke into not just hundreds but thousands of different pieces. And we haven't had visible outward unity since.

Now, I want to ask a simple question in light of these major historical and theological issues: Are you really a Protestant? What are you specifically *protesting*? Do you understand what the issues are in your time?

IS THE PROTEST NOW OVER?

These questions will simply not go away. In recent months I have heard that the protest is now over for modern evangelicals. Now the time has come, we are repeatedly being told, to make peace with people, to end the reformation process begun by the sixteenth-century Protestant Reformation. Please don't misunderstand me at this point—I desire peace with everyone who believes in the Lord Jesus Christ, with everyone who believes the Gospel of Jesus Christ. But if anybody claims to be a Christian and preaches or teaches *another gospel* from the one God has declared in Jesus Christ, I cannot be at peace with him or her regarding this message and its implications for the church. To make peace with such, in this message of the gospel, is to make war with Christ.

That is precisely how Luther saw it in the sixteenth century. If you read his letters you can feel the very agony of his soul. Virtually all of his good friends would say to him, "Martin, Martin, you're being bigoted, you're being narrow-minded, you're being tenacious; certainly you can't be right. Everybody else can't be wrong. Give this up, Martin." But we must observe his response. He repeatedly argued that this was not his cause. It was the cause of Christ. This is the gospel, he said. This does matter. God does care whether you believe that you're justified *solely* by the imputation of the righteousness of Christ. You can't believe in imputation and also believe that you're justified by your own participation in an inward grace that Christ pours into your heart—a grace that you cooperate with and assent to and then do works of satisfaction by which you have merit acceptable to God. The difference in these two messages is huge. The gulf is immense. We can't gloss it over with modern rhetoric that simply does away with centuries of major theological concern.

There simply cannot be two differing gospels. This is the obvious point Paul is making to the Galatians. It was also the obvious point made by our Protestant forefathers, who had real confidence in the total sufficiency of the biblical gospel. Now we have come to the place, it seems, where we no longer have this deep concern. You might say we have come to be indifferent in large measure. But our very indifference will land us in great difficulty, for as one Puritan aptly put it, "Indifference in religion, is the first step to apostasy from religion."[6]

The gospel message is nonnegotiable. I wonder if evangelicals still understand this in the face of postmodern criticism and philosophical relativism. As Cyprian, the third-century Bishop of Carthage, stated plainly, "The gospel cannot stand in part or it will fall in part."

In the middle of the sixteenth century, the Roman Catholic Church responded to Luther's uprising by convening the Council of Trent. At this council, Rome not only went to great pains to define their own view of justification—their view of the gospel that saves—but they included twenty canons on justification, each one beginning with the same formula—"If anyone says . . ." Then they fill out the formula with specific beliefs that might be expressed at their time in history. At the conclusion of each of these canons, it says: "Upon him anathema sits."

In a way, I admire Rome very much for the way they did this and the way they continue to say it in the recent *Catechism of the Catholic*

Church.[7] At least the Roman Catholic Church understood in the sixteenth century that the doctrine of justification touched the very heart of the gospel. It seems to me, implicitly at least, that they agreed with Luther that justification is the article of faith upon which the church stands or falls. Sadly, they disagreed, and still disagree, with Luther's understanding of what the gospel is. This much we can say, however—at least they had the courage of their convictions and said, in effect, "Luther is preaching a different gospel. Calvin is preaching a different gospel. These Protestants, with their doctrine of *sola fide*, justification by faith alone, are teaching a different gospel; therefore they are under the anathema of God." If Rome was right in the sixteenth century, then you can be sure of one truth—we are under the anathema of God, because the apostle Paul preaches that in Galatians 1:9: "If any man is preaching to you a gospel contrary to what you have received, he is to be accursed."

As a Bible student, and as one who has confidence in the full sufficiency of the gospel itself, I believe that Luther, Calvin, and the Protestant Reformers had it right. They were preaching the biblical gospel. The great, great tragedy is this—when Rome put justification by faith alone under her anathema, she put herself as a visible teaching body under the anathema of God. And the world is still waiting, more than five centuries later, for her repentance. Nothing in the modern teaching of the Roman Catholic Church has fundamentally altered this.

Don't misunderstand. I know that there are people within the Roman Catholic Church, thousands and perhaps millions, who personally believe the biblical gospel. But they do so in spite of their church's response over the past five centuries. And if they believe the Gospel of Jesus Christ, they're going to be saved by Jesus Christ alone, not by or through their church. But the Roman Catholic Church does not believe and does not teach the biblical gospel. It openly and persistently denies the salvation of *sola gratia* (grace alone), *sola fide* (faith alone), and *solus Christus* (Christ alone).

All of this being said, it is an immense tragedy when in our day people are making a mad rush to bring peace, seemingly at any price, when there is no real peace. I have frequently felt the burden of pressure to cooperate in this move away from the sufficiency of the gospel now going on in evangelicalism. I feel this burden for the sake of relationships, for the sake of peace among evangelicals, and for the sake of simply getting along and not being perceived as a troublesome person. But the gospel and its sole sufficiency demands much more of me than simply "getting along" with everyone.

Some time ago I came early for a church service and sat down. I opened my Bible to pray and meditate in preparation for the service. The first thing I did was read Romans 3 and 4 again. I said to myself, *I want to make sure I understand what the New Testament is teaching about the gospel.* The second thing I did that morning was to read this first chapter of Galatians afresh. What struck me was something I never really noticed before, because every time I've ever spoken from Galatians 1, I've always quit reading at the end of verse 9. Consequently, I didn't see the connection with verse 10: "For am I now seeking the favor of men, or of God? Or am I striving to please men? If I were still trying to please men, I would not be a bond-servant of Christ."

Paul says clearly that, if I strive to please God, then I risk every human relationship in order to do so. He endured this loss rather than compromise for one second the sufficiency of the Gospel of Jesus Christ. He understood the crisis in Galatia, and he knew that only a grasp of the total sufficiency of the gospel would solve the problem.

It bothers me at meetings of the presbytery of my own denomination when I see people arguing and fussing over doctrines that are not essential. At the same time I believe, and I urge you to believe, that justification by faith *alone* is absolutely essential to the Gospel of Jesus Christ. And when the word *alone* is left out in modern formulations, as it often is, the essential essence of this truth is fundamentally lost. To depart from this doctrine in any way is to betray the Gospel of Jesus Christ. We simply cannot do this, no matter what it costs, no matter how many friends we may lose, no matter how many people become angry with us.

As I talk with friends who are theologians, I am amazed at much of what is happening in our generation. The thing I can't understand is how quickly and easily people who make a sound public profession of evangelical, even Reformed, theology are deserting it for other movements and issues that take us away from confidence in the utter sufficiency of Christ and His grace. What's going on in our time? I'm convinced that many of these people actually believe justification by faith alone, but something is happening to make them equivocate. It is almost as if something is in the air.

A friend of mine, another theologian, said to me recently, "R. C., there's a strange thing going on today. What we have is people who are willing to be evangelicals and to say, 'Yes, I believe in the gospel of the free grace of Christ, and that justification is by Christ and Christ alone, by faith and by faith alone, by grace and by grace alone.' These theologians and leaders are willing to say this in their discussions of theology. What they're not willing to do is to speak out against an opposite view." To put it another way, they are willing to affirm, but they are not as willing to deny. They're willing to be positive, but they're not willing to say anything negative. I have appreciated the way in which theologians involved in the lordship debate of the last ten years or so have frankly admitted that one side or the other is preaching *another* gospel. At least we are admitting that this issue is as important as it really is.

The way we teach justification by faith alone can result in the preaching of a different gospel, one that is under the anathema of God. We must be just as candid about this. I appreciate it when people on both sides have been willing to admit, "One of us is not preaching the gospel of the New Testament."

This whole issue does matter. I think it matters very significantly, and I think it matters eternally. It is very important these days for every professor of Bible and theology, for every Christian, to sit down by himself or herself and ask the questions "What is the gospel? Is this what I really believe? Is what I teach really the biblical gospel or *another* gospel?" Your response may well bring you into the freedom of grace and light, or it may put you directly under the curse of God. You cannot be neutral to the matter of the gospel and its authority. The present crisis will not allow you to absent yourself from the careful consideration of these critical matters, not if you truly love the Lord Jesus Christ.

We need the kind of perspective that the great reformer John Calvin expressed in his last will and testament. He understood the authority of the gospel and the sufficiency of its message. He understood that the gospel itself required earnest disputation, in both affirmation and denial, if he was to be faithful to it. Wrote Calvin (25 April 1564), "In all the disputes I have had with the enemies of the truth, I have never made use of subtle craft nor sophistry, but have gone to work straightforwardly in maintaining [God's] quarrel."[8]

Notes

1. Timothy George, *Galatians*, The New American Commentary (Nashville: Broadman/Holman, 1994), 90.

2. Ibid.

3. William Hendriksen, *Galatians*, New Testament Commentary (Grand Rapids: Baker, 1968), 39.

4. J. Gresham Machen, *Machen's Notes on Galatians*, ed. John H. Skilton (Phillipsburg, N.J.: Presb. & Ref., 1972), 47–48.

5. Martin Luther, *What Luther Says*, comp. Ewald M. Plass (St. Louis: Concordia, 1959), 568.
6. I. D. E. Thomas, comp., *The Golden Treasury of Puritan Quotations* (Chicago: Moody, 1975), 20. This quotation is taken from William Secker.
7. *Catechism of the Catholic Church* (New York: Catholic Book Pub., 1994), 481–87. This much-heralded catechism is considered the definitive work of the modern post–Vatican II magisterium of the church. Note especially the material on grace and justification, as well as the discussion of merit. Sadly, Rome has not changed one essential iota of its doctrine on these vital points.
8. Graham Miller, *Calvin's Wisdom: An Anthology Arranged Alphabetically* (Edinburgh: Banner of Truth, 1992), 65–66.

CHAPTER
7

BEHOLD THE LAMB: THE GOSPEL AND SUBSTITUTIONARY ATONEMENT

S. Lewis Johnson, Jr.

At the heart of evangelical theology for centuries has been the theme that the message of the gospel is centered in the preaching of "Jesus Christ, and Him crucified" (1 Cor. 2:2). And it has been argued validly that in this message is found the essence of the orthodox doctrine of the Atonement.

In further defense of its message, the church, especially in its Reformed branches, has contended that the proper understanding of the *nature* of the atonement of our Lord settles the major questions that the Atonement raises. To be specific, if the Atonement is sacrificial, penal, and substitutionary, other matters, such as its extent and reference, find easier solution.

It is my conviction that the proper emphasis upon the substitutionary aspect of the Atonement has been mislaid in our day. We must recover this if we are to regain deep confidence in the message of the gospel as "the power of God to salvation for everyone who believes" (Rom. 1:16 NKJV). And we emphasize that its benefits do accrue to all who believe.

In addition, even in professing evangelical circles, a saddening omission of stress upon the Atonement's penal aspect may be found. "Who wants to hear about sin?" is a question heard from mouths other than Robert Schuller. Therefore, to the historically orthodox doctrine of penal substitution this chapter is addressed.

THE DOCTRINE OF PENAL SUBSTITUTION

Objections to penal substitution are not new. This grand truth has been mislaid in the past. And it has been attacked, even in the house of those who profess evangelical religion. Almost a century ago the great Southern Presbyterian theologian Robert L. Dabney expressed succinct-

119

ly the perennial objection to the claim that Jesus Christ died a penal substitutionary death for sinners: "This cardinal conception is rejected by the multitudes of rationalizing nominal Christians through every party, from Socinians upward. They say that they must reject it as essentially unjust, as thus obnoxious to necessary moral intuitions, and so impossible to be ascribed to a righteous God."[1]

Dabney made some important points in his small but useful book. He distinguished "potential guilt" (the sense of wrongdoing that springs up immediately from our consciences after sin) from "actual guilt" (*reatus*, "the state of an accused person, or guilt"). Actual guilt is, thus, the obligation to punishment because of sin, the penal decision of the lawgiver. When, then, the Scriptures speak of imputation or substitution, the reference is not to potential guilt or to our sinful nature but to actual guilt. It is the latter alone that God's forgiveness removes in this life, although the saving work of Christ ultimately removes our sinfulness, too.

It must be kept in mind that the penal substitution of Christ at Calvary removes actual guilt.[2] Dabney concludes, "The whole question between us and the objectors is this: May the sovereign Judge righteously provide for such a substitution, when the free consent of the substitute is given, and all the other conditions are provided by God for good results?"[3]

Much hinges on these matters. Recent theological history indicates that the denial of penal substitution has led to a modification or perversion of several orthodox doctrines. The divine attributes are brought under direct attack when we eliminate penal substitution. Among those doctrines directly affected are (1) retributive justice based on God's perfections, (2) God's immutability, and (3) the proper biblical emphasis on the infiniteness of sin's evil.

It is not hard to find contemporary illustrations of the views that Dabney deplored when he wrote a hundred years ago. John Hick, whose views of the Atonement lie within the commonly accepted Abelardian model,[4] rejects fundamentally, almost out of hand, the orthodox view. He calls it "the old Protestant penal-substitutionary atonement theory."[5] He finds this viewpoint "morally and spiritually repugnant,"[6] thus informing us that Dabney's opponents are still with us in the twentieth century. And their influence on evangelical theology is not hard to detect in the modern milieu.

The two most common biblical texts cited as denying substitution are Deuteronomy 24:16 and Ezekiel 18:20, the former affirming personal responsibility and family solidarity, while Ezekiel asserts the principle that "retribution is not communicated by generation but is borne only by the individual involved."[7]

It is easy to see that the human situations differ from the divine, and it must be admitted that human analogies are not inspired, but occasionally we are forced to use them. In the imagined human situation of the broken law, excluding the guilty criminal (who is a murderer), there are four distinct parties: the wronged family of the murdered man and society, the judge, the proposed innocent substitute, and the Supreme Court (the king in other societies).

Let us agree that it would be wrong to sentence an innocent person, although willing, to suffer death in the place of a guilty murderer. The teaching of Scripture is quite different: "There is the condemned criminal, the guilty sinner," H. E. Guillebaud notes.

> But beside him there is only One, Who is Judge, Wronged Party, King (or Law), and Substitute. God was not administering someone else's law, but His own, and the sin was not committed against someone else but against Him: and above all He did not take someone else and accept him as substitute for the condemned sinner (He refused an offer of this kind when made by Moses, Ex. xxxii. 30–35), but He came Himself, took upon Him the nature of the guilty ones, and bore the penalty of His own Law. The Substitute who died on Calvary expressly declared Himself to be the Judge of the world (Matt. xiii. 41–43; xxv. 31–46).[8]

Who, then, are we poor humans to rail against a divine Trinitarian work?

Although some critics of the teaching have seen it as self-evident that one person's sin cannot be transferred to another, is it not remarkable, as Dabney says,

> that not only the most devout Christians, but the greatest thinkers and philosophers of all ages—a Lactantius, an Augustine, an Anselm, an Aquinas, a Luther, a Calvin, a Pascal, a Claude, a Turretin, a Butler, a Newton, a Chalmers, an Edwards, a Wesley, an Archibald Alexander, a Thornwell [and, we might add for the twentieth century, a Bavinck, a Warfield, a Machen, and others]—saw no difficulty in this proposition which our Socinianizers find so unspeakably absurd?[9]

Thus, a simple biblical, exegetical, and theological survey of the concept of penal substitution with its application to the doctrine of the atonement of Christ would appear to be in order. But, first, we will consider some objections to penal substitution.

OBJECTIONS TO PENAL SUBSTITUTION

This great doctrine of Christ's penal substitutionary sacrifice is not popular today. Even in churches that joyfully and fruitfully affirmed and disseminated this doctrine far and wide in earlier centuries, the loss is quite noticeable. Several objections have been offered against this vital truth. I mention only three common ones.

First, this view of the work of Christ assumes a schism in the Trinity, a "monstrous" idea.[10] God, it is claimed, is the stern judge insisting on the execution of justice, and Christ is the merciful Savior who interposes and satisfies the legal demand of the Father, appeasing His wrath against sinners. The members of the Trinity are not at one in their attitude toward humanity: God is propitiated, while Christ propitiates. How can there be one impulse in God to punish and another impulse not to punish? The impulse to save can only be an impulse of love and not at all of justice.

Occasionally evangelicals aid this view by speaking as if Christ, and not the triune God, is the sole author of salvation. This nontrinitarian concept of salvation produces a room full of serious problems that undermine the sufficiency of the gospel itself. Modern preachers and teachers need to return to a more faithful exposition of the message that is God's power to save.

The objection that God has two contradictory impulses has no substance. There is no schism in the Trinity when redemption and its application is understood properly. Rather, there is a perfect harmony, the Father sacrificing His Son, the Son willingly offering Himself, and the Spirit applying the benefits of the satisfaction to God's elect. And as for the view that God is being only a just and wrathful deity, let us remember that it is the love of God that leads to the gift of the redeeming Son. There is no antagonism between God's love and justice, as John plainly affirms: "In this is love, not that we loved God, but that He loved us and sent His Son to be the propitiation [the satisfaction, a word from which the saving import cannot be removed, as Hodge says[11]] for our sins" (1 John 4:10). The psalmist puts it this way: "Lovingkindness and truth have met together; righteousness and peace have kissed each other" (Ps. 85:10).

Second, some have recently argued that the Bible does not make use of the concept of punishment in connection with the atonement. Hendrikus Berkhof claims that the idea of punishment, though found in Western orthodoxy since Anselm, "is foreign to the NT."[12] I am compelled to ask, "Can anyone maintain this position in light of Isaiah 53:5-6, 2

Corinthians 5:21, and Galatians 3:13?" Listen to Isaiah: "But He was pierced through for our transgressions, He was crushed for our iniquities; the chastening for our well-being fell upon Him, and by His scourging we are healed. All of us like sheep have gone astray, each of us has turned to his own way; but the Lord has caused the iniquity of us all to fall on Him" (53:5–6). The apostle adds,

> He made Him who knew no sin to be sin on our behalf, so that we might become the righteousness of God in Him. (2 Cor. 5:21)

> Christ redeemed us from the curse of the Law, having become a curse for us—for it is written, "Cursed is everyone who hangs on a tree." (Gal. 3:13; cf. Deut. 21:23)

Many other passages affirm the same truth and, furthermore, actually trace the just bearing of our punishment to the justifying love of God (cf. Rom. 3:24–26).

Third, some claim that penal satisfaction makes God inferior to people, for people freely forgive, but God cannot do so. Hence, it is argued, God is less charitable, merciful, and good than humans. This is to forget that God is the just judge of the universe. A judge may be very kind and forgiving as a private individual, but in his official duties he must see that the law is followed to the letter. As a famous judge once said, "When I have been tempted to relax my duty to be true to the law, I have reminded myself that I have a duty to my country." The ultimate end of God's own works is God Himself and not His creature's well-being. If we are to render to Him all worship and reverence, should He not receive it (1 Cor. 10:31)?

These objections—that there is a schism in the Trinity and that people freely forgive whereas God cannot—ultimately turn stubbornly away from the glorious truth of merciful satisfaction. Listen to the nineteenth-century theologian William G. T. Shedd: "There is mercy in permitting another person to do for the sinner what the sinner is bound to do for himself; and still greater mercy in providing that person; and greater still, in becoming that person."[13]

In speaking of Christ's sacrifice, James Stalker, the eminent Scottish minister and professor, said, "The dignity of the act is, however, chiefly brought out in the claim that He gave His life 'for many.'" When prisoners were bartered at the conclusion of a war, the exchange was not always simply man for man. An officer was of more value than a common soldier, and several soldiers might be redeemed by the surrender of one officer. For a woman of high rank or extraordinary beauty, a still greater number of prisoners might be exchanged; and by the giving up of a king's son many might be redeemed. So the sense of His own unique dignity and His peculiar relation to God is implied in the statement that His life would redeem the lives of many.[14]

THE OLD TESTAMENT ROOTS
OF PENAL SUBSTITUTION

The apostle Paul declared that our Lord "died for our sins according to the Scriptures" (1 Cor. 15:3), a statement that indicates that His death was not fortuitous. It was, as C. K. Barrett says, "willed and determined by God, and that it formed part of the winding up of his eternal purpose."[15] Barrett goes on to say that a death that took place in accordance with the Scriptures invites interpretation in Old Testament categories—for example, "of sacrifice, of punishment and atonement."[16] I would like to look at several of the passages from the Old Testament that surely would, or could, have been in the apostle's mind when he wrote of the sacrificial death of the Savior.

GENESIS 15:7–21

In the remarkable ratification of the Abrahamic covenant by an ancient form of sacrifice it is the Lord alone who passed between the pieces of the sacrificial animals. In other such covenantal procedures both parties walked between the pieces of the animals, but here God in symbol form walks between the pieces, and Abram is not invited to follow. The meaning is clear: This covenant is not a conditional covenant in which duties must be fulfilled by people. It is one in which God undertakes to fulfill the conditions Himself, thus guaranteeing by the divine fidelity to His Word and by His power the accomplishment of the covenantal promises.

C. F. Keil points out that the representation indicated that Abram was only bound to receive the gracious gifts of the Lord.[17] Gerhard Von Rad agrees: "The ceremony proceeded completely without words and with the complete passivity of the human partner."[18] And finally, Herman Ridderbos puts it vividly: "Abraham is deliberately excluded—he is the *astonished spectator* (Gen. 15:12, 17)"[19] (italics added).

An important point we must not miss is that the ratification is accomplished by the sacrifice of the animals, the death looking forward typically to the obedient death of the Seed of Abraham (Jesus), who would truly pass through the pieces, suffering for the sins of His people, and come out in victory with the promises in His hands. Clearly a penal substitution is reflected here.

GENESIS 22:1–14

In one of the greatest scenes in the history of salvation, surpassed only by the Greatest Father's offering up of His "Isaac" at Golgotha, where this story found its proper climax and antitype, Abraham obediently offered up his son Isaac as a sacrifice. All of the important features of Christ's penal substitutionary sacrifice are typically foreshadowed in the sacrifice of Isaac. The son is bound and placed upon the altar and prepared for a death interrupted only by the voice of the Angel of the Lord (v. 11); the substitution of a ram for Isaac is plainly a type of Christ. The apostle Paul, borrowing language from verses 12 and 16, finds the antitype to Isaac's "altar experience" in our Lord's cross death.[20] That Abraham offered up the ram "in the place of his son" (v. 13) further stresses the substitutionary aspect of the offering.[21]

EXODUS 12:1–13

It is certain that one of the passages the apostle Paul had in mind was Exodus 12:1–13, for the apostle says in 1 Corinthians 5:7, "For Christ, our Passover lamb, has been sacrificed" (NIV).[22] The reference, of course, is a typical one to the death of Christ. The shedding of the lamb's blood was the means of the deliverance of Israel's sons from the judgment of death. The lamb was a substitute whose death prevented the destroying angel from slaying Israel's firstborn sons. The Passover, thus, was part of the series of events in Israel's history that left them a pictorial pattern of expiation and propitiation by a substitute in their salvation history, aiding them in preparing for the coming of the Lamb of God.

THE CEREMONIAL LAW AND THE DAY OF ATONEMENT (cf. Lev. 16:1–34; 23:26–32; Heb. 9:1–10:18)

The sacrifices of animals had their beginning in the Garden of Eden (cf. Gen. 3:21) and were enshrined in the law of Moses as emblems and types intended to teach men and women that forgiveness of sin was impossible without the satisfaction of divine justice in the payment of the penalty of death. This payment was ultimately impossible for guilty men and women to make; thus, it could be made only by a divinely provided substitute to whom guilt was transferred.

The law was a God-given exposition of the nature of sin and pardon. The guilty worshiper brought his sacrificial victim, laid hands upon it in token of identification and confession of sin, and the animal was slain by the priest to obtain the blood (Heb. 9:22), which was then sprinkled on the altar. The required parts of the animal were committed to the fire to be burnt as "a pungent emblem of divine justice."[23] The truths of expiation, the imputation of sin and righteousness, and substitution were the unending message. The Messiah was to die for the ungodly (Rom. 5:6), for sinners (5:8), and for the unjust (1 Peter 3:18).

The climactic Day of Atonement, which Israel called *Ha Yom* (lit. "the day"), contained an elaborate ritual that proclaimed the same truth. The author of the stately epistle to the Hebrews, against the typical background of the ritual of that day, asserts of Jesus Christ that "now once at the consummation of the ages He has been manifested to put away sin by the sacrifice of Himself" (9:26).

ISAIAH 52:13–53:12

In the last and most important of the songs of the Servant of the Lord (part of a chapter called by Emil Brunner "the quintessence of the Old Covenant"[24]), Isaiah depicts the triumph of God's great Servant in His sin-bearing, suffering, death, and victorious exaltation. Evangelical commentators are united in affirming that the Servant's sufferings are substitutionary and penal.[25] J. A. Motyer incisively comments, "Verse 4 demands the noun 'substitution,' and verse 5 adds the adjective 'penal.'"[26]

THE NEW TESTAMENT EXPOSITION OF SUBSTITUTION

THE TEACHING OF OUR LORD

Matthew 20:28. The interpretation of our Lord's death as a penal and substitutionary sacrifice is found in almost all forms of New Testament teaching. The language of the text before us, "just as the Son of Man did not come to be served, but to serve, and to give His life a ransom for many" (cf. Mark 10:45), is fully in line with the affirmation. It represents, in this instance, the teaching of our Lord Himself. Here three great truths cry out for emphasis.

In the first place, we can see that He came *voluntarily*. The word *come* points to His entry into life, and the word *gave* points to His exit. As someone has said, they stress His volition in two things concerning which we are not consulted—our birth and our dying. The word *came* stresses His sovereignty in His service. It was the word He used of His coming, except when He modifies it to "was sent." With only one exception (cf. John 18:37) He never uses the term *born*, which Pilate used in the one instance because he was an unbelieving Roman official. Even then Jesus adds, "I have come into the world." He alone is the master of His fate.

The Son came to "give His life," death being the goal of His life. The "ransom" is the "price of release,"[27] the price paid for culprits under judgment. The ransom is the satisfaction of divine justice, which requires a life—a life with infinite value—for lives. In other words, Christ's death was *propitiatory* (cf. Rom. 3:24–26).

John Calvin was the first to clearly recognize the vitally important distinctions in the offices of Christ (i.e., Prophet, Priest, and King) and to gather the discussion of His mediatorial work around them. He was followed in this by the Lutherans. The priest, representing people before God, made the reconciling offering, called a *satisfactio*, or satisfaction. The satisfaction accomplished by our Lord on the cross effected an expiation of sin and a propitiation of the Father. This work of the Son rendered the Father able, consistent with His own perfections, to reconcile us in His mercy, to renew us, and finally to exalt us to the dignity, excellence, and blessedness of sons of God. It was not our merits in any sense but rather our misery that brought Him in grace to redeem us. As one older hymn has it—pity was joined with power.

It is remarkable that the professing Christian church today finds the idea of penal satisfaction by substitution so distasteful. "No two words in the theological vocabulary of the cross," John Stott has said, "arouse more criticism than 'satisfaction' and 'substitution.'"[28] Charles Hodge devotes three pages in his theology to the symbols of the Lutheran and Reformed churches that indicate their agreement on the necessity of Christ's satisfaction of God's justice. Even in the Roman Catholic Council of Trent the descriptive phrase is "Christ Jesus, who for our sins has made satisfaction" (*Christus Jesus, qui pro peccatis nostris satisfecit*).[29]

Finally, He came to give Himself a ransom "for many." The Greek preposition *anti*, which ordinarily has the force of "in place of," may have the force of "in behalf of" (Matt. 17:27), but it more commonly has the former sense. It is the preposition that most clearly expresses the idea of substitution, as it does here. Incidentally, would a man who was only a great teacher make such majestic statements?

Matthew 26:27–28. We by reason of space only briefly consider two other of our Lord's statements. In the midst of the Last Supper He took the cup, offered thanks, gave it to them, and said, "Drink from it, all of you; for this is My blood of the covenant, which is poured out for many for forgiveness of sins." As Klaus Schilder has pointed out,

> Two lines meet in the guest chamber where Jesus is seated: that of the Old and that of the New Testament. Now the switch is thrown over. Fleshly Israel will no longer go up to celebrate the Passover according to the old law. Instead spiritual Israel (and, we add, believing Gentiles) will rise from the table presently, will go out to celebrate a better Passover of fulfillment, the Holy Supper.[30]

The altar of the old covenant vanishes, and the table of the new is prepared, but both exist on account of the blood. Up to this time every eye looked forward, but soon they will look backward. In this holy context our Lord broke the bread and gave His men the cup.

The language of verse 28 with its "blood" that is "poured out" is sacrificial language,[31] as in 20:22 with its "cup," symbolic of death and judgment. The "covenant," coupled with the expression "forgiveness of sins," alludes to Jeremiah 31:34 and the new covenant. The expression "My blood of the covenant, which is poured out for many for forgiveness of sins" may be our Lord's most important atonement statement. His death is a violent sacrificial death to ratify the new covenant and its promises (Jer. 31:31–34).[32]

The sense, then, of the passage is that our Lord's death is sacrificial and concerns "many."[33] In view of the violent death in sacrificial blood, it is fair to speak again of His death as the penalty paid for sin, and the payment is in behalf of many; that is, many benefit from His death. This text, with the Markan parallel, justifies the use of the term *substitutionary* with reference to His death in the words of the Supper. The term *remission,* referring to the remitting of merited punishment, is a judicial term, consonant with the satisfaction rendered to the Father's justice.

Matthew 27:46. Our Lord's cry of dereliction—"My God, My God, why have You forsaken Me?"—is the inevitable sequel to the horror that He experienced in the Garden of Gethsemane (see Mark 14:33–34, 36). I shall mention only a few things to underline the claim that the cry itself, in its context, shrieks penal substitution.

In the first place, Jesus' "why" implies conscious innocence of any sin or wrongdoing on His part. Who else among men could honestly take the same position? Further, consider the following questions: (1) Would a loving God forsake the only good man who ever lived (Ps. 37:25; Matt.

3:17)? (2) Would a loving God injure the only innocent man? (3) Why were His prayers answered elsewhere (see John 11:42; Ps. 22:2)? In fact, David's "Yet You are holy" (Ps. 22:3) may be the answer: the Son has become at the moment He utters David's ancient anticipation of Calvary the Unholy One, the sin offering, the curse (Gal. 3:13; 2 Cor. 5:2).

THE TEACHING OF PAUL

Romans 3:21–26. This is the normative New Testament text on justification by grace alone through faith alone and is a passage described by more than one older commentator as containing "the marrow of theology" or a "brief summary of divine wisdom."[34] The important focus is on verse 25 and the phrase "a propitiation in His blood."

The commentator C. E. B. Cranfield's sense of this passage is that God "purposed" that Christ "be by the shedding of his blood a propitiatory sacrifice."[35] The language is again clearly that of a penal sacrifice, as the term *blood* specifically indicates. Cranfield notes that there is no "cheap" forgiveness to be seen here, nor forgiveness given "lightly."[36] Against His Son, God directed the "full weight of that righteous wrath which [people] deserved."[37] Thus, He bears the judgment of others. The picture is that of a substitutionary sacrifice.

Further, the use of the term *propitiation* (or *propitiatory sacrifice*)— the Old Testament term used for the mercy seat[38] of the ark of the covenant of the tabernacle—indicates that the Day of Atonement ritual is in Paul's mind.[39] Since, as we have previously seen, the ritual looks at the death of the Redeemer to come as a penal sacrifice, this observation plainly strengthens that viewpoint. In the ritual itself the laying on of hands upon the second goat pointed to the transference of the guilt of Israel to the animal. The animal was the substitutionary sacrifice that stood typically for the Messiah to come.

Romans 8:32. When Paul comes to the climax and conclusion of his magnificent outline of God's eternal purpose, stretching from divine foreknowledge and predestination,[40] there is a moment of awed silence, such as when one catches a first glimpse of the Atlantic or Pacific, or when one reaches the summit of a majestic mountain. It is not surprising that commentators are quite reserved here. Even the apostle reflects this with a reverent exclamation: "What then shall we say to these things?" (v. 31). The next clause, "If God is for us," may be rendered "Since God is for us," thus making the clause an apt summary of the first eight chapters of the letter.

Verse 32 substantiates the sentiments of verse 31, declaring that the

God who gave His Son for us, the greatest gift of all, cannot logically withhold from us any spiritual blessing. Having given His best and most, will He withhold the rest and the lesser? The verse, it should be noticed, leans heavily on the Old Testament incident of the offering up of Isaac, as the language suggests. The verb translated here as "spare" is taken from Genesis 22:16 (cf. v. 12), where the Septuagint reads, "and you have not spared your beloved son for my sake."[41]

The phrase "for us all" (v. 32), with the Greek preposition *hyper*, meaning "in behalf of," refers to the believers.[42] It is evident that the statement of Paul here is harmonious with ideas of penal sacrifice and substitution.[43]

1 Timothy 2:4–6. The important clause here is the first of verse 6: "who gave Himself as a ransom for all." This is very similar in its sense to Matthew 20:28 and Mark 10:45. The language, however, is different.[44] It expresses clearly that the one Mediator died as a substitute. The noun *antilytron* is formed from the word meaning "ransom" and the preposition *anti*, meaning "instead of, in place of." Thus, He gave Himself as a redeeming sacrifice in place of and in behalf of all (cf. Titus 2:14). As the context makes plain (see vv. 1–2, 7), redemption was accomplished for *all kinds of people*, as Augustine,[45] Calvin, and many others have noted.

THE TEACHING OF JOHN

In a scene that can only be described as sublime, John describes a vision in which heaven invests the Lion of Judah with authority to establish His dominion over the earth through His coming advent and judgment (Rev. 5:9–10; see Heb. 2:5–9). It has been said that the Apocalypse is a long polemic against Domitian, whom Pliny called "the beast from hell," the first Roman emperor to have himself officially entitled "God the Lord."[46] Here is the answer of heaven to Domitian's proud claims.

The real "God the Lord," it turns out, is a slaughtered lamb, who survives and stands, as if risen from the dead (v. 6). The seven-sealed book is a testamentary disposition of earth's affairs and the goal of history—a prewritten history of the manner in which Christ accomplishes His royal office of universal dominion for us, described in chapters 6–20.

The living creatures and the elders sang when the Lamb took the book from the hand of the one who sat on the throne in token of His right to worldwide rule. The song extols the Lamb's worth in relation to the past, the present, and the future. The source of the Lamb's power and worth is the atonement that He has accomplished. Its features are clear.

In the first place, it is *penal*. The death that He has died is by violence, as the word "slain"[47] and the phrase "with Your blood" indicate. The death is the death of one under judgment. It is, as the connection with Isaiah 53:7 indicates (which in turn refers to Exodus 12 and the Passover), the death of God's Passover Lamb.

In the second place, the death is clearly *substitutionary*, as I have pointed out previously.

Third, it is *particular*. The partitive expression "from [lit., out from[48]] every tribe and tongue and people and nation" indicates that the scope of this purchase is *not* universal.[49] The NASB appropriately translates it "*men* from every tribe."

One significant thing should be added: This purchase is an *effective* purchase. All who were purchased became royal priests (v. 10). None are lost in the process of redemption. The substitution is, therefore, effective. The chapter concludes with a chorus of praise from all heaven that climaxes in what someone has called "an unparalleled fortissimo" to the Father and to the Lamb, who also is worshiped as God (cf. 22:9).

Robert Browning, in a letter published after his death, cited several utterances of men of genius as to the Christian faith. Among them is one from Charles Lamb, the well-known nineteenth-century English essayist:

> In a gay fancy with some friends, as to how he and they would feel if the greatest of the dead were to appear suddenly in flesh and blood once more—a final suggestion, "And if Christ entered this room?" he changed his manner at once and stuttered out, as his manner was when moved, "You see, if Shakespeare entered we should all rise; if He appeared, we must kneel."

Yes, we must, and we would.

THEOLOGICAL REFLECTIONS ON SUBSTITUTION AND ATONEMENT

CONCERNING THEORIES OF THE ATONEMENT

The vicarious repentance theory. John McLeod Campbell (1800–1872), Scottish Presbyterian minister, later deposed from the Christian ministry for heresy (1831), is the author of a theory of the Atonement that is still regarded highly by several prominent British theologians, including R. S. Franks, Thomas F. Torrance, and his brother, James B. Torrance. This view, sometimes called the vicarious repentance theory, has had some influence in various circles of thought.

Rejecting the penal substitutionary theory, Campbell took his clue from a statement by Jonathan Edwards (who supported the penal substitutionary viewpoint) that atonement might be accomplished by "either an equivalent punishment or an equivalent sorrow and repentance."[50] Campbell fashioned his unorthodox theory as follows: the Son, in His perfect oneness with the Father, must have made a repentant confession, and it must have been "a perfect Amen in humanity to the judgment of God on the sin of man."[51] I am surprised at Jonathan Edwards's words. Emil Brunner rightly questions, "What has my present repentance to do with my previous guilt?"[52] The guilt necessitates the atonement.

The weaknesses of the theory are many, beginning with the fact that there is no support for it at all in specific Scripture. Second, the heart of the Atonement is no longer the Cross but the Incarnation. Although the apostles in their writing give the Incarnation the high regard it deserves, they have built their teaching solidly on the redemptive Cross (cf. 1 Cor. 2:2; Gal. 3:1; etc.). Third, and most devastating of all, if our Lord's so-called vicarious repentance is sufficient for atonement, then the necessity of the Cross is destroyed (Gal. 2:21, "Christ died needlessly"). "Campbell," Robert Letham writes, "leaves us with the overwhelming centre of the Christian faith (the cross) as little more than a frightening charade."[53]

The governmental theory. Evangelicals have also shown a fascination with the governmental theory of the Atonement. The great Dutch jurist, Hugo Grotius (1583–1645),[54] denied substitution and contended that Christ's death served as a way to prevent human moral corruption and to promote the common good. It is possible for God to relax the law so that an exact penalty is not necessarily enacted for each violation. Grotius used the term *penal substitution*, but he actually gave it the sense of a substitute for the penalty that should have been attached for humanity's sins.[55]

This device for avoiding penal substitution's perceived evils is characteristic of Arminian theology. It may be reflected in the theological sojourn of Clark Pinnock. Pinnock confesses that he began his theological life as a Calvinist[56] but now has come to an Arminian position, although historic Arminianism would clearly reject his denial of divine omniscience, and perhaps even more so his more recent deviations.[57] He has explained his transformation from Calvinism to Arminianism as related to his former belief in substitution:

> What kind of substitution, if unlimited in scope, does not entail absolute universalism in salvation? Obviously it required me to reduce the precision in which I understood the substitution to take place. Christ's death on behalf of the race evidently did not automatically secure for anyone an actual reconciled relationship with God, but made it possible[58] for people to enter into such a relationship by faith. . . . It caused me to look again first at the theory of Anselm and later of Hugo Grotius, both of whom encourage us to view the atonement as an act of judicial demonstration rather than a strict or quantitative substitution as such.[59]

So, instead of turning to the overwhelming evidence for substitution from the Scriptures, only a part of which we have tried to expound in this chapter, Pinnock has turned to another interpretation of the Atonement in which the historic orthodox penal substitutionary sacrifice of Christ for sins is discarded.

CONCERNING PROCLAMATION

Substitutionary atonement powerfully affects the message we preach. If the preaching of Paul to the Corinthians is a model for us (1 Cor. 2:2), and if that preaching is centered in an atonement by penal substitution, then may we not conclude that the message of the Cross is the declaration that Jesus Christ has discharged all the debts of sin and guilt on behalf of those who have believed (cf. 1:30–31; 6:11)?

In the discharging of all our debts, is the Lord not bound by His own promises to grant believers all the blessings of salvation—such as faith (Eph. 2:8–9; Phil. 3:9), effectual grace (John 6:44, 65; Acts 16:14), justification, sanctification, and redemption (1 Cor. 1:30)? There are two passages in the New Testament that appear to demand that, if He has died for us, all the things remaining for eternal life are a divine warrant for us. The passages are Romans 5:9–10 and 8:32–34, the latter passage being further strengthened to the place of absolute certainty by the prayers of our great High Priest to that end (see v. 34).

We are thus led to the dilemma expressed so well by J. I. Packer:

> If we are going to affirm penal substitution for all without exception we must either infer universal salvation or else, to evade this inference, deny the saving efficacy of the substitution for anyone; and if we are going to affirm penal substitution as an effective saving act of God we must either

infer universal salvation or else, to evade this inference, restrict the scope of the substitution, making it a substitution for some [but] not all.[60]

The serious present-day attack on penal substitution, which includes not only Clark Pinnock's views but also in a much milder form an apparently wavering Peter Toon,[61] is a return in part to Socinianism's argument that Christ's substitution is ultimately impossible, because it is unjust.[62]

Romans 5:8–10 and 8:32 appear to me to be unanswerable texts for those who deny the scriptural teaching of Christ's substitutionary atonement. These passages state plainly that, if Jesus gave Himself for us in atonement, everything else must follow because, having done the most that He could do in dying as our substitute, the lesser things—such as conviction of sin, repentance, effectual grace, faith—must inevitably follow. God's great eternal purpose, expressed so beautifully in 8:28–30, must reach its fruition in glorification for all those for whom He died.

The reality of Christ's substitutionary death for believers should increase our wonder, inspire our worship, and thrill our souls. The Christian who would understand the gospel and present it to others effectively must more fully appreciate this central theological truth, which is at the heart of the preaching of the Cross.

NOTES

1. Robert L. Dabney, *Christ Our Penal Substitute* (Richmond: Presbyterian Committee of Publication, n.d.), 5.
2. Ibid., 10–14.
3. Ibid., 14.
4. I say "commonly accepted" because the term *moral influence theory* may not really be fair to Abelard (1079–1142), for in the same context in which he expresses his view that redemption is "love in us" is another statement referring to redemption by the blood of Christ. See his *Exposition of the Epistle to the Romans* and his comments on Rom. 3:19–26. Cf. Robert Letham, *The Work of Christ* (Downers Grove, Ill.: InterVarsity Press, 1993), 166–67; Alister McGrath, "The Moral Theory of the Atonement: An Historical and Theological Critique," *Scottish Journal of Theology* 38 (1985): 205–20.
5. John Hick, "An Inspiration Christology for a Religiously Plural World," in *Encountering Jesus: A Debate on Christology*, ed. Stephen T. Davis (Atlanta: John Knox, 1988), 6.
6. Ibid. What strikes an evangelical at once is Hick's sparse use of Scripture in building his Christology.
7. John W. Wevers, ed., "Ezekiel," in *New Century Bible* (London: Thomas Nelson & Sons, 1969), 144.
8. H. E. Guillebaud, *Why the Cross?* (London: Inter-Varsity Fellowship, 1946), 146–47. My indebtedness to him is evident.

9. Dabney, *Christ Our Penal Substitute*, 73.

10. Louis Berkhof, *Systematic Theology* (Grand Rapids: Eerdmans, 1953), 372.

11. Charles Hodge, *Systematic Theology* (Grand Rapids: Eerdmans, 1952), 2:540.

12. Hendrikus Berkhof, *Christian Faith: An Introduction to the Study of the Faith*, trans. Sierd Woudstra (1973; reprint, Grand Rapids: Eerdmans, 1979), 305.

13. William G. T. Shedd, *Dogmatic Theology* (1888; reprint, Grand Rapids: Zondervan, n.d.), 1:377–78.

14. James Stalker, *The Christology of Jesus: Being the Teaching Concerning Himself According to the Synoptic Gospels* (London: Hodder & Stoughton, 1899), 179–80.

15. C. K. Barrett, *A Commentary on the First Epistle to the Corinthians* (New York and Evanston, Ill.: Harper & Row, 1968), 338.

16. Ibid.

17. C. F. Keil and F. Delitzsch, *Biblical Commentary on the Old Testament*, trans. James Martin (Grand Rapids: Eerdmans, 1971), 1:217.

18. Gerhard Von Rad, *Genesis: A Commentary*, rev. ed. (Philadelphia: Westminster Press, 1972), 188.

19. Herman N. Ridderbos, *The Epistle of Paul to the Churches of Galatia* (Grand Rapids: Eerdmans, 1953), 131.

20. The LXX uses the same verb for "spare" in verses 12, 16 that Paul uses in Romans 8:32. "Isaac was rescued by divine intervention," C. E. B. Cranfield says, "but for Jesus there was no such intervention, no other lamb could take the place of the Lamb of God; and the delivering up meant making to drink to the very dregs the cup of wrath." Cranfield (*A Critical and Exegetical Commentary on the Epistle to the Romans* [Edinburgh: T & T Clark, 1975], 1:217, 436) regards the death of Christ as both penal and substitutionary. James D. G. Dunn (*Romans 1–8*, Word Biblical Commentary 38 [Dallas: Word, 1988], 38:501) agrees.

21. I leave the details of this beautiful typical incident that looks on to the greater eternal Father's gift of His eternal Son to the expositor. That it took place in the land of Moriah, where centuries later the temple sacrifices would take place (2 Chron. 3:1), highlights the fact that, as Keil (*Biblical Commentary on the Old Testament*, 1:253) says, "The heavenly Father would perform what it had demanded of Abraham, but oh! how infinitely greater was His sacrifice!" (cf. H. C. Leupold, *Exposition of Genesis* [Grand Rapids: Baker, n.d.], 2:630–31).

22. The *hyper hēmōn* of the Majority Text (cf. NKJV "for us") is probably not genuine.

23. Dabney, *Christ Our Penal Substitute*, 90.

24. Emil Brunner, *The Mediator: A Study of the Central Doctrine of the Christian Faith*, trans. Olive Wyon (London: Lutterworth, 1934), 508.

25. Cf. J. Ridderbos, *Isaiah*, trans. John Vriend (1950–51; reprint, Grand Rapids: Zondervan, 1985); Edward J. Young, *The Book of Isaiah* (Grand Rapids: Eerdmans, 1972), 3:347–49; J. Alec Motyer, *The Prophecy of Isaiah: An Introduction & Commentary* (Downers Grove, Ill.: InterVarsity Press, 1993), 429–31; B. B. Warfield, "Christ Our Sacrifice," in *The Works of Benjamin B. Warfield* (Grand Rapids: Baker, 1981), 2:421–22.

26. Motyer, *The Prophecy of Isaiah*, 430.

27. BAGD, 482.

28. John R. W. Stott, *The Cross of Christ* (Downers Grove, Ill.: InterVarsity Press, 1986), 111.

29. Session XIV; chap. VIII. Cf. Hodge, *Systematic Theology*, 2:480–82.

30. K. Schilder, *Christ in His Suffering*, trans. Henry Zylstra (Grand Rapids: Eerdmans, 1938), 157–58. The discerning reader will note my modifications of Schilder's fine insight.

31. W. F. Albright and C. S. Mann, *Matthew: Introduction, Translation, and Notes* (Garden City, N.J.: Doubleday, 1971), 322.

32. Cf. David Hill, *The Gospel of Matthew* (London: Oliphants, 1972), 339. Matthew's *peri* here approaches *hyper* in sense. Mark 14:24 does have *hyper* (Robert H. Gundry, *Matthew: A Commentary on His Literary and Theological Art* [Grand Rapids: Eerdmans, 1982], 528). He takes the "many" to be the elect. Space limitations prevent the writer discussing the reference of "many" in the debate over the intent of the Atonement. After noting the connection with Isaiah 53, Jeremias concludes that Jesus "died for all, for reconciliation of the world" (*TDNT*, 6:543). He is followed in this by I. Howard Marshall (*The Work of Christ* [Palm Springs: Ronald N. Haynes, 1969], 42). Tom Wells (*A Price for a People: The Meaning of Christ's Death* [Edinburgh: Banner of Truth, 1992], 73–75, 137–45), in response to Jeremias, has argued deftly and persuasively that Jeremias's data may just as easily refer to the totality of the community referred to in Isaiah 53, that is, the community of the godly remnant there, who confess their sin and acknowledge the Servant's suffering for them.

33. It is likely that the term *many* is an echo, an allusion, to Isaiah 53:11–12, indicating that our Lord thought of Himself as the Servant of the Lord (v. 12, "many"), "about whose substitution for sinners such wonderful things are said by Isaiah" (Stalker, *The Christology of Jesus*, 187–88).

34. F. Godet, *Commentary on St. Paul's Epistle to the Romans*, trans. A. Cusin (Edinburgh: T & T Clark, 1881), 1:252.

35. Cranfield, *Commentary on the Epistle to the Romans*, 1:201.

36. Ibid., 1:213.

37. Ibid., 1:217.

38. The debate over the meaning of the Greek term *ilastērion* here continues. Cranfield (*Commentary on the Epistle to the Romans*, 1:216–17) prefers "a propitiatory sacrifice." J. M. Gundry-Volk has mounted recently a vigorous defense of the meaning of "mercy-seat" for the term. I do not have the space to discuss the question, although it may be difficult for some to think of Christ as part of a piece of furniture. It is interesting for this paper that Gundry-Volk also considers the Day of Atonement ritual to be before the reader in the passage. See "Expiation, Propitiation, Mercy Seat," *DOPAHL*, 279–84. Cf. also Douglas Moo, *Romans 1–8*, Wycliffe Exegetical Commentary (Chicago: Moody, 1991), 232–36.

39. Cf. Dunn, *Romans 1–8*, 172.

40. The two words refer to divine election, the one stressing the special personal knowledge of God in electing grace (cf. Gen. 18:19; Jer. 1:5; Amos 3:2) and the other its destination, eternal glory (cf. Eph. 1:4; 2 Tim. 1:9).

41. The LXX reads *kai ouk epheisō tou uiou tou tou ayattētou di' eme*; it may be rendered, "and you have not spared your beloved son for My sake." A further connection might be made. In Romans 8:32 Paul says that God "delivered Him over for us all." The clause is an allusion to Isaiah 53:12 and its LXX rendering "His soul was delivered over to death." In other words, there is a connection between Romans 8:32, Genesis 22:16, and Isaiah 53:12. This would link the Isaac-Christ typology of Genesis 22:16 and the figure of the Servant of Jehovah we have discussed previously in connection with Isaiah 52:13–53:12, both contexts of penal sacrifice by substitution.

42. Moo, *Romans 1–8*, 583. For *hyper* Moo likes "on our side," although granting that it may refer to "the vicarious work of Christ" (Rom. 5:6–8). "In behalf of" is its usual meaning, but it is not easy to see how His sacrifice can be in our behalf without being in our place. An Abelardian type of atonement cannot ultimately deliver us. We need a more complete and fundamental remedy for our plight; we need a substitute to bear our sin and guilt. The comment of G. C. Berkouwer (*The Work of Christ*, trans. Cornelius Lambregtse [Grand Rapids: Eerdmans, 1965], 309) is accurate: "The sacrifice was fully 'in behalf of' because it took place 'in the stead of'" (cf. *TWNT*, 1:372–73).

43. Moo, *Romans 1–8*, 582–83. It is evident that the statement of Paul is harmonious with ideas of penal sacrifice and substitution. For further discussion of issues connected with Christ's death, see J. B. Green, "Death of Christ," *DOPAHL*, 201–9, and "Death of Jesus," *DOJATG*, 148–63; Leon Morris, "Atonement" and "Theories of Atonement," *EDOT*, 97, 100–102.

44. Gordon D. Fee (*1 and 2 Timothy, Titus*, New International Biblical Commentary [Peabody, Mass.: Hendrickson, 1984], 66) suggests that 1 Timothy 2:6 might be a "Hellenized form" of the parallel in Mark 10:45.

45. Augustine, *Enchiridion*, XXIV.97, XXVII.103.

46. Cf. Ethelbert Stauffer, *Christ and the Caesars: Historical Sketches* (1952; reprint, London: SCM, 1955), 142–91.

47. The verb *sphattō* is used to refer to our Lord's death only in Revelation (5:6, 9, 12; 13:8), and its use is taken from the familiar Servant Song of Isaiah 52:13–53:12 (see 53:7). In fact, the phrase "a new song" from this verse is a further connection with the Servant of the Lord in Isaiah, for the phrase is found in the first of the Servant songs (42:10; see G. R. Beasley-Murray, *Revelation*, New Century Bible [Grand Rapids: Eerdmans, 1974], 126–27). Cf. R. H. Charles, *A Critical and Exegetical Commentary on the Revelation of St. John* (Edinburgh: T & T Clark, 1920), 1:146–47.

48. Cf. Acts 21:16 (note the partitive expression).

49. See Charles, *Commentary on the Revelation of St. John*, 1:147; Henry Barclay Swete, *The Apocalypse of St. John: The Greek Text with Introduction*, Notes, and Indices, 3d ed. (Grand Rapids: Eerdmans, 1951, 1909), 81.

50. Jonathan Edwards, "Remarks on Important Theological Controversies," Chap. V.3 in *The Works of Jonathan Edwards* (1834; reprint, Edinburgh: Banner of Truth, 1974), 2:567.

51. John McLeod Campbell, *The Nature of the Atonement and in its Relation to Remission of Sins and Eternal Life*, 4th ed. (London: James Clarke, 1959), 135–36.

52. Brunner, *The Mediator*, 447.

53. Letham, *The Work of Christ*, 170.

54. John Owen referred to Grotius as "that Ishmael" (*The Works of John Owen* [London: Banner of Truth, 1967], 10:380).

55. Cf. Millard J. Erickson, *Christian Theology* (Grand Rapids: Baker, 1984), 2:790.

56. Clark H. Pinnock, "From Augustine to Arminius: A Pilgrimage in Theology," in *A Case for Arminianism: The Grace of God, the Will of Man*, ed. Clark H. Pinnock (Grand Rapids: Zondervan, 1989), 16–18.

57. Ibid., 25. Pinnock in a recent book ("Systematic Theology," in *The Openness of God*, ed. Clark Pinnock, Richard Rice, John Sanders, William Hasker, and David Basinger [Downers Grove, Ill.: InterVarsity Press, 1994], 117–18) has drifted so far as to deny the historic doctrine of God's immutability.

58. I do not have the space in this chapter to deal with the position that Christ's sub-stitutionary sacrifice did not secure an actual salvation for anyone but only made salvation possible to believers. B. B. Warfield (*The Plan of Salvation* [Boonton: Simpson, 1989], 97) has dealt convincingly with the claim. This is the type of substitution that was taught me by my first instructors in systematic theology. Lewis Sperry Chafer, who was a strong spiritual influence on me in my early years and who was, indeed, a man of faith and a lover of grace, spoke of his beliefs as "moderate Calvinism." It was, in fact, something similar to Amyraldianism. Con-sistent Calvinism to him was full of "strained interpretations." And yet Chafer (*Systematic Theology* [Dallas: Dallas Seminary Press, 1948], 3:184–88) called the seeming inequity of judgment falling upon a person for whom Christ had borne eternal judgment by substitution "one more mystery which the finite mind can-not understand"! This system, Warfield said, was logically inconsistent, unstable, and thus untenable. How profitable it would have been to have had John Owen's famous conundrum in my school days. (The "conundrum" is an argument con-structed by Owen in support of particular redemption. It has often been summa-rized and printed for handy distribution by those who support Owen's viewpoint. It is an argument that has not yet received an answer. For a summary of it, see Owen's *Works*, 10:249.)

59. Pinnock, *A Case for Arminianism*, 23.

60. J. I. Packer, "What Did the Cross Achieve?" *Tyndale Bulletin* 25 (1974): 37.

61. Peter Toon, *Justification and Sanctification* (Westchester, Ill.: Crossway, 1983), 140–44.

62. Cf. Berkouwer, *The Work of Christ*, 310–11.

CHAPTER
8
WHAT DOES
GOD KNOW?

Robert B. Strimple

O ther chapters in this volume have shown how contemporary evangelicalism's failure to submit to the Scriptures as the church's only sufficient and final authority for faith and life has resulted in the eclipse of the central doctrines of the Protestant Reformation. With regard to the issue before us in this chapter, however, the challenge brought today by some popular evangelical teachers is more radical still. Here Christians face the denial not simply of one of the distinctives of Reformation theology but of a fundamental truth held in common by every historic branch of the Christian church.

This denial relates to the most basic element of our Christian faith, namely, our doctrine of God Himself, especially His omniscience. This doctrine has historically taught that God is the One who declares the end from the beginning (Isa. 46:10), the God who perfectly knows not only the present and the past but also the future. For this reason the psalmist can confidently trust that "all the days ordained for me were written in your book before one of them came to be" (Ps. 139:16).

THE PRESENT CRISIS

The attacks on the doctrine of God's all-inclusive foreknowledge have been spearheaded by Richard Rice and Clark Pinnock.[1] Their boldness (chutzpah?) in denying this universally held Christian doctrine is truly remarkable, because they themselves recognize that, although Christian theologians have held differing views of the relationship between God's foreknowledge and His foreordination, and between God's foreordination and human responsibility, the entire broad historical stream of orthodox Christian faith has affirmed the comprehensive character of God's foreknowledge. They refer to the view they are rejecting as "traditional theism"[2] or "classical theism"[3] and readily acknowledge that this has been the theism of Roman Catholicism (whether Augustinian, Thomistic, or Molinist), Eastern Orthodoxy, Lutheranism, Calvinism, and, yes, Arminianism.[4]

These "new model" evangelicals state this quite clearly: "Like Calvin, Arminius affirms God's absolute foreknowledge, but unlike Calvin, he has no coherent explanation for it."[5] Nevertheless, Rice and Pinnock continue to speak of themselves as Arminians[6] and of their writings as presenting "a case for Arminianism,"[7] a "consistent Arminianism."[8] One may appreciate their recognition of the theological difficulties of historic Arminianism at this point (Rice: "Traditional Calvinists have a strong case when they argue that absolute foreknowledge excludes the freedom to do anything other than what God knows will occur"[9]; Pinnock: "I agree with the traditional Calvinists that strong omniscience entails strong predestination and also with Luther who argued precisely this against Erasmus"[10]), but it is unhelpful and even misleading to speak of a doctrine that denies God's absolute foreknowledge as Arminian. What that doctrine is (to put the correct historical label on it) is *Socinianism.*

OLD SOCINIANISM OR NEW EVANGELICALISM?

Many readers may never have heard of the Socinians. They were a small splinter group that arose shortly after the Reformation. Socinian churches were especially influential in Poland for a time; later the Socinian movement spread to England, where it was soon absorbed into Deism and disappeared as a separate movement.[11] Socinianism is usually remembered for (1) its denial of the deity of Christ and (2) its denial of the need for a substitutionary atonement and for justification by the imputed righteousness of Christ. Socinianism, therefore, was considered a heresy regarding the person and the work of Christ.

But Socinianism also held to a heretical doctrine of God. The Socinian doctrine can be stated very briefly, and it must be contrasted with both Calvinism and Arminianism. Calvinism (or Augustinianism) teaches that the sovereign God has *foreordained* whatsoever comes to pass, and therefore He *foreknows* whatsoever comes to pass. Arminianism denies that God has foreordained whatsoever comes to pass but wishes nevertheless to affirm God's foreknowledge of whatsoever comes to pass. Against the Arminians, the Socinians insisted that logically the Calvinists were quite correct in insisting that the only real basis for believing that God *knows* what you are going to do next is to believe that he has *foreordained* what you are going to do next. How else could God know ahead of time what your decision will be? Like the Arminians, however, the Socinians insisted that it was a contradiction of human freedom to believe in the sovereign foreordination of God. So they went "all the way" (logically) and denied not only that God has foreordained the free decisions of free agents but also that God fore-knows what those decisions will be.

That is precisely the teaching of the "free-will theism" of Pinnock, Rice, and other like-minded "new model evangelicals." They want their doctrine of God to sound very "new," very modern, by dressing it up with references to Heisenberg's uncertainty principle in physics and to the insights of process theology (although they reject process theology as a whole because it "tends to stray from any biblical moorings and . . . returns us to Hellenism, where the world is not created but is eternally dependent on God"[12]). But it is just the old Socinian heresy rejected by the church centuries ago.

Right down to some of its most basic arguments, it is Socinianism all over again. For example, the oft-repeated affirmation by Rice and Pinnock is that they believe in God's omniscience, yes; but, after all, *omniscience* means knowing all that is knowable, and the free decisions of free creatures (and the consequences of those decisions) are not knowable.[13] This is not only an argument from Richard Swinburne (often cited[14]) but also a direct echo of the Socinian argument.[15]

Nowhere in the writings of the contemporary exponents of the "open view" of God, however, do we find a reference to the Socinian roots of their doctrine.[16] In Pinnock's narration of his theological pil-grimage "From Augustine to Arminius," he nowhere acknowledges that his doctrine of God has gone "beyond" Arminius to Socinus. Why not? Pinnock continues to speak of his thinking as "Arminian thinking,"[17] never as "Socinian thinking." Why? One cannot help but wonder if it is because the label "Arminian" has less objectionable theological conno-tations to evangelical ears.

Why is it important to recognize that this allegedly "new" doctrine of God is not new at all? Certainly not because being an old view makes it a wrong view, but that we might guard against the false notion that the "new model" evangelicals are presenting now for the first time some cre-ative new idea and that perhaps if our Reformation forefathers had only known these ideas they would have rethought their doctrine of God. Quite the contrary, our Reformation forefathers were presented with the modern Rice/Pinnock arguments in the form of Socinianism and clearly rejected them. Lelio Socinus pestered Calvin and Melanchthon with let-ter after letter in which he set forth such views,[18] and the Reformers rejected Socinus's views as untrue to the biblical witness.

GOD'S SOVEREIGNTY AND HUMAN FREEDOM

It is tempting to enter into a point-by-point rebuttal of the arguments presented for the so-called "open view of God."[19] Instead, I would like to present a brief, positive statement of the biblical doctrine regarding God's sovereignty and human freedom. I shall do that by making just *two points* (the first at some length, the second briefly).[20]

GOD'S SOVEREIGNTY IS NOT THE PROBLEM

The Bible never presents the fact that God orders all things according to the purpose of His sovereign will as a threat to human freedom. Rice and Pinnock see a great tension, even an impossible contradiction, between any affirmation of God's sovereign foreordination and an affirmation of man's[21] true freedom. The Bible does not. The insistence by these "free-will theists" that there is an irrational tension here—and thus we must choose which truth we shall affirm, God's absolute sovereignty or genuine human freedom—strangely echoes the concern that has been the driving motivation of modern atheism, whether in Ludwig Feuerbach (who influenced Karl Marx so strongly) or in Friedrich Nietzsche or in twentieth-century existentialist Jean Paul Sartre. We might call this a seesaw (teeter-totter) conception: if humans are to "go up" (be recognized for all that they are, as significant and valuable), then God must "go down." God is viewed by such thinkers as the greatest imaginable threat to the dignity and freedom of man.[22] But the biblical perspective is diametrically opposed to that notion.[23]

Modern atheism answers the alleged threat (solves the supposed tension) by declaring that God does not exist. Deism had earlier handled the alleged threat to human freedom by removing God from His creation once He had "gotten the ball rolling." Rice and Pinnock, on the other hand, present a supposedly reduced or "limited" removal of God from the picture. They refer over and over again to the fact that God does not know all the "details" of the future, that "some" actions are not under God's control, namely, those actions that result from human decisions and the consequences of such actions. Rice emphasizes that

> God knows a great deal about what will happen. . . . He knows infallibly the content of his own future actions, to the extent that they are not related to human choices. . . . And he knows the ultimate outcome to which he is guiding the course of history. All that God does not know is the content

of future free decisions and this is because decisions are not there to know until they occur.[24]

He even suggests that

> the openness that genuine freedom entails may actually constitute a small proportion of what will happen. . . . [Those future events that are certain to occur] would include divine actions that are not dependent upon circumstances in the creaturely world but arise solely from God's personal decision . . . [unrelated to] free creaturely decisions. . . . Genuine freedom in particular requires only that the future be open to some extent.[25]

Similar assurances that God knows much about future events and that it is only some "details" that remain unknown to God until they actually happen appear repeatedly in Pinnock's argument. But are Rice and Pinnock being candid with us when they emphasize the "modest" character of their proposal? Either they are disingenuous, or they have not thought through sufficiently the implications of their position.

Think about it. Just how "limited" is the part of this world's ongoing history that we are asked to see as not under God's control, nor even within His present knowledge? How many truly significant occurrences in our world are *not* the actions of human beings or the consequences of such actions? Pinnock and Rice give us surprisingly few specific examples of such occurrences—preferring to speak vaguely of "divine actions that are not dependent upon circumstances in the creaturely world." Perhaps the fact that the sun will shine on my picnic tomorrow would be one such event. But even a "natural" phenomenon such as whether or not tomorrow will be sunny in Southern California may well be determined by how much smog has been produced by how many automobiles whose drivers decided to turn the ignition key in the past several days. And, of course, at a global level, how could God know it as absolutely certain that someone would not have made this planet uninhabitable before tomorrow by recklessly unleashing a nuclear holocaust?[26]

Since this world, created and governed by a personal God, is personal to the core, that realm to which God's response could only be *reactive* to personal human decisions (in Rice's view[27]) is far more pervasive than Rice suggests—so pervasive, indeed, that his confidence that God will eventually work all things out for good, even though He cannot ordain by His eternal plan *any* action of man, woman, angel, or demon, seems without solid foundation. Rice speaks much about God's love: "God's unswerving commitment to the welfare of his creatures and his profound sensitivity to their experiences."[28] But his God can do nothing, in the final analysis, to ensure the welfare of any one of His creatures, either temporally or eternally. Pinnock insists that "if Plan A fails, God is ready with Plan B,"[29] but remember that in none of those plans is God free (according to Pinnock) to sovereignly and effectually call and regenerate the sinner. It is because God, on Pinnock's model, must wait for the sinner to do what the Bible tells us the sinner is *unable* to do (John 6:44, 65; Rom. 8:7) that marks out *every* plan for failure.

Other contributors to the book *The Openness of God* reflect further on the kind of confidence free-will theism can offer in the final triumph of the God of love. One thing, of course, is clear: no assurance can be offered to individual sinners. Any certainty must remain general at best, never personal. According to contributor William Hasker, "God governs the world according to *general strategies* which are, as a whole, ordered for the good of the creation but whose detailed consequences are not foreseen or intended by God prior to the decision to adopt them."[30] Therefore, David Basinger acknowledges that he "naturally find[s] prayers requesting even noncoercive divine influence in the lives of others to be very problematic."[31] And there is a poignant sadness to his conclusion at the end of the volume:

> There are certain risks involved. Things do not always turn out as expected or desired. But the God to whom we are committed is always walking beside us, experiencing what we are experiencing when we are experiencing it, always willing to help to the extent consistent with our status as responsible creations of his.[32]

The role of the God of free-will theism thus seems to be reduced to that of a well-meaning but essentially powerless grandparent, who desires the best for his grandchildren but can do little to bring it about.

In a response to *The Openness of God*, Timothy George speaks of "the vague hope that somehow good will triumph over evil," and he makes this comment: "But the 'open God' cannot guarantee that it will. He can only struggle with us against the chaos and keep on trying harder."[33] The argument that because God has a *limitless* number of plans (A, B, *ad infinitum*) we can be certain that His loving purpose for humankind will ultimately be fulfilled is guilty of the same logical fallacy as the evolutionist's insistence that given drafts of time sufficiently vast, mere chance could have produced everything, including human persons, who are the image of God. If a cause sufficient to produce the desired result is not at work at some point—and remember that the fundamental premise of free-will theism is that God must never "overpower" human freedom by transforming the hard hearts of sinners—that result will never be accomplished.

In order to emphasize the sharp contrast between the popular contention that, if God were truly sovereign and ultimately in control, genuine human freedom would be destroyed, and the *biblical* perspective, a little fish story may be helpful.[34] One day it occurred to this fish as he swam in the vast ocean with water all around him, on every side, that this water was hemming him in, cramping his style, limiting his freedom and his opportunity to fulfill the full potentialities of his "fishness." So he swam over near the shore, and he huffed and he puffed and he threw himself up on the beach. And he shouted out: "I'm *free* at last!"

But you and I know what was really the case. Almost with that very shout he was not free but *dead!* The water all around him had not been limiting his freedom as a fish or making it impossible for him to fulfill all the potentialities of his fishness. On the contrary, that water was the very element in which he lived and moved and had his being as a fish. It was the necessary and perfect environment in which to fulfill his fishness.

For us as human beings created in God's image it is, as the apostle Paul emphasized, in God that we live and move and have our being (Acts 17:28). It is a common misunderstanding to think that our "problem"—as far as being free and fulfilling our full potential as women and men created in God's image—is that God is sovereign, that He works all things according to the purpose of His will. *The truth is that the absolute sovereignty of God, far from rendering meaningless the freedom and personality of men and women, guarantees that their actions will be full of meaning.* The atheist, for example, has every reason to conclude that human actions are meaningless, ultimately of no significance, given his philosophic premise. But the fact is that men and women do not live in that kind of universe—an impersonal, chance-is-ultimate universe in which human actions take place in the vacuum of the unknown. They live in *God's* world in which God has ordained that the decisions and actions of His image (men and women) shall have *eternal* significance.

The ultimate test of any doctrinal formulation is to be found in its consistent faithfulness to the evidence of Scripture. Only in submitting, truly, to the authority of Scripture does evangelical theology honor the evangel itself. That is the test, ultimately, of this new "openness" proposal. What does the Word of God say? The simple fact is this: *The rela-*

tionship between God's sovereignty and human responsibility is never presented in the Bible as a problem. In Romans 9, it is true that the objector
to Paul's teaching tries to set it up as a problem: "One of you will say to
me: 'Then why does God still blame us? For who resists his will?'" (v.
19). If even Pharaoh was "raised up" by God (v. 17) so that through his
hardness of heart God's power might be displayed and God's name proclaimed in all the earth, who can be said to be doing anything other
than the will of God? Pharaoh certainly was doing God's will. Judas
Iscariot was also. Pharaoh and Judas were two of the greatest servants
God ever had! How then can God justly find fault with them?

But to think this way, of course, is to confuse the *decretive* will of
God, by which He has indeed foreordained everything that happens
(including Pharaoh's stubbornness and Judas's treachery), with the *preceptive* will of God (the moral commands of God), the revealed law of
God that tells us what our holy God delights in.[35] It is God's preceptive
will, found in the Bible, that is to be the guide for our life. It is that
which we are responsible to obey and justly held guilty for disobeying.
This is an important principle to remember as we seek to "know God's
will for our lives."

Our Lord Jesus Christ announced in Luke 22:22 that He, the Son of
Man, would go from that last supper with His disciples to His arrest and
crucifixion "*as it has been decreed*" by God. But does this fact of God's
sovereign foreordination in any way lessen human responsibility and
guilt? Not at all! Our Lord makes this quite clear as He immediately
adds, "but woe to that man who betrays him." Woe to him because he
will be held *accountable* for his sin; he will be judged by God, the holy
Judge; and he will be punished.

In Acts 2:23 the instructive conjunction of the two truths of divine
sovereignty and human responsibility again appears. The handing over
of Jesus of Nazareth to those responsible for His execution was "by
God's set purpose and foreknowledge"—a most clear and strong affirmation of the sovereign divine ordination of this evil act, the arch-crime
of human history, the crucifixion of the Lord of glory. But immediately
we read that it was through the agency of "wicked men"—*wicked*,
notice, because *responsible* for their action and *guilty* of the sin—that He
was put to death.

Acts 4:28 is quite similar. Herod, Pontius Pilate, the Gentiles, and
the people of Israel, when they met together to conspire against God's
holy servant, Jesus, "did what [God's] power and will had decided
beforehand should happen." But there is absolutely no suggestion that

those wicked sinners were anything but responsible and guilty for their evil conspiracy and heinous actions, and it is for that reason that they will suffer the penalty spoken of in that second Psalm to which Peter appeals here.

The objector whom Paul brings into the "debate" in Romans 9 asks, "Why does God still blame us?" Why does God hold us responsible? "For who resists his will?" (v. 19). If by His decretive will God has fore-ordained (and thus foreknown) whatsoever comes to pass, then none of us has ever done anything but what God has willed! What is Paul's response to this logic? He does not say something like this: "You know, you have a good point there. I never thought of that. I guess God's fore-ordination and foreknowledge cannot include the free actions of free creatures because, if they did, those actions would not be truly free and human beings would not be responsible before God for them." The answer the apostle Paul gives, by the inspiration of the Holy Spirit, is "But who are you, O man, to talk back to God? Shall what is formed say to him who formed it, 'Why did you make me like this?'" (v. 20).

Now, it is true that for our limited, creaturely understanding it does present us with an ultimate *mystery* in the sense that we cannot perfect-ly see through the way in which our acting as free, responsible agents is interrelated to God's acting. In reality, here is where the true *limitation* comes into the picture. It is not *God's* knowledge but *our* finite human understanding that is limited. The ultimate mystery exists for our limit-ed minds. That is true because of the two doctrines that the Bible every-where sets before us, sometimes in the same verse, as we have already noticed in Luke-Acts: (1) God is the eternal God who has foreordained (and therefore foreknows) whatsoever comes to pass; and (2) a man or a woman, His creature, is a *person*, that is, a free agent who acts on the basis of decisions that are his own and for which he and he alone is therefore responsible. And those two truths are the truths that "light up," so to speak, all reality and all our experience so that this mystery does not puzzle us or distress us but rather reveals to us what we need to know in order to worship and serve our God aright.

Consider the biblical doctrine of inspiration. The Holy Spirit's "car-rying along" the prophets so that they spoke from God (2 Peter 1:21), God's "breathing out" the Scriptures (2 Tim. 3:16), clearly reveals to us that there is absolutely no tension between the complete sovereign con-trol of God and complete human freedom. Indeed, the biblical writers were most perfectly free when they were most totally controlled by the Holy Spirit.

It is unclear how the inspiration of the Bible is to be understood from a "limited omniscience" perspective. Did God have to wait to see what the prophet or the apostle would pen next in order to decide whether that could be included in His inerrant, authoritative Scripture? Are we to picture God peering over Paul's shoulder and saying, "Oh, I like that! That's good! I want that in my New Testament"? John Sanders asks, "What sort of relationship can we have with a God who cannot act or communicate clearly?"[36] A good question. But how can the God of free-will theism communicate clearly through human words if He cannot control human decisions regarding word choice any more than other human decisions?

This is our first point, then. The fact that God is truly sovereign is not our problem. That is not what limits our freedom and our fulfillment of all that we should be as God's children. The all-embracing sovereignty of God is as much our proper element, as God's creatures, as the sea is the proper element of the fish. Our problem, as the Bible consistently sees it, is *our sin*, and this is my second point.

THE PROBLEM IS SIN

For our Reformation forefathers in the faith, the "problem" for man's free will was a *theological* (ethical) one, not a *philosophical* (metaphysical) one. When Luther and Calvin spoke of the human will being not free but in bondage, they did not at all mean that it was not free because the sovereign Creator and Sustainer of the universe has foreordained whatsoever comes to pass. Not at all! Rather, they were speaking of the fact that man, who was created holy and good (according to Gen. 1:31; Eccl. 7:29; Eph. 4:24; Col. 3:10), by the bad use of his free will lost both himself and it (as Augustine put it). That is, by his willful, voluntary sin, his rebellion against the sole authority of his Creator and Lawgiver, man became guilty before his God, incurring the penalty for his sin—death (psycho-physical, spiritual, and eternal death)—and sinners are in slavery now to sinful, depraved hearts.

We must emphasize as clearly as possible that it is not the fact of God's sovereignty but rather the fact of *man's fall* that has cost humanity freedom of will. But, again, this must not be misunderstood. Even the Fall did not alter the fact that man is a free agent, a person, not a robot or a merely instinct-driven animal. His decisions are from-within-determined by a decision of his own will. This is true of fallen men and women just as much as it was true of Adam. You see (as Luther put it), there is a vast difference between an *enslaved* will and an *annihilated* will.

Luther and Calvin preferred, however, to use the term *freedom* the way the Bible uses it when Jesus says, "If the Son sets you free, you will be free indeed" (John 8:36). Luther and Calvin preferred to speak of that freedom which is freedom indeed: freedom to do the good, freedom to do that in which God delights. That is what we mean when we speak of the freedom of God or the freedom of the saints in final glory. It is obvious that we cannot define the essence of their freedom as the so-called ability to do good or evil, right or wrong. True freedom is the power to do the truly good.

And that is what fallen men and women have lost and need to have restored by the grace of God and the power of the risen Christ. Yes, fallen men and women are still human, still persons, still "free" in that sense. But since their decisions are from-within-determined, from-the-"heart"-determined (in the biblical sense of that term), and since that heart is now a sinful heart, "deceitful above all things and beyond cure" (Jer. 17:9), the decisions of that heart may be many and various; but they are all tainted by sin and *cannot*, apart from God's saving grace, be anything different:

> The sinful mind is hostile to God. It does not submit to God's law, nor can it do so. (Rom. 8:7)

> The man without the Spirit does not accept the things that come from the Spirit of God, for they are foolishness to him, and he cannot understand them, because they are spiritually discerned. (1 Cor. 2:14)

As our Lord taught (for example, in His parable of the good tree and the good fruit and the bad tree and the rotten fruit, Matt. 7:17–18; 12:33–35), what is needed is a new heart. And a new heart is God's gracious gift, not man's attainment (see Ezek. 36:26–27).

This is the second of our two points, then. As the Bible sees it, our problem is sin, and our need is for the Savior and for His liberating, life-giving Spirit. True freedom is not simply a metaphysical human attribute. True freedom is God's gracious gift to those whom He, by the Spirit, makes His bondslaves in union with Christ.

It is nothing short of amazing—and most distressing—that the lengthy discussions by Rice and Pinnock concerning the freedom of the human will are totally silent on both these counts. They simply do not speak about the effects of sin or about the need for a Savior. They do not reflect on the fact that men and women as they are, apart from the special grace of God, apart from Christ, apart from the Holy Spirit, *cannot* make the right decisions. Reading their presentations, one would think

149

that sinners on their own can do all that is necessary to please and obey God. As a matter of fact, pleasing God and obeying God do not seem to be in the forefront of concern.

BUT WHAT DIFFERENCE DOES THIS REALLY MAKE?

Some readers may still want to ask, "After all is said and done, what difference does it make whether I view God as foreknowing all things or not? Perhaps this matter of whether or not God's omniscience is 'limited' is one of those esoteric questions that professional theologians get paid to debate but that 'regular people' need not concern themselves with." As many of the essays in this volume have emphasized, the importance of any single point of biblical doctrine is that biblical theology "hangs together." Pinnock himself recognizes that "no doctrine is more central than the nature of God. It deeply affects our understanding of the incarnation, grace, creation, election, sovereignty and salvation."[37]

In a 1989 essay tracing his personal "pilgrimage in theology," Pinnock describes the way in which he has had to rethink the atoning work of Christ.[38] In his 1990 book *Tracking the Maze*, he insists that such "orthodox doctrines" as "belief in plenary inspiration, vicarious atonement, the deity of Christ, etc." should not be "the litmus test" of what is true evangelicalism.[39]

The Reformers, on the basis of their biblical doctrine of God, presented a biblical doctrine of salvation. A Socinian view of God leads inevitably to a Socinian view of salvation, which is not the good news of salvation by God's free grace—by grace alone, through faith alone, in Christ alone, to the glory of God alone—but rather a message of salvation by one's own efforts, a false gospel that is not good news at all. It is the *gospel* that is at stake in this debate.

NOTES

1. See especially Richard Rice's works: *God's Foreknowledge & Man's Free Will* (Minneapolis: Bethany House, 1985); "Divine Foreknowledge and Free-will Theism," in *The Grace of God, the Will of Man: A Case for Arminianism*, ed. Clark H. Pinnock (Grand Rapids: Zondervan, 1989); and "Biblical Support for a New Perspective," in *The Openness of God*, ed. Clark Pinnock, Richard Rice, John Sanders, William Hasker, and David Basinger (Downers Grove, Ill.: InterVarsity Press, 1994). Also see Clark H. Pinnock's works: "God Limits His Knowledge," in *Predestination & Free Will*, ed. David Basinger & Randall Basinger (Downers Grove, Ill.: InterVarsity Press, 1986); "From Augustine to Arminius: A Pilgrimage in The-

ology," in *The Grace of God, the Will of Man*; and "Systematic Theology," in *The Openness of God*.

2. Rice, "Biblical Support for a New Perspective," 51. Rice (*God's Foreknowledge & Man's Free Will*, 10) presents his view as "an alternative to the traditional Christian understanding of God's relation to the world."

3. Pinnock, "Systematic Theology," 107.

4. Therefore, Pinnock ("Systematic Theology," 104) can understand why "some critics may speak . . . as if we were advocating a God other than the God of historic Christianity."

5. Rice, "Divine Foreknowledge and Free-will Theism," 122.

6. See *The Openness of God*, 192 n. 28.

7. This is the subtitle of *The Grace of God, the Will of Man*.

8. Rice, "Divine Foreknowledge and Free-will Theism," 123, 134. Given the significant difference between the two theologies, it seems surprising that true Arminians would join Rice and Pinnock in presenting "a case for Arminianism" instead of taking great pains to clearly distance their doctrine of God from what is now being called "free-will theism." See, for example, Jack W. Cottrell's chapter in *The Grace of God, the Will of Man*:

   > What enables God to monitor people's plans and include such permission in his eternal decree? The answer is his foreknowledge. . . . God has a true foreknowledge of future free-will choices without himself being the agent that causes them or renders them certain. . . . This is how God maintains sovereign control over the whole of his creation, despite the freedom he has given his creatures. . . . Unless God is in *total* control, he is not sovereign. . . . Now our question is, *How* does God maintain such control over a relatively free world? The answer is, through his *foreknowledge* and through his *intervention* in creaturely affairs whenever this is necessary to accomplish his purposes. . . . Nothing takes God by surprise." (pp. 111–12)

9. Rice, "Divine Foreknowledge and Free-will Theism," 128.

10. Pinnock, "God Limits His Knowledge," 156–57.

11. For convenient treatments of Socinian history and theology, see Thomas M. Lindsay, *A History of the Reformation* (New York: Scribner's, 1938), 2:470–83; Earl Morse Wilbur, *A History of Unitarianism: Socinianism and Its Antecedents* (Cambridge, 1945); Kenneth Scott Latourette, *A History of Christianity* (New York: Harper, 1953), 792–96; *The Polish Brethren: Documentation of the History and Thought of Unitarianism in the Polish-Lithuanian Commonwealth and in the Diaspora, 1601–1685*, ed. and trans. George Huntson Williams (Missoula, Mont.: Scholars Press, 1980); and Francis Turretin, *Institutes of Elenctic Theology*, trans. George Musgrave Giger, ed. James T. Dennison, Jr. (Phillipsburg, N.J.: Presb. & Ref., 1992), 1:208–12.

12. John Sanders, "Historical Considerations," in *The Openness of God*, 93–94. In the same volume Rice speaks of the "similarities and differences between process theism and the idea of God developed in this book" (p. 33); Pinnock concludes that "the problem in process theology seems to be the fact that it requires us to view the world as necessary to God" (p. 108).

13. See, for example, Rice, *God's Foreknowledge & Man's Free Will*, 32, 54, his chapter in *Predestination & Free Will*, 157, and "Divine Foreknowledge and Free-will Theism," 130; see also Pinnock, "From Augustine to Arminius," 25.

14. Richard Swinburne, *The Coherence of Theism* (Oxford: Clarendon, 1977), 175.

15. Francis Turretin (*Institutes of Elenctic Theology*, 1:208) noted, "They openly withdraw from him the knowledge of future contingencies as not being in the class of knowable things, saying either that he does not know them absolutely or only indeterminately and probably . . . (*Praelectionis theologicae* 11 [1627], p. 38). . . . And Smalcius in opposition to Frantzius." "But how can that be true which destroys itself and is repugnant to the Scriptures or does great violence to them? To say that God knows those things which are in no manner, such as future contingencies are, is to contradict himself; for what is knowable is not properly contingent, and what is properly contingent cannot be known (*Refutatio Thesium D. Wolfgangi Frantzii*, Disp. XXII* [1614], 436–37)."

16. For example, in his chapter in *The Openness of God* dealing with "Historical Considerations," John Sanders moves from a review of Augustine, Luther, Calvin, and Arminius to a survey of "modern" theology (divided into three categories: progressives, moderates, and conservatives), with no mention of Socinianism.

17. Pinnock, "From Augustine to Arminius," 28. This characterization of his theology as "Arminian thinking" comes near the end of a chapter in which Pinnock has rejected not only the Arminian view of God's eternal foreknowledge but also "the standard Arminian" explanation of election as being based on the foreknowledge of God, Wesley's view of total depravity, and the need for universal prevenient grace.

18. Lindsay, *A History of the Reformation*, 2:471.

19. Many helpful treatments of the biblical doctrine of God's foreknowledge are available, including such recent publications as Paul Helm, *The Providence of God* (Downers Grove, Ill.: InterVarsity Press, 1994), and S. M. Baugh, "The Meaning of Foreknowledge," in *The Grace of God, the Bondage of the Will*, ed. Thomas R. Schreiner and Bruce A. Ware (Grand Rapids: Baker, 1995). The latter volume contains valuable discussions of many other aspects of the biblical doctrine of divine sovereignty. Although William Lane Craig (*The Only Wise God* [Grand Rapids: Baker, 1987]) espouses the Molinist concept of "middle knowledge" that I myself find ultimately unsatisfactory, his discussion of many specific passages establishing the fact that "the biblical conception of God's omniscience includes foreknowledge of future free acts" (p. 37) is especially stimulating.

20. Some of this material appeared in the author's article on "God's Sovereignty & Man's Free Will," *Modern Reformation* (January/February 1993): 3–7.

21. The word *man* is used here and in what follows in the generic sense of "human being," "a human person," whether male or female.

22. Robert D. Brinsmead, formerly editor of the journals *Present Truth* and *Verdict*, whose own theological pilgrimage has taken him from Seventh Day Adventism through evangelicalism and Barthianism to arrive now at a humanism that extols "human freedom . . . a freedom grounded in the supremely human God," insists that "one of the greatest enemies of freedom is the old theism of traditional Christianity" (*Quest: A Publication of Human Freedom*, Essay 4, 1990, 2, 1). He also writes an essay entitled "Dare to Blaspheme and Dare to Be Free" in which he speaks of "The Tyranny of the Vertical Dimension" (*Quest*, Essay 1, 1989, 5–9).

23. Pinnock ("God Limits His Knowledge," 144) notes, "In the minds of certain atheists belief in divine sovereignty rules out human freedom and makes it impossible to account for evil in the world." What is disturbing to the Christian reader is that Pinnock *agrees* with those atheists.

24. Rice, "Divine Foreknowledge and Free-will Theism," 134.

25. Rice, *God's Foreknowledge & Man's Free Will*, 55, 56, 65.
26. It is not clear how Pinnock can even affirm that God controls all purely "natural" events, since he does not find it rational to say that the God who is love has ordained, or even "permitted," evil events in our lives, such as destructive earthquakes or ravaging floods.
27. Rice, *God's Foreknowledge & Man's Free Will*, 63.
28. Rice, "Biblical Support for a New Perspective," 57–58.
29. Pinnock, "Systematic Theology," 113.
30. William Hasker, "A Philosophical Perspective," in *The Openness of God*, 152.
31. David Basinger, "Practical Implications," in *The Openness of God*, 161.
32. Ibid., 176.
33. Timothy George, "Has God Been Held Hostage by Philosophy?" *Christianity Today* 39 (9 January 1995): 34.
34. I first heard this story told by my teacher at Westminster Seminary, Cornelius Van Til.
35. Paul Helm (*The Providence of God*, 132) has helpfully noted that a distinction between two senses in which we speak of "the will of God" appears not only in traditional theism but in free-will theism also:

    > Suppose for the moment that God's providence is "risky" and there are areas of human action (including human evil action) which God not only does not will, but which he does not know will happen until the events occur. Nevertheless, the events in these areas are *permitted* by God, albeit in a very loose and weak sense. For if God did not allow them, and in some sense support them, then they would not occur. . . . God then wills (permits) what he does not will (command). . . . So it is not an advantage of that view that it avoids having to think of God having two "wills."

36. Sanders, "Historical Considerations," 94.
37. Pinnock, "Systematic Theology," 8.
38. Pinnock, "From Augustine to Arminius," 22–23. In that essay he offers this apt illustration: "Just as one cannot change the pitch of a single string on the violin without adjusting the others, so one cannot introduce a major new insight into a coherent system like Calvinian theology without having to reconsider many other issues" (p. 18).
39. Clark H. Pinnock, *Tracking the Maze* (New York: Harper & Row, 1990), 184.

CHAPTER
9

EVANGELICALISM, CONVERSION, AND THE GOSPEL: HAVE WE SOLD OUR HERITAGE FOR RELEVANCE?

John D. Hannah

Something is out of focus in the life of the modern church. This is an observation that requires little reflection. A host of scholars—from sociologists, with their statistical and cultural analyses, to theologians, who are concerned over the loss of truth—have written about this. Pastors are increasingly providing more popular "jeremiads." Although the description of this malaise is disturbing, the discovery of the root causes that have brought it about are mind-boggling. The age-old truism is, I fear, proven correct once again: "We have met the enemy and he is us."

Michael S. Horton has stated my point succinctly: "The problem is, evangelical theology has become less evangelical and more modern."[1] In the past several centuries, and most particularly in this one, the church has struggled against the direct opposition of the Enlightenment[2] by developing a particular kind of polemics and by seeking to better present the gospel to the enhanced democratic sensibilities of modern man in a context of market-driven, pragmatic views of life and its meaning. In the process the church has adopted, quite unwittingly perhaps, the very assumptions of the Enlightenment. I believe the crisis that we face has been correctly observed by David Wells: "The stream of historic orthodoxy that once watered the evangelical soul is now dammed by a worldliness that many fail to recognize as worldliness because of the cultural innocence with which it presents itself."[3]

THE INFLUENCE OF THE ENLIGHTENMENT

Symptomatic of the influence of the Enlightenment is *the penchant to systematize and organize information*, which on the surface appears commendable. The problem is this: It often leads to distortions of the complexity of the problem through both simplicity and naïveté. It also leads to a mechanical, often lifeless, view of the Christian experience. James Davidson Hunter has suggested that, as a result of these influences, the church has increasingly become mechanistic in its approach to spirituality: "The spiritual aspects of Evangelical life are increasingly approached by means of and interpreted in terms of 'principles,' 'rules,' 'steps,' 'laws,' 'codes,' 'guidelines,' and such."[4] The result is a spiritual bareness of soul devoid of inner dynamic, namely, a personally profound experience of the life of God. It is a confusion of the historic facts of the faith without their spiritual meaning. It is the mind without the heart.

A second heritage of the Enlightenment is what Hunter calls *cultural pluralism*. Os Guinness denominates this as secularism.[5] The fruit of this, says Hunter, is the pressure to be tolerant, nonconfrontative, and concessive. "This has entailed a softening and a polishing of the more hard-line and barbed elements of the orthodox Protestant world view. . . . It has been culturally edited to give it the qualities of sociability and gentility."[6] To parrot David Wells's judgment of the church at large, and I have in mind the evangelical one, theology is fast becoming "an embarrassing encumbrance." The doctrine of the utter otherness, or holiness, of God has been replaced by the idol of the moral self. God is slick and slack, happiness is the opposite of righteousness, sin is self-defeating behavior, morality is a trade-off of private interests, worship is entertainment, and the "church is a mall in which the religious, their pockets filled with the coinage of need, do their business."[7]

Thomas Oden describes the current state of the church as an "ecclesiastical swamp" produced by three intellectual sources. First, there is an intellectual immune deficiency syndrome (a marked decline of Christian content, with a hightened emphasis on the emotive elements). Second, there is an acceptance by many of the premises of modernity. Third, there is an obvious ignorance of the traditions' roots in classic orthodoxy.[8] Mark Noll laments the Manichean, Gnostic, and Docetic tendencies in evangelicalism that have produced an intellectual scandal by separating the mind from the heart, leaving the latter without moorings or direction.[9]

A third realm of influence, which a host of writers have picked up on, is *structural pluralism*, or *privatization*. This circumstance "creates a situation that limits the relevance of religious symbols and meaning to certain sectors of social experience."[10] The Enlightenment reduced the world of "reality and truth" to the private sphere of the individual self and at the same time suggested that individual well-being and pleasure are the key elements in spiritual maturity. It gave birth to a number of descriptive phrases prevalent in our day, such as the Therapeutic State or the Psychological Man. This has become the Age of Self-Esteem and Self-Fulfillment, the Golden Era of Exoneration. It seems to many to be a grand new period in church history. I think it is an unprecedented one, where exalted feelings and a positive, overconfident, narcissistic view of the self are perceived as spirituality.[11]

David Wells is eloquent in describing the socialization and moralization of evangelical life and thought. He suggests that evangelicalism is "losing its character, if not its soul," as theological content is substituted with psychological insight in the pulpits. The clergy strive to be relevant while Christianity is continually being conceived of as "one more expression of the self movement." All this is tragic, for evangelicalism increasingly appears to stand under the same judgment as turn-of-the-century liberalism, which also berated doctrine while stressing morals and culture.[12]

The root of modernity, the Enlightenment, which we have been conditioned to despise publicly and to embrace privately, calls for sobriety and reflection. Statistics give us a confusing medley of conflicting impressions. There seems to be vast numerical strength in the churches, yet an appalling ignorance and superficiality at the same time. After studying the spiritual perspectives of Americans, George Barna concluded that "they do not take these [religious] perspectives so seriously as to integrate them into the fabric of their lives. . . . Most Americans have little depth to their religious reflections. . . . The average American . . . is neither a deep theological thinker nor worries about the importance of developing life-shaping religious convictions."[13] Barna adds, "Many who call themselves Christians have no clue as to the truth about sin and salvation, about the Resurrection and Redemption. . . . Look beyond people's words to the spiritual fruit of their lives."[14]

One writer, observing the current state of the church, could only repine, "Given Evangelicalism's accommodation to modernity, can it seriously maintain its claim of falling in the line of orthodox succession?"[15] Hunter, writing in the early 1980s, wondered if cultural concessions would ultimately lead to real doctrinal compromise; it would seem that in the 1990s it has. It is David Wells's judgment that "we need reformation, not revival. The habits of the modern world, now so ubiquitous in the evangelical world, need to be put to death, not given new life. They need to be rooted out, not simply papered over with fresh religious enthusiasm."[16]

It is now the time, if God should grant us mercy, to seek recovery from the "enlightened" secularism that has rushed headlong into the church. Yet, where do we go for examples and models of saints who have actively engaged in the defense of the Christian faith? Personally, I can think of no better model for the recovery of our roots in classic orthodoxy than the works of Jonathan Edwards. Here we find the greatest evangelical American mind in our history. He was one of the truly profound thinkers of the last several centuries. His thinking was anything but anti-intellectual. And he never made a dichotomy between the heart and the mind, between piety and theology.

To put forward Edwards as a paradigm for the church in our present crisis, I will focus on his understanding of the gospel. I will stress how he understood the miracle of true conversion, both its meaning and its experience. Lacking in evangelical theology today is the centrality of the Cross of Christ and the dethronement of the self. In the judgment of the contemporary church, self-esteem is often the focus of our worship. Whereas Christ, Calvary, and sin are deliberately treated as subjects to be approached with caution, political correctness, user-friendliness, and nonconfrontation are all contemporary essentials. One Christian philosopher has struck a responsive chord concerning these issues: "The newer language of Zion fudges: 'Let us confess our problem with human relational adjustment dynamics, and especially our feebleness in networking.'. . . 'Peanut Butter Binge' and 'Chocolate Decadence' are sinful; lying is not. The measure of sin is caloric."[17]

JONATHAN EDWARDS, GOD'S BEAUTY, AND CONVERSION

As a historical theologian I am convinced that Jonathan Edwards, arguably America's greatest theologian and the eighteenth-century pastor of the congregational church in Northampton, is a fitting mirror to put before evangelicalism today. The contrast between his view and ours is so utterly distinct. Though Edwards wrote a vast amount touching on a wide range of social disciplines—from psychology to ethics, from philosophy to metaphysics—he always wrote as a pastor-polemicist. As a pastor, the chief goal of his intellectual endeavor was the preaching of the gospel. Biographer Patricia Tracy has noted that "his chief professional concern was the saving of souls."[18] It seems strange by today's standards that the pastorate could once have been the most fruitful setting for the pursuit of the mind. It seems equally unimaginable in contemporary American culture to identify the life of the mind with the pastorate.

EDWARDS AND THE BEAUTY OF GOD

At the very center of Edwards's understanding of God and life is his concept of beauty, an aesthetic quality. The revelation of God to sinful creatures is a disclosure of Himself; thus, what God reveals is what God is, as far as His willingness to reveal Himself goes. Hence, the key to understanding his view of religion is to grasp his perception of God. This can only be expressed, properly, in the word *beauty*. Roland André Delattre has noted that "beauty is fundamental to Edwards' understanding of being."[19] God is beautiful to behold, full of excellence in symmetry and proportion. His divine essence consists of moral perfection, or holiness. He alone is lovely, tender, full of mercy. In one of his earliest sermons, Edwards exclaims, "God is an infinite excellency, infinite glory, and beauty itself; he is infinite, eternal, and immutable excellency; he is not only an infinitely excellent being, but a being that is infinite excellency, beauty, and loveliness."[20]

To know God is to know Him as He is. This knowledge consists in a cognitive and affective awareness of God. It was actually not the darker side of God's immutable attributes that Edwards sought to explain with his immense literary and mental skills in the pulpit at Northampton. (That side is known to all through natural revelation and conscience.) It was this overwhelming sense of the beauty and altogether loveliness of the Great Being that compelled Pastor Edwards to labor so arduously for the souls of his listeners. Delattre has captured this point well:

> Although some of Edwards' impact on his own age and even more so much of his reputation in ages since his own rested upon his capacity to make the terrors of hell and separation from God real and apparent to his hearers, it was the divine beauty and the real good in God rather than the horrors following upon sin that he tried most passionately to make apparent to those in his spiritual care. It was the beauty of God and of all things in God rather than the fires of hell that most moved his mind to dialectics and his tongue to eloquence.[21]

From this fundamental starting point, that God is beauty, comes several crucial deductions that form the heart of Edwards's perception of reality.

First, God is triune (not singular), contrary to the contemporary insights of Unitarians and Deists. Beauty and excellency can only be a result of relationship, communication, and excellency (which is seen in proportion and expression). God is singularly lovely and ravishing to the intellect because of the complexity of His repetition.

Second, since God created the material universe, including mankind, to glorify Himself, creation is an extension and manifestation of God. This means that creation is a revelation of Himself so that He might behold the beauty of Himself. This is Edwards's profound insight into the meaning of the belief that man was created for the glory of God. In one of his early miscellanies, he noted,

> For God to glorify himself is to discover himself in his works, or to communicate himself in his works, which is all one. . . . He loves to see himself, his own excellencies and glories, appearing in his works, loves to see himself communicated. And it was his inclination to communicate himself that was a prime motive of his creating the world. His own glory was the ultimate [end], himself was his end; that is, himself communicated."[22]

Third, both creation and Jesus Christ, who is revealed by the Spirit in and through the Bible, are mirrors, in varying degrees, of the perfections of God. Nature is the beauty of God in shadowed form; Christ is the perfection of the shadows and the ultimate revelation of beauties.

EDWARDS AND CONVERSION

The very essence of being a Christian, according to Edwards, has to do with the knowledge of God in the innermost part of the human soul. It is this perception of God as beauty that utterly ravishes the soul with delight.

> The highest end and happiness of men is to view God's excellency, to love and receive expressions of his love and that therefore their greatest business is to meditate [on] and use means to understand God's bounty, and to express suitably their love; this love including all those other affections which depend upon it, and are necessarily connected with it, which we call worship.[23]

This knowledge is mediated through the gospel[24] and is a great divine miracle of the revelation of God in Christ to the heart and the mind. First, there must be the revelation of God to the mind; then there is this affective, delightful, and willful submission of the soul, the inward being, to this God-given revelation in the gospel itself.

The disclosure of beauty. Grace, in the soul, is a matter of having it put there by the sovereign mercies of God. It is the act of receiving grace that must be preceded by the principle of grace. Natural man cannot have a principle of the beauty and the amiableness of holiness simply because he has no idea of its existence. The natural man cannot see because "he has not the ideas in the mind," that is, any awareness of the beauty and loveliness of God.[25] The disclosure of the moral beauties of God is a matter of a "divine and supernatural light" revealed in the innermost recesses of the soul. It enraptures, ravishes with desire, and floods the soul with true delight. The lost individual is not in this desperate condition because he/she is without sufficient faculties of reason and will. No, it is because, in the state of adversity to God and His beauty, he/she responds with vileness and contempt. Humanity is without a true mental awareness of the true God. People do not have a knowledge of God as He truly is, so they simply cannot embrace what, to them at least, is nonexistent!

The problem is not in the ability to embrace Christ; it is in an ignorance that is completely due to moral blindness. This category of beauty really does exist, but sinful people crave the shadow of it in all the wrong places (i.e., selfishness, pleasure).

> 'Tis no wonder the wicked man sees not the amiableness of holiness; for he has not that idea that is expressed by the [word] "holy," by the name holiness. 'Tis not because their minds are not apt to be delighted with harmony and proportion as others, but because they have not those ideas in which the sweet harmony exists; and it's impossible they should, because they never obtained them by internal sense and experience.[26]

The miracle of *category creation* (i.e., the dawning of the idea of God as beauty), the revelation of God's holiness and beauty in the soul, comes through the preaching, or heralding, of the gospel of Christ. It is only in the preaching of Christ that true spiritual light will ever fill the soul (for the mind must have the data to evaluate and choose). This Edwards describes as the doctrine of regeneration, which must precede conversion (or turning) precisely because one must have an object to turn to in order to properly turn away from something else. Regeneration is, spiritually, "an opening of the eyes"—an opening of the eyes to the beauty of Christ and God found in the gospel.

The perception of beauty. The disclosure of light to the soul is the revelation of the marvelous mercies and provisions of Christ for the sinner. Shadows of beauty become beauty itself, combining both perception and true experience. The new birth occurs in an instant. In it the sinner is granted a spiritual perception of the beauty of a dying substitute and willingly embraces God's grace. This regeneration of the soul is an aesthetic experience.[27]

161

Hence we learn that the prime alteration that is made in conversion, that which is first and the foundation of all, is the alteration of the temper and disposition and spirit of the mind; for what is done in conversion is nothing but conferring the Spirit of God. . . . Indeed the first act of the Spirit of God or the first that this divine temper exerts itself in is in spiritual understanding or in the sense of the mind its perceptions of glory and excellencies &c—in ideas it has of divine things and this is before any proper acts of the will.[28]

Terrance Erdt, another Edwards biographer, defines conversion in this context: "The feeling of love, the sense of the heart, that the saint experiences when in a certain frame of mind, is God the Holy Spirit. The saint's new disposition is itself the Holy Spirit, of the inclination of God, of God's love."[29] Edwards described the experience of conversion in several of his sermons to his Northampton congregation. For example, preaching on Romans 2:10 in 1735, he said,

When a person is converted, he has the image of God stamped on him. . . . They have their eyes opened, and are led into such a sight of God and acquaintance with him, as changes the soul into the image of God's glory . . . . For though the image of God in Christians in this world is very imperfect, yet it is real. The real image of God is most excellent, though it be most imperfect. . . . The image of God is a greater beauty in [the angels'] eyes than the brightness and glory of the sun in the firmament. . . . This holy spark is put into the soul in conversion, and God maintains it there.[30]

The act of embracing Christ, who is revealed in the soul, is an act that engages the entirety of man's being: the intellect, emotion, and will. This means that man is not in the least a passive agent. As Edwards defines ability or power (i.e., the ability to do as one pleases), the sinner's difficulty is not in a proper inability to embrace the Savior; it is in a proper unwillingness to do so. That unwillingness is not because of a lack of ability to function willfully; it is because the will is without a holy, beautiful object to embrace. His assumption is that a person makes choices, freely based on self-interest or the potential for pleasurableness. The real difficulty is not in a person's inability to will or choose; it is his utter blindness to Christ. How can one choose what he does not perceive as extant?

Salvation entails a pleasurable vision of Christ that at once causes the sinner to desire to come to its beauty; thus, the sinner freely and willingly comes to his Savior. Edwards describes faith as "our voluntary delegation of Christ to represent us, a hearty choosing of him as Mediator."[31] Elsewhere, he defines faith this way: "As in other things 'tis the dictate of the understanding, in conjunction with the clearness and liveliness of the idea, that determines the will, so it is in heavenly things: 'tis the determination of the understanding that the offer of the gospel is true, in conjunction with a clear and sensible idea of the excellence of it, that is true faith."[32] Conrad Cherry defines Edwards's concept of faith as "loving the God who reveals himself in the Word."[33]

As God is by nature beauty and as the experience of redemption is the relishing experience of amiableness and loveliness, true religion must be experienced at the affectional level. To be a Christian means, very genuinely, that one has fallen in love with God; that he or she has come to an intellectual and personal experience of the reality of God's presence as beauty and delight. The positive experience of God is a rational and emotional delight in the beauty of His holiness; the negative experience is that of conviction and repentance. Edwards wrote: "There are these three things necessary: (1) to see our danger of eternal misery, (2) to see the absolute necessity of a savior, and (3) to see the sufficiency and excellency of the Savior that is offered. The first is given in conviction, the second in humiliation, the third in conversion."[34]

The unbeliever is able to perceive the idea of the greatness of God but not the excellencies of His being. His greatness, when understood, may lead to the conviction of the justice of condemning and punishing sin but never to the discovery of God's mercies. Conviction is designed to cause the troubled sinner to flee to God, pleading for His mercy. Of repentance Edwards wrote, "'Tis God's manner, before the bestowal of some signal blessing and remarkable manifestation of his favor, to humble men by showing them the evil of their own hearts and how little they deserve his favor, and to teach them their dependence upon him."[35] Cherry summarizes the point: "One must still distinguish between faith and repentance since their immediate objects are different: repentance has reference primarily to the evil to be delivered from (sin), while faith has reference to both evil to be delivered from and good to be obtained (salvation)."[36] It is an experience that transforms the entirety of the person!

The manifestation of beauty. To embrace Christ is an activity of the entire being. The sight of the beauty of God will be revealed in the altogether loveliness of Christ. This is done in faith, which is a bond between the soul and Christ, wherein the saint becomes a partaker of the very character of Christ through the Spirit. How can one be genuinely moved to embrace a person as the highest object of pleasure and delight and not be morally changed and motivated toward that object in the process? How can anyone receive the Holy Spirit, who is love, and not manifest that characteristic?

In the 1738 work *Charity and Its Fruits*, Edwards states, "The Spirit of God is the spirit of love. And therefore when the Spirit of God enters the soul, love enters. God is love, and he who has God dwelling in him by his Spirit will have love dwelling in him."[37] To know the Lord Jesus in His redemptive office is to earnestly seek conformity to Him in this life, while being pained by every act of disconformity or sin. Or, if true religion consists in holy affections, as Edwards insists in *A Treatise Concerning Religious Affections*,[38] how can one have a true, biblical faith without a moral striving to express that love for the beauty of Christ, which is the essence of it?

In one of Edwards's New York sermons, "The Way of Holiness," which Wilson Kimnach cites as a paradigm of his earliest reflections on the meaning of conversion,[39] he sought to explain to his congregation the reality of salvation. The criteria is clearly a delighting in the Lord that is both mental and moral.

> Meditate on the holiness of God and see if you cannot see a conformity, a likeness in your mind. There is no likeness or comparison in degree—we speak not of that—but yet there is a likeness in nature between God and the soul of the believer. . . . See if you see any resemblance in your life to the life of Christ. It is not supposed that ever any copy comes near this original, nor ever will; but yet they may perceive whether the same spirit, the same temper and disposition, in a lesser degree be in them, that was manifested by the life and conversation of Jesus Christ. . . . Is there an agreeableness between your souls and the Word of God? The Bible is the epistle of Christ that he has written to us; now, if the same epistle is also written in our hearts that is written in the Scriptures, it may be found out by comparing.[40]

Edwards, unlike many in the modern church, did not segment or separate the mind from the spirit, the intellect from the will, desire from the actual doing. Man is a wholistic being that operates as a unit. He cannot be said to love the Lord with his passions, yet be devoid of actions that are consistent with them. Conrad Cherry has written, "Human violation is not to be broken into distinct and possibly contrary internal and external acts. . . . The body and the soul are a unity; the outer and the inner are united in the work. . . . The willing in practice is the performance of the act willed."[41] Actions are determined by an inward disposition, the heart; the external is the barometer of the invisible.

The Northampton cleric pondered the ground of true conversion, particularly in the context of the Great Awakening. The pulls and tugs of enthusiasm, on the one hand, were significant. Here was stressed the role of the internal, invisible, and subjective. On the other extreme was rationalism, with its emphasis on the cognitive, visible, and moral. Edwards worked through these issues, and his thought seems to culminate in *A Treatise Concerning Religious Affections*. Here he is, properly, the defender of neither enthusiasm nor rationalism. Three of his major works actually touch upon this subject, not to mention sermonic material, short works, and the *Miscellanies*. In this material we are given witness to the importance of the evidence of a true work of God in all of His endeavors. The essence of Edwards's argument is captured well by Cherry: "The deed is the best test of religious sincerity."[42]

In an unpublished notebook, "Signs of Grace or Signs of Godliness," assembled by Edwards in the 1730s, he includes "bridling the tongue," "thirsting after spiritual food," and "a merciful spirit & practice" as evidence of a true profession of faith in Christ.[43] He notes in cryptic lines: "We know whether we have the Spirit of X by the fruit of it we are told what they be Gal 5; . . . The fruit of grace in the life must be the proper evidence of it"; and "There must be a change in man; he in heart and life must be changed."[44] This early evidence indicates that Edwards would have found it incredible to suggest that the Spirit of God, the Spirit who is love, could dwell in the recesses of the heart and not leave an indelible trace of His character on the life. Simply put, it is utterly impossible that a renovated willingness would be unwilling to conform to the object of its highest and dearest affection.

The publication of the 1741 sermon delivered at Yale College titled "The Distinguishing Marks of a Work of the True Spirit" is an Edwardsean defense of the Great Awakening, which was, at that time, still in progress. Though Edwards does not explicitly take up the evidence of an individual's state in grace but seeks to vindicate the Awakening as a movement of God, he does touch upon evidences that relate to the subject of individual assurance. The assumption is that redemption has more than internal evidences—as the root so the fruit. Humility and love are not qualities that one can fail to manifest if he is in possession of them, and the devil cannot counterfeit them, says Edwards. Of this fifth sign of a true work of God, he comments:

The surest character of true divine supernatural love, distinguishing it from counterfeits that do arise from a natural self-love, is that Christian virtue shines in it, that does above all others renounce and abase and annihilate self, viz. humility. Christian love, or true charity, is a humble love.
. . . When therefore we see love in persons attended with a sense of their own littleness, weakness, and utter insufficiency; and so self-diffidence, self-emptiness, self-renunciation, and poverty of spirit, there are the manifest tokens of the Spirit of God.[45]

Edwards's major treatise on the subject of proper evidence of true Christian profession is *A Treatise Concerning Religious Affection* (1746). This work is "his most acute and detailed treatment of the central task of defining the soul's relation to God."[46] Although Edwards clearly states that there are no infallible evidences[47] of the gracious state or the possession of spiritual life, there are evidences—the chief among them, the twelfth positive sign, is Christian practice: "Passing affections easily produce words; and words are cheap; and godliness is more easily feigned in words than in actions. Christian practice is a costly, laborious thing. . . . Godliness consists not in a heart which intends to do the will of God, but in a heart that does it."[48]

The sight of the beauty of God in the soul is not only a conforming light; it is a reflecting light as well. The light that has shone in the soul of a person of necessity shines forth from it revealing the quality and character of that light. One cannot desire to love and embrace God with the mind and not also will and desire conforming and submissive obedience.

THE BEAUTY OF GOD AND CONVERSION DISPLAYED

That Edwards was primarily a pastor-polemicist, rather than a theologian, philosopher, or ethicist, is evident in his use of personal narratives. The story of experience is used as an illustrative device to further the validity of his argument. Daniel Shea, commenting on Edwards's use of his own personal conversion narrative, states what might be applied to his use of others as well: "By narrative example he will teach what is false and what is true in religious experience, giving another form of argument he carried on elsewhere; and he hopes to affect his readers by both the content and the presentation of his experience."[49]

In "A Faithful Narrative of Surprising Conversions," an account of the Awakening in the Connecticut River valley in the 1730s, Edwards selected the experiences of Abigail Hutchinson and Phebe Bartlett to demonstrate his argument. In the recounting of the former's experience of conversion, he speaks of "a sweet sense of the excellency and loveliness of Christ" and "a constant ravishing view of the glory of God and Christ."[50] The four-year-old Phebe exclaims, following her sudden alteration, "Mother, the kingdom of heaven is come to me" in the midst of an effusion of love.[51]

In the diary of David Brainerd, Edwards found some of his most extensive material to define the experience of conversion, both what it is and is not, as well as what it does and does not. Perry Miller refers to his use of the missionary as "another case history,"[52] while Norman Pettit states, "His use of the diary must be seen as part of a larger effort to answer a basic theological question: 'What are the distinguishing qualifications of those that are in favor with God and entitled to his eternal life?'"[53] Brainerd describes the instant of conversion as "a new inward apprehension I had of God," "divine glory that I then beheld," and "My soul was so captivated and delighted with the excellency, the loveliness and the greatness and other perfections of God."[54]

Sarah Edwards's spiritual experience is used by her husband in the defense of the Awakening in *Some Thoughts Concerning the Revival*. Although the description of her experiences do parallel those of a conversion narrative (i.e., a vision of the excellencies of Christ), they also rehearse the psychological experiences of a saint.[55] His description of her relationship with God as a thirteen-year-old girl provides keen insight into the experience of conversion since he wrote it in a period of his own intense attempt to describe it in his own experience. He speaks of her as "beloved of that great being" who "comes to her and fills her mind with exceeding sweet delight" "to be ravished with his love and delight forever."[56]

The most important description of the subjective experience of conversion in the Edwards material is perhaps that of his own, which is found both in his diary, which he wrote in the months surrounding his own conversion, and in his "Personal Narrative," which he crafted in the 1740s. Wilson Kimnach, writing of the conversion experience in 1721 during his earliest pastorate, where the issue was uppermost in his mind, states, "The New York period was, by his own account, the time of Edwards's greatest religious intensity. He might subsequently have become more learned, wiser and deeper, but he was never again to have had 'inward burning' in his own heart."[57] Though citing several stirrings of God that proved momentary and inconsequential, Edwards's conversion path was never as tortured as that of Brainerd's. He described the moment of conversion as follows:

The first that I remember that I ever found anything of that sort of inward, sweet delight in God and divine things, that I have much in sense, was on reading those words [in] 1 Tim 1.17 ["Now, to the King eternal, immortal, invisible, the only God, be honor and glory forever and ever. Amen"]. . . . As I read the words, there came into my soul, and was as it were diffused through it, a sense of the glory of the divine Being; a new sense, quite different from any thing I ever experienced before. I thought with myself, how excellent a Being that was, and how happy I should be, if I might enjoy that God, and be wrapt up to God in heaven, and be swallowed up in him.[58]

The description of his experience is the same in phraseology as in the other narratives cited. He speaks of "a new sort of affection," "a sweet burning in my heart, an ardor of soul," and of the perception of the "beauty and excellency of his person."[59] The experience is the perception by the entirety of one's being—the intellect, heart, emotion, and will—of the very being and character of God. It is nothing less than the revelation of the holiness of God in the inner being of the recipient. Says Shea: "At its center the 'Personal Narrative' focuses on the experiential realization that holiness is the divine attribute which primarily elicits the love of the saint. God's underived mercies could not, of course, be encompassed by words, it could only be loved."[60] Such an insight makes Robert Jensen's statement apropos: "Edwards' religion was from its root . . . a sheer adoration of God's majesty . . . a sheer beholding of God's beauty."[61]

CONCLUSION

Could it be that the "evangelical world," which has been so much defined by its opposition to the Enlightenment, has become lost in the very ideas it has sought to repel? The emphasis on "getting theology right," and with it the reduction of the immensely difficult and complex into quick and easy steps, seems to have considerably affected modern evangelical views of the gospel and its sufficiency. The stress upon the rationality and provability of the evangelical faith has seemingly robbed us of much of the inner dynamic of mystery and wonder, of reverential awe, and of our own littleness. In the quest to make the modern church more important to society, the church is finding itself less appealing to an increasingly apathetic world because it has little to offer that is distinctive. Our growing accommodation of the gospel message to immediate, felt needs, with the hope of attracting the less interested, may well cause the church to forget that its true work is about an indescribable miracle of God's grace and that its message is ultimately about something we can neither explain nor cause by self-effort and exertion.

The truth of the matter is this: In the seemingly irrelevant exercise of testimony and witness, in the weakness of a message preached, God still performs true miracles, even in a day when we are told that this does not happen because miracles have ceased. It is not too far from the reality of our situation to say that we seem cursed by God with a living fulfillment of the promise that He issued long ago through Amos: "'Behold, days are coming,' declares the Lord God, 'when I will send a famine on the land, not a famine for bread or a thirst for water, but rather for hearing the words of the Lord'" (8:11).

My plea is that Christians would again discover the importance and centrality of the gospel itself, that the message of Christ crucified would become the focus of the evangelical pulpit once again. Might it be said of the church today what was written of the experience of conversion in the life and ministry of Jonathan Edwards, the Northampton cleric:

> The importance of this experience goes far beyond the changes it wrought in his personal life, for it became the cornerstone of his whole structure of thought, determining the basis not only of his revival preaching, but also his religious philosophy. He first endeavored to search out the innerness of the experience and to understand it himself; then he endeavored to translate it into doctrine. The task was lifelong. One might almost say that out of a personal, emotional experience of his seventeenth year he built a theological system.[62]

NOTES

1. Michael S. Horton, *Beyond Culture Wars* (Chicago: Moody, 1994), 214.
2. The "Enlightenment" was an eighteenth-century movement regarded by Karl Barth, the famous theologian, as a reaction to Christianity's too strident insistence on the sinfulness of mankind, not originally an attack upon either the integrity of the Scriptures or the biblical record of Christ's life, death, and resurrection.
3. David F. Wells, *No Place for Truth; Or, Whatever Happened to Evangelical Theology?* (Grand Rapids: Eerdmans, 1993), 11.
4. James Davidson Hunter, *American Evangelicalism: Conservative Religion and the Quandary of Modernity* (New Brunswick, N.J.: Rutgers Univ. Press, 1983), 75; also see p. 76.
5. Os Guinness, "Sounding Out the Idols of Church Growth," in *No God But God: Breaking with the Idols of Our Age*, ed. Os Guinness and John Seel (Chicago: Moody, 1992), 163.
6. Hunter, *American Evangelicalism*, 87.

7. Wells, *No Place for Truth*, 300.

8. Thomas C. Oden, "On Not Whoring After the Spirit of the Age," in *No God But God*, 196.

9. Mark A. Noll, *The Scandal of the Evangelical Mind* (Grand Rapids: Eerdmans, 1994), 35–36.

10. Hunter, *American Evangelicalism*, 91.

11. Paul C. Vitz, "Leaving Psychology Behind," in *No God But God*, 97.

12. Wells, *No Place for Truth*, 137–38.

13. George Barna, *The Barna Report, 1992–93* (Ventura, Calif.: Regal, 1992), 44.

14. Ibid., 58.

15. Hunter, *American Evangelicalism*, 99.

16. Wells, *No Place for Truth*, 301.

17. Cornelius Plantinga, Jr., "Natural Born Sinners: Why We Flee from Guilt and the Notion of Sin," *Christianity Today* 38 (14 November 1955): 26.

18. Patricia J. Tracy, *Jonathan Edwards, Pastor* (New York: Hill & Wang, 1979), 4.

19. Roland André Delattre, *Beauty and Simplicity in the Thought of Jonathan Edwards* (New Haven, Conn.: Yale Univ. Press, 1968), 1.

20. Jonathan Edwards, "God's Excellencies," in *Sermons and Discourses, 1720–1733*, vol. 10 of the *Works of Jonathan Edwards*, ed. Wilson H. Kimnach (New Haven, Conn.: Yale Univ. Press, 1992), 421.

21. Delattre, *Beauty and Simplicity*, 130.

22. Jonathan Edwards, *The 'Miscellanies,'* a-500, vol. 13 of the *Works of Jonathan Edwards*, ed. Thomas A. Schafer (New Haven, Conn.: Yale Univ. Press, 1994), 360–61 [#247].

23. Ibid., 291 [#127].

24. In a sermon preached prior to 1733 entitled "Great Guilt No Obstacle to the Pardon of the Returning Sinner," Edwards defined the content of the saving message of God as having three components: first, "That we should see our misery, and be sensible of our need of mercy"; second, "they must be sensible that they are not worthy that God should have mercy on them"; and third, "they come to God for mercy in and through Jesus Christ alone" (*Works of President Edwards*, ed. Isaiah Thomas, Jr. [1808; reprint, Worcester, Mass.: Isaac Sturtewart, printer, 1856], 4:423–24).

25. Edwards, *Miscellanies*, 289–91 [#126].

26. Ibid., 287 [#123].

27. Terrance Erdt, *Jonathan Edwards: Art and the Sense of the Heart* (Amherst, Mass.: Univ. of Massachusetts Press, 1980), 2.

28. Edwards, *Miscellanies*, 462–63 [#397].

29. Erdt, *Jonathan Edwards*, 40.

30. Jonathan Edwards, "Sermon on Romans 2:10," in *Seventeen Sermons*, vol. 8 of the *Works of President Edwards*, ed. Sereno E. Dwight (New York: S Converse, 1829–30): 228–29.

31. Edwards, *Miscellanies*, 218 [#33].

32. Ibid., 342 [#212].

33. Conrad Cherry, *The Theology of Jonathan Edwards* (Garden City, N.Y.: Anchor, 1968), 71.

34. Edwards, *Miscellanies*, 400 [#317].

35. Ibid., 385 [#295].

36. Cherry, *Theology of Jonathan Edwards*, 67.

37. Jonathan Edwards, *Charity and Its Fruits, in Ethical Writings*, vol. 8 of the *Works of Jonathan Edwards*, ed. Paul Ramsey (New Haven, Conn.: Yale Univ. Press, 1989), 132.

38. Jonathan Edwards, *A Treatise Concerning Religious Affections*, vol. 2 of the *Works of Jonathan Edwards*, ed. John E. Smith (New Haven, Conn.: Yale Univ. Press, 1959), 95.

39. Edwards, *Sermons and Discourses, 1720–1733*, 10:466.

40. Ibid., 477.

41. Cherry, *Theology of Jonathan Edwards*, 129.

42. Ibid., 133.

43. Jonathan Edwards, "Signs of Grace or Signs of Godliness," unpublished work from the 1730s (New Haven, Conn.: Yale Univ., Beinecke Rare Book and Manuscript Collection), [3].

44. Ibid., [3], [5], [9].

45. Jonathan Edwards, "The Distinguishing Marks," in *The Great Awakening*, vol. 4 of the *Works of Jonathan Edwards*, ed. C. C. Goen (New Haven, Conn.: Yale Univ. Press, 1972): 257–58.

46. Edwards, *Religious Affections*, 2:1.

47. Ibid., 2:340.

48. Ibid., 2:332, 348.

49. Daniel B. Shea, Jr., "The Art and Instruction of Jonathan Edwards' *Personal Narrative*," in *The American Puritan Imagination: Essays in Revaluation*, ed. Sacvan Bercovitch (New York: Cambridge Univ. Press, 1874), 160.

50. Edwards, "A Faithful Narrative," in *Works of Jonathan Edwards*, 4:195.

51. Ibid., 4:200.

52. Perry Miller, *Jonathan Edwards* (1949; reprint, Amherst, Mass.: Univ. of Massachusetts Press, 1981), 246.

53. Norman Pettit, ed., *The Life of David Brainerd*, vol. 7 of the *Works of Jonathan Edwards* (New Haven, Conn.: Yale Univ. Press, 1985), 22.

54. Ibid., 138–39.

55. Edwards, "Some Thoughts Concerning the Revival," in the *Works of Jonathan Edwards*, 4:331–41.

56. Ibid., cited in the introduction, 4:68–69.

57. Edwards, *Sermons and Discourses, 1720–1733*, 10:267.

58. Jonathan Edwards, *An Account of the Conversion and Religious Experience* (London: Printed by J. Matthews, 1780), 7.

59. Ibid., 8–9.

60. Shea, "The Art and Instruction of Jonathan Edwards' *Personal Narrative*," 169.

61. Robert W. Jensen, *America's Theologian: A Recommendation of Jonathan Edwards* (New York: Oxford Univ. Press, 1988), 15.

62. Ola Elizabeth Winslow, *Jonathan Edwards, 1703–1758. A Biography*. (New York: Macmillan, 1940), 74.

PART
4
FLASH POINTS
IN THE CRISIS

CHAPTER
10
HOW SHALL WE THEN WORSHIP?

John F. MacArthur, Jr.

Comedian Flip Wilson used to have a character in his repertoire named Reverend Leroy, who pastored The Church of What's Happenin' Now. In the early 1970s Reverend Leroy and his church were an outrageous parody. But, truthfully, the evangelical community these days is swarming with Reverend Leroys and churches that might aptly be named The Church of What's Happenin' Now.

There is almost no limit to how far some churches will go to be "relevant" and "contemporary" in their worship services. And nothing, it seems, is too profane or too outrageous to be fused with "worship."

The *Los Angeles Times Magazine* recently reported on one Lutheran church in Southern California that distributes flyers advertising their church service as "God's Country Goodtime Hour." The flyers boldly promise "line dancing following worship." According to the magazine article, "the pastor is dancing, too, decked out in Wrangler boots and Levis." The pastor credits the campaign with revitalizing his church. The article describes Sunday morning at the church:

> Members listen to sermons whose topics include the pastor's '70 Ford pickup, and Christian sex (rated R for "relevance, respect, and relationship," says [the pastor], "and more fun than it sounds"). After the service, they dance to a band called—what else?—the Honkytonk Angels. Attendance has been steadily rising.[1]

You might think such a scene is merely an aberration from an obscure or offbeat church. Sadly, that is not the case. Current church-growth theory has opened the door wide for such antics. It sometimes seems as if P. T. Barnum is the main role model for many practitioners of church growth these days. In fact, the following ad for a Sunday evening service appeared in the bulletin of one of the largest and best-known churches in the heart of America's "Bible belt":

Circus
See Barnum and Bailey bested as the magic of the big top circus comes to The Fellowship of Excitement! Clowns! Acrobats! Animals! Popcorn! What a great night!

This same church once had their pastoral staff put on a wrestling match during a Sunday service, even going so far as to have a professional wrestler train the pastors to throw one another around the ring, pull hair, and kick shins without actually hurting one another.[2] Again, these are not extraordinary incidents. Scores of churches are following similar methods, employing every means available to spice up their services.

Clearly, the corporate worship of the Lord's Day is undergoing a revolution that has few parallels in all of church history. The resulting crisis within evangelicalism cannot help but be profound in its direct bearing upon the health of thousands of our churches.

TRUE WORSHIP

A few years ago while preaching through the gospel of John, I was struck by the depth of meaning in John 4:23: "An hour is coming, and now is, when the true worshipers will worship the Father in spirit and truth; for such people the Father seeks to be His worshipers." I saw as clearly as I had ever seen before the implications of that phrase "worship . . . in spirit and truth."

The phrase suggests, first of all, that true worship involves the intellect as much as the emotions. It underscores the truth that worship is to be focused on God, not on the worshiper. The context also indicates that Jesus was saying that true worship is more a matter of substance than of form. And He was teaching that worship embraces what we do in life, not just what we do in the formal place of worship.

I interrupted the John 4 series at that point and did an extended topical study on worship. Moody Press graciously asked me to compile those messages in a book, which they published in 1983 as *The Ultimate Priority*. That survey of worship affected me as profoundly as any sermon series I have ever prepared. It forever changed my perspective on what it means to worship.

That series also signaled the beginning of a new era for our church. Our corporate worship took on a whole new depth and significance. People began to be conscious that every aspect of the church service—the music, the praying, the preaching, and even the offering—is worship rendered to God. They began to look at superficialities as an affront to a holy God. They saw worship as a participant's activity, not a spectator sport. Many realized for the first time that worship *is* the church's ultimate priority—not public relations, not recreation and social activities, not boosting attendance figures, but worshiping God.

Furthermore, as our congregation began to think more earnestly than ever about worship, we were continually drawn to the only reliable and sufficient worship manual—Scripture. If God desires worship in spirit and *truth*, then surely all true worshipers must fashion their worship in accord with the truth He has revealed. If worship is something offered to God—and not just a show put on for the benefit of the congregation—then every aspect of it must be pleasing to God and in harmony with His Word. So the effect of our renewed emphasis on worship was that it heightened our commitment to the centrality of Scripture.

SOLA SCRIPTURA

A few years after that series on worship, I preached through Psalm 19. It was as if I saw for the first time the power of what the psalmist was saying about the absolute sufficiency of Scripture:

> The law of the Lord is perfect, restoring the soul;
> The testimony of the Lord is sure, making wise the simple.
> The precepts of the Lord are right, rejoicing the heart;
> The commandment of the Lord is pure, enlightening the eyes.
> The fear of the Lord is clean, enduring forever;
> The judgments of the Lord are true; they are righteous altogether.
> They are more desirable than gold, yes, than much fine gold;
> Sweeter also than honey and the drippings of the honeycomb.
> (Ps. 19:7–10)

The point of that passage is, quite simply, that Scripture is *wholly sufficient to meet every need of the human soul*. It suggests that *all essential spiritual truth* is contained in the Word of God. Think of this: The truth of Scripture can restore the sin-damaged soul, confer spiritual wisdom, cheer the downcast heart, and bring spiritual enlightenment. In other words, the Bible sums up everything we need to know about truth and righteousness. Or, as the apostle Paul wrote, Scripture is able to equip us for every good work (2 Tim. 3:17).

That series on Psalm 19 marked another decisive moment in our church's life. It brought us face-to-face with the Reformers' principle of *sola Scriptura*—Scripture alone. In an age when many evangelicals seem to be turning en masse to worldly expertise in the areas of psychology, business, politics, public relations, and entertainment, we were pointed back to Scripture as the only source for infallible spiritual truth. That had an impact on every aspect of our church life—including our worship.

THE SUFFICIENCY OF SCRIPTURE
TO REGULATE WORSHIP

How does the sufficiency of Scripture apply to worship? The Reformers answered that question by applying *sola Scriptura* to worship in a tenet historically called the *regulative principle*. John Calvin was one of the first to articulate it succinctly:

> We may not adopt any device [in our worship] which seems fit to ourselves, but look to the injunctions of him who alone is entitled to prescribe. Therefore, if we would have him approve our worship, this rule, which he everywhere enforces with the utmost strictness, must be carefully observed. . . . God disapproves of all modes of worship not expressly sanctioned by his word.[3]

Calvin supported this principle with a number of relevant biblical texts, including 1 Samuel 15:22: "To obey is better than sacrifice, and to heed than the fat of rams." He also appealed to Matthew 15:9, which says, "In vain do they worship Me, teaching as doctrines the precepts of men."

An English Reformer and a contemporary of Calvin, John Hooper, stated the same principle in this way: "Nothing should be used in the Church which has not either the express Word of God to support it, or otherwise is a thing indifferent in itself, which brings no profit when done or used, but no harm when not done or omitted."[4] And nineteenth-century Scottish church historian William Cunningham defined the regulative principle in these terms: "It is unwarrantable and unlawful to introduce into the government and worship of the church anything which has not the positive sanction of Scripture."[5]

The Reformers and Puritans applied the regulative principle against formal ritual, priestly vestments, church hierarchy, and other remnants of medieval Roman Catholic worship. The regulative principle was often cited, for example, by English Reformers who opposed elements of high-church Anglicanism that had been borrowed from Catholic tradition. It was the Puritans' commitment to the regulative principle that caused hundreds of Puritan pastors to be ejected by decree from Church of England pulpits in 1662.[6]

Furthermore, the simplicity of worship forms in Presbyterian, Baptist, Congregational, and other evangelical traditions is the result of applying the regulative principle. Evangelicals today would do well to recover their spiritual ancestors' confidence in *sola Scriptura* as it applies to worship and church leadership. A number of harmful trends that are gaining momentum these days reveal a diminishing evangelical confidence in the sufficiency of Scripture. On the one hand, there is, as we have noted, almost a circus atmosphere in some churches, where pragmatic methods that trivialize what is holy are being employed to boost attendance. On the other hand, growing numbers of former evangelicals are abandoning simple worship forms in favor of high-church formalism. Some are even leaving evangelicalism altogether and aligning with Eastern Orthodoxy or Roman Catholicism.

Meanwhile, some churches have simply abandoned virtually all objectivity, opting for a worship style that is turbulent, emotional, and devoid of any rational sense. Perhaps the most talked-about movement currently sweeping Christendom is a phenomenon known as the "Toronto Blessing," where whole congregations laugh uncontrollably for no rational reason, bark like dogs, roar like lions, cluck like chickens, or jump, run, and convulse. They see this as evidence that the power of God has been imparted to them.

None of these trends is being advanced for solid biblical reasons. Instead, their advocates cite pragmatic arguments or seek support from misinterpreted proof texts, revisionist history, or ancient tradition. This is precisely the mind-set the Reformers fought against.

A new understanding of *sola Scriptura*—namely, the sufficiency of Scripture—ought to spur us to keep reforming our churches, to regulate our worship according to biblical guidelines, and to desire passionately to be those who worship God in spirit and truth.

APPLYING *SOLA SCRIPTURA* TO WORSHIP

Immediately, practical questions arise about how *sola Scriptura* should be used to regulate worship. Someone will point out that no less than Charles Spurgeon used the regulative principle to rule out the use of any musical instruments in worship. Spurgeon refused to allow an organ in the Metropolitan Tabernacle because he believed there was no biblical warrant for instrumental music in Christian worship. Indeed, there are Christians even today who oppose instrumental music on the same grounds. In the church I pastor, however, we employ instruments of all kinds, from the trumpet and the harp to loud cymbals (cf. Ps. 150).

Obviously, not all who affirm the soundness of the regulative principle necessarily agree in every detail about how it should be applied. Some would point to such differences in matters of practice and suggest that the whole regulative principle is untenable. William Cunningham noted that critics of this principle often try to debunk it by resorting to the tactic of *reductio ad absurdum*:

> Those who dislike this principle, from whatever cause, usually try to run us into difficulties by putting a very stringent construction upon it, and thereby giving it an appearance of absurdity. [But] the principle must be interpreted and explained in the exercise of common sense. . . . Difficulties and differences of opinion may arise about details, even when sound judgment and common sense are brought to bear upon the interpretation and application of the principle; but this affords no ground for denying or doubting the truth or soundness of the principle itself.[7]

Cunningham acknowledged that the regulative principle is often employed in arguing against things that may be seen as relatively unimportant, such as "rites and ceremonies, vestments and organs, crossings, kneelings, bowings," and other trappings of formal worship. Because of that, Cunningham said, "some men seem to think that it partakes of the intrinsic littleness of things."[8] Many therefore conclude that those who advocate the regulative principle do so because they actually enjoy fighting over small matters.

Certainly no one should take delight in disputes over minor points. It is undoubtedly true that the regulative principle has occasionally been misused in this way, but concern for correct worship is not, ultimately, a minor issue. An obsession with applying any principle down to the smallest detail can easily become a destructive form of legalism, though that is not inherent in the actual concern for sound worship.[9] But the principle of *sola Scriptura* as it applies to worship is nevertheless worth defending fiercely. The principle itself is by no means trivial. After all, failure to adhere to the biblical prescription for worship is the very thing that plunged the church into the darkness and idolatry of the Middle Ages.

I have no interest in igniting a debate about musical instruments, pastoral robes, sanctuary decorations, or other such matters. If there are those who want to use the regulative principle as a springboard for such debates, please leave me out. The issues that spark my concern about contemporary worship are far larger than these matters. They seem to me to go to the very heart of what it means to worship in spirit and in truth. My concern is this: The contemporary church's abandonment of *sola Scriptura* as the regulative principle has opened the church to some of the grossest imaginable abuses—including honkytonk church services, the carnival sideshow atmosphere, and wrestling exhibitions. Even the broadest, most liberal application of the regulative principle would have a corrective effect on such abuses.

Consider for a moment what would happen to corporate worship if the contemporary church took *sola Scriptura* seriously. Four biblical guidelines for worship immediately come to mind that have fallen into a state of tragic neglect. Recovering them would surely bring about a new Reformation in the modern church's worship.

PREACH THE WORD

In corporate worship, the preaching of the Word should take first place. All the New Testament instructions to pastors center on these words of Paul to Timothy: "Preach the word; be ready in season and out of season; reprove, rebuke, exhort, with great patience and instruction" (2 Tim. 4:2). Elsewhere, Paul summed up his advice to the young pastor, "Until I come, give attention to the public reading of Scripture, to exhortation and teaching" (1 Tim. 4:13). Clearly, the ministry of the Word was at the heart of Timothy's pastoral responsibilities.

In the New Testament church, the activities of the believing community were totally devoted to "the apostles' teaching and to fellowship, to the breaking of bread and to prayer" (Acts 2:42). The preaching of the Word was the centerpiece of every worship service. Paul once preached to a congregation past midnight (20:7–8). The ministry of the Word was such a crucial part of church life that before any man could qualify to serve as an elder, he had to prove himself skilled in teaching the Word (cf. 1 Tim. 3:2; 2 Tim. 2:24; Titus 1:9).

The apostle Paul characterized his own calling this way: "Of this church I was made a minister according to the stewardship from God bestowed on me for your benefit, *so that I might fully carry out the preaching of the word of God*" (Col. 1:25, italics added). You can be sure that preaching was the predominant feature in every worship service he took part in.

Many people see preaching and worship as two distinct aspects of the church service, as if preaching has nothing to do with worship and vice versa. But that is an erroneous concept. The ministry of the Word is the platform on which all genuine worship must be built. In *Between Two Worlds*, John Stott says it well:

> Word and worship belong indissolubly to each other. All worship is an intelligent and loving response to the revelation of God, because it is the adoration of his Name. Therefore acceptable worship is impossible without preaching. For preaching is making known the Name of the Lord, and worship is praising the Name of the Lord made known. Far from being an alien intrusion into worship, the reading and preaching of the word are actually indispensable to it. The two cannot be divorced.[10]

Preaching is an irreplaceable aspect of all corporate worship. In fact, the whole church service should revolve around the ministry of the Word. Everything else is either preparatory to, or a response to, the exposition of Scripture.

When drama, music, comedy, or other activities are allowed to usurp the preaching of the Word, true worship inevitably suffers. And when preaching is subjugated to pomp and circumstance, that also hinders real worship. A "worship" service without the ministry of the Word is of questionable value. Moreover, a "church" where the Word of God is not regularly and faithfully preached is no true church.

EDIFY THE FLOCK

Scripture tells us that the purpose of spiritual gifts is for the edification of the whole church (Eph. 4:12; cf. 1 Cor. 14:12). Therefore all ministry in the context of the church should somehow be edifying— building up the flock, not just stirring emotions. Above all, ministry should be aimed at stimulating genuine worship. To do that it *must* be edifying. This is implied by the expression "worship . . . in spirit and truth."

As we noted earlier, worship should engage the intellect as well as the emotions. By all means worship should be passionate, heartfelt, and moving. But the point is not to stir the emotions while turning off the mind. True worship merges heart and mind in a response of pure adoration, based on the truth revealed in the Word.

Music may sometimes move us by the sheer beauty of its sound, but such sentiment is not worship. Music by itself, apart from the truth contained in the lyrics, is not even a legitimate springboard for real worship. Similarly, a poignant story may be touching or stirring, but unless the message it conveys is set in the context of biblical truth, any emotions it may stir are of no use in prompting genuine worship. Aroused passions are not necessarily evidence that true worship is taking place.

Genuine worship is a response to divine *truth*. It is passionate because it arises out of our love for God. But to be true worship it must also arise out of a correct understanding of His law, His righteousness, His mercy, and His being. Real worship acknowledges God as He has revealed Himself in His Word. We know from Scripture, for example, that He is the only perfectly holy, all-powerful, all-knowing, omnipresent source from which flows all goodness, mercy, truth, wisdom, power, and salvation. Worship means ascribing glory to Him because of those truths. It means adoring Him for who He is, for what He has done, and for what He has promised. It *must* therefore be a response to the truth that He has revealed about Himself. Such worship cannot rise out of a vacuum. It is prompted and vitalized by the objective truth of the Word.

Neither rote ceremonies nor mere entertainment are able to provoke such worship—no matter how moving such things may be. Those things cannot edify. At best they can arouse the emotions. But that is not true worship.

HONOR THE LORD

Hebrews 12:28 says, "Let us show gratitude, by which we may offer to God an acceptable service with reverence and awe." That verse speaks of the attitude in which we should worship. The Greek word for "service" is *latreuōmen*, which literally means "worship." The point is that worship ought to be done reverently, in a way that honors God. In fact, the King James Version translates it this way: "Let us have grace, whereby we may serve God acceptably with reverence and godly *fear*" (italics added). And the next verse adds, "For our God is a consuming fire" (v. 29).

There is certainly no place in the corporate worship of the church for the kind of frivolous, shallow, giddy atmosphere that often prevails in modern churches that seek to be "relevant." To exchange the worship service for a circus is about as far from the spirit of biblical worship ("in reverence and awe") as it is possible to get. "Reverence and awe" clearly refers to a solemn sense of honor as we perceive the majesty of God. It demands a sense of both God's holiness and our own sinfulness. Everything in the corporate worship of the church should aim at fostering such an atmosphere.

Why would a church replace preaching and worship with entertainment and comedy in its Lord's Day services? Many who have done it say they do so in order to reach non-Christians. They want to create a "user-friendly" environment that will be more appealing to unbelievers. Their stated goal is usually "relevance" rather than "reverence." Their services are intentionally designed to reach unbelievers with the gospel, not for believers to come together for worship and edification. Many of these churches give little or no emphasis to the New Testament ordinances. The Lord's Supper, if observed at all, is relegated to a smaller, midweek service. Baptism is virtually deemed optional, and baptisms are normally performed somewhere other than in the Sunday services.

What's wrong with all of this? Is there a problem with using the Lord's Day services as evangelistic meetings? Isn't the church to reach the lost week by week? Is there really a biblical reason Sunday should be the day believers gather for worship?

Both biblically and historically there are a number of reasons for setting aside the first day of the week primarily for worship and fellowship among believers. Unfortunately, an in-depth examination of all these arguments would be far outside the scope of this brief chapter. But a simple application of the regulative principle will yield ample guidance.

We learn from Scripture, for example, that the first day of the week was the day the apostolic church came together to celebrate the Lord's table: "And upon the first day of the week, when the disciples came together to break bread, Paul preached unto them" (Acts 20:7 KJV). Paul instructed the Corinthians to do their giving systematically, on the first day of the week, clearly implying that this was the day they came together for worship. History reveals that the early church referred to the first day of the week as the Lord's Day, an expression found in Revelation 1:10.

Furthermore, Scripture suggests that the regular meetings of the early church were not for evangelistic purposes but primarily for mutual encouragement and worship among the community of believers. That's why the writer of Hebrews made this plea: "Let us consider how to stimulate one another to love and good deeds, not forsaking *our own assembling together*, as is the habit of some, but encouraging one another" (Heb. 10:24–25; italics added).

Certainly there were times when unbelievers came into an assembly of believers (cf. 1 Cor. 14:23). First-century church meetings were essentially public meetings, just as most are today. But the service itself was intentionally designed for worship and fellowship among believers. The corporate preaching of Christ would sometimes bring unbelievers to acknowledge Jesus as Lord savingly, but normally it seems evangelism took place in the context of everyday life, as believers went forth with the gospel (Acts 5:42; 6:7). First-century believers gathered for worship and fellowship and scattered for evangelism. When a church makes all its meetings evangelistic, believers lose opportunities to grow, be edified, and worship.

More to the point, there is simply no warrant in Scripture for adapting weekly church services to the preferences of unbelievers. Indeed, the practice seems to be contrary to the spirit of everything Scripture says about the assembly of believers. When the church comes together on the Lord's Day, that is no time to entertain the lost, amuse the brethren, or otherwise cater to the "felt needs" of those in attendance. This is when we should bow before our God as a congregation and honor Him with our worship.

PUT NO CONFIDENCE IN THE FLESH

In Philippians 3:3 the apostle Paul characterizes Christian worship this way: "We are the true circumcision, who worship in the Spirit of God and glory in Christ Jesus and *put no confidence in the flesh*" (italics added).

Paul goes on to testify about how he came to see that his own pre-Christian Pharisaical legalism was worthless. He describes how he was once obsessed with external, fleshly issues—such as circumcision, lineage, and legal obedience—rather than the more important issue of the state of his heart. Paul's conversion on the Damascus road changed all that. His eyes were opened to the glorious truth of justification by faith. He realized that the only way he could stand before God and be accepted was by being clothed with the righteousness of Christ (v. 9). He learned that merely complying with religious rites—such as circumcision and ceremony—is of no spiritual value whatsoever. In fact, Paul labeled those things as rubbish or, more literally, as "dung" (v. 8 KJV).

To this day, however, when the average person speaks of "worship," it is usually the external things that are in view—liturgy, ceremony, music, kneeling, and other formal issues. I recently read the testimony of a man who left evangelical Christianity and joined Roman Catholicism. One of the primary reasons he gave for abandoning evangelicalism was that he found Roman Catholic liturgy "more worshipful." As he went on to explain, it became apparent that what he actually meant was that Rome offered more of the accoutrements of formal ritual—candle burning, statues, kneeling, reciting, crossing oneself, and so on. But those things have nothing to do with genuine worship in spirit and truth. In fact, as human inventions—not biblical prescriptions—they are precisely the sort of fleshly devices Paul labeled "dung."

Experience and history show that the human tendency to add fleshly apparatus to the worship God prescribes is incredibly strong. Israel did this in the Old Testament, culminating in the religion of the Pharisees. Pagan religions consist of nothing *but* fleshly ritual. The fact that such ceremonies are often beautiful and moving do not make them true worship. Scripture is clear that God condemns all human additions to what He has explicitly commanded: "In vain do they worship Me, teaching as doctrines the precepts of men" (Matt. 15:9). We who love the Word of God and believe in the principle of *sola Scriptura* must diligently be on guard against such a tendency.

WORSHIP *IS* THE ULTIMATE PRIORITY

To Martha, troubled to distraction with the chores of being a hostess, our Lord said, "Martha, Martha, you are worried and bothered about so many things; but only one thing is necessary" (Luke 10:41–42). The point was clear. Mary, who sat at His feet in adoration, had "chosen the good part, which shall not be taken away from her" (v. 42). Mary's worship had eternal significance, whereas all Martha's busy activity meant nothing beyond that particular afternoon.

Our Lord was teaching that worship is the one essential activity that must take precedence over every other activity of life. And if that is true in our individual lives, how much more weight should we give it in the context of the assembly of believers?

The world is filled with false and superficial religion. We who love Christ and believe that His Word is true dare not accommodate our worship to the styles and preferences of an unbelieving world. Instead, we must make it our business to be worshipers in spirit and in truth. We must be people who worship in the Spirit of God and glory in Christ Jesus and put no confidence in the flesh. And to do that we must allow Scripture alone to regulate our worship.

Notes

1. Judy Raphael, "God and Country," *Los Angeles Times Magazine*, 6 November 1994, 14.

2. E. Gustav Niebuhr, "Mighty Fortress: Megachurches Strive to Be All Things to All Parishioners," *Wall Street Journal*, 13 May 1991, A:6.

3. John Calvin, *The Necessity of Reforming the Church* (reprint, Dallas: Protestant Heritage Press, 1995), 17–18.

4. John Hooper, "The Regulative Principle and Things Indifferent," in Iain H. Murray, ed., *The Reformation of the Church* (Edinburgh: Banner of Truth, 1965), 55.

5. William Cunningham, *The Reformers and the Theology of the Reformation* (reprint, Edinburgh: Banner of Truth, 1989), 27.

6. The Act of Uniformity (1661) was given royal assent by Charles II shortly after the restoration of the English monarchy. It required every minister in the Church of England to declare unfeigned support of everything prescribed in the new edition of the Book of Common Prayer. Many ministers dissented and objected to the use of vestment and other extrabiblical prescriptions for how worship services were to be conducted. These men were summarily ejected from their pulpits and their livelihoods because of their stand for the principle of *sola Scriptura*.

7. Cunningham, *The Reformers and the Theology of the Reformation*, 32.

8. Ibid., 35.

9. At the same time, it is helpful to remember that some of the disputes we read about in church history were not as trivial as they may seem at first sight. There was a heated debate among early Protestants, for example, about the appropriate posture for receiving communion. Some felt that the elements should be taken from a kneeling position, but the followers of Calvin insisted that communion should be administered to people who are seated. The real debate had to do with an issue far more significant than posture. Roman Catholicism taught that the elements were the actual body and blood of Christ and therefore they should be lifted up before the people to be worshiped by them. During the Catholic Mass, when the elements are elevated, people are expected to kneel in worship. The Calvinists correctly saw this as a form of idolatry, and in order to make their own position clear they taught that the elements were the sign and seals of Christ's presence, not the actual physical body of the Lord Jesus. This meant that the elements were not to be worshiped and that the people should receive them while seated. The context of this debate is often forgotten by contemporary evangelicals, who sometimes wrongly characterize the Reformers as arguing about trifles.

10. John Stott, *Between Two Worlds: The Art of Preaching in the 20th Century* (Grand Rapids: Eerdmans, 1982), 82.

CHAPTER
11
HOW SHALL WE SING TO GOD?

Leonard Payton

We are, more times than not, a people defined by our music. We fight over it in the church. We change congregations because of worship music style, with little concern for the theology of the new or the old congregation. Whole denominations are embroiled in debate over worship music style with no clear outcome in sight.

We who are church music directors and worship pastors are being asked to become administrators of activities with ever-increasing diversity. Some of us have actually become intoxicated by the apparent power that we wield. After all, well-performed music, large performing ensembles, and large listening audiences do touch a desire for glory in all of us. The postmodern life is often so gray and futile that we would gladly escape to the glory of the fourth chapter of Revelation every Sunday, and we demand that music serve this goal.

There is nothing intrinsically wrong with well-performed music, large performing ensembles, and large listening audiences. Still, other church musicians sense that we are in a runaway train headed straight for a broken bridge. I am one of the latter, and thus much of my purpose in this chapter will be to encourage ecclesiastical authorities and thoughtful laity to reflect soberly on the crisis before us. My prayer is for a deep reformation in church music—that all alike will be led to insist, within their own spheres of influence, that comprehensive biblical principles be brought to bear on every detail of worship music.

Indeed the real crisis is this: *Ecclesiastical authorities, while recognizing that music is important to congregational life, usually fail to see that its biblical role puts it squarely within the ministry of the Word as a partner to preaching.* For, as the apostle Paul told us, the word of Christ dwells richly within us with all wisdom when we teach and admonish one another *with psalms, hymns, and spiritual songs* and sing with gratitude in our hearts to God *with psalms, hymns, and spiritual songs* (Col. 3:16).

We church musicians are not likely to lead the charge simply because we run a perpetual seven-day treadmill with our tongues hanging out. There is little time to get off the treadmill, and, in fact, this is the way most of our congregations apparently want it. Our congregations are concerned that we make them feel a certain way when they come to church. In the rampant uncertainty of the postmodern world, parishioners understandably want stability in church life (even though they claim to want diversity). If we church musicians paused for a moment and realized how much music belonged within the ministry of the Word, we might alter our practices in a way that would disrupt the general bonhomie.

Ours will be a difficult task because music literacy in our surrounding culture is at an all-time low, even though we hear more music in our day-to-day existence than in any culture preceding ours. This task requires, clearly, that we understand both the Bible and music. Although this chapter is primarily about *sola Scriptura* and how it affects worship music, the musician with a full quiver of musical skills will be in the best position to implement the necessary changes. There is simply no substitute for hard-won musical skills, and this comes only with thousands of hours of ongoing study.

If we are to recover the authority of Scripture in our worship, then we must likewise recover it in our music, which is an important element of true God-centered worship conforming to the principle of *sola Scriptura*. Just as the sixteenth-century Reformers gave major attention to this area, so must we. Indeed, it was Martin Luther who said, "We should not ordain young men as preachers, unless they have been well exercised in music." This, of course, is that same Luther who was so adamant about the restoration of biblical preaching. He saw no sharp division between the role of worship music and preaching or between the role of the church musician and the preacher.

THE SCRIPTURES AND MUSIC

If we were to ask people what the purpose of music in worship is, the answers would be as varied as if we asked them to name their favorite baseball team. But the problem is not that Scripture is not sufficient. The Bible gives clear marching orders in this area, as well as a plethora of applied examples. Some of our present confusion may arise from a peculiar translation issue. In the *New American Standard Bible*, Colossians 3:16 reads, "Let the word of Christ richly dwell within you, with all wisdom teaching and admonishing one another with psalms and hymns and spiritual songs, singing with thankfulness in your hearts to God." Other translations, such as the *New International Version*, remove the "psalms, hymns and spiritual songs" from the "teaching and admonishing one another," placing them squarely and exclusively with "sing . . . with gratitude in your hearts to God." Depending on one's casual reading of this text, worship music could vary considerably.

The real clue, however, is not so much in the word order as in the words "psalms and hymns and spiritual songs." Here we need to think a bit about the intended first-century readers of this text. The addressee of this book is "the saints and faithful brethren in Christ who are at Colossae" (Col. 1:2). At the end of the book (4:16), Paul commands them to pass the letter on to the church in Laodicea. The church at Ephesus was also acquainted with the formulation "psalms and hymns and spiritual songs" (Eph. 5:19). In each case, not only did Paul write to them in Greek, but they were primarily Greek readers, and their Old Testament most likely would have been the Greek Septuagint, which labeled the 150 Psalms alternatively as "Psalms" or "Hymns" or "Spiritual Songs." Taken by itself, this detail speaks strongly for the old Reformed practice of singing the entire Psalter on a regular basis, a practice we would do well to reconsider.

I once examined the entire worship music repertoire of my congregation, most of which I had inherited, placing each song under one of three biblical categories: (1) "teaching"; (2) "admonition"; and (3) "singing with thankfulness in your hearts to God." Of some four hundred praise choruses and hymns, I found that most of them fit within category three, with about thirty in category one, and fewer than ten in category two. This may reflect our American spirit—the notion that we are free and that nobody can tell us what to do, least of all a worship leader. A new gnosticism[1] has crept in, convincing us that feeling good is an inextricable component of orthodoxy. Admonition just does not fit "orthopathos," an orthodoxy of shared feelings and experiences.[2]

Having stumbled onto this feature of my own congregation's worship music diet, I then went to the 150 Psalms to see what the proportions of these categories would be. I read the Psalms with three colored highlighters in hand. I used one highlighter to mark teaching, one for admonition, and one for gratitude to God. More skillful Bible scholars than I will anticipate what I found: There was simply no way to separate the categories. Consider Psalm 103. The way we "bless the Lord" is to reel off a *long* list of blessings:

- He forgives all our iniquities
- He heals all our diseases
- He redeems our lives from destruction
- He crowns us with lovingkindness and compassion
- He satisfies our years with good things, and so on

Later in this psalm, it becomes clear that these blessings are given to those who fear the Lord. Taken together, we have a song of gratitude to God that teaches us about God's provision and further admonishes us to fear the Lord. This is the nature of true biblical worship music. The glorification of God and the edification of the saints occur concurrently. Worship music functions as an integral part of the teaching ministry. Pulpit preaching has greater power to explain the text logically, but music has greater power to *inculcate* the text, to take the text more profoundly into other parts of the hearer's being.

WORSHIP MUSIC AND THEOLOGY

Until the time of King David, the role of music in worship was somewhat incidental. It was no accident that "the man after God's heart" institutionalized the Levitical musicians. But just what did the Levitical musicians do? There is no clearly detailed description of the Levitical musician's responsibilities, but, as with many other issues in the Bible, a vivid picture begins to emerge by putting together several loose particulars.

In 1 Chronicles 6, we learn that the chief musicians Heman, Ethan, and Asaph came from the three separate clans of Levi. It may be that musical skill and wisdom necessitated drawing from the whole tribe rather than from a narrower pool, as was the case with the priests. Toward the end of the same chapter, we find that the Levites were given towns and accompanying fields scattered throughout the entire land of Israel. Thus, the land of Israel would have been sprinkled with "local" Levitical musicians.

First Chronicles 24 and 25 indicate that the priests and the musicians had two-week tours of duty at the temple in Jerusalem. This raises the fascinating question, "What were they doing the rest of the year?" Part of this is answered in the authorial ascription of some of the psalms. It was Asaph who thundered that God owns "the cattle on a thousand hills" (Ps. 50:10). If a modern church musician wrote a worship text like Psalm 50, he would probably not get it published in the contemporary Christian music industry. And Heman's Psalm 88 is incontestably the bleakest of all the psalms. In short, Levitical musicians wrote psalms, and those psalms plainly were not obligated to accommodate the gnostic, emotional demands of the twentieth-century evangelical church.

We know Solomon composed 1,005 psalms, most of which are lost (1 Kings 4:32). Nevertheless, this demonstrates that the writing of psalms was apparently a flourishing activity at the time. We also know that Solomon "was wiser than Ethan the Ezrahite, Heman, Calcol and Darda, the sons of Mahol" (v. 31). If Solomon had not existed, *two of the wisest men in Israel would have been musicians!* They were teachers of the highest order. This leads me to suspect that Levitical musicians, scattered throughout the land, served as Israel's teachers. Furthermore, the book of Psalms was their textbook. And because this textbook was a songbook, it may well be that the Levitical musicians catechized the nation of Israel through the singing of psalms.

A Levitical musician reached maturity at age thirty, not age twenty as in the case of the unspecialized Levite (1 Chron. 23:3, 5, 24). One wonders what the state of church music today would be were musical leadership withheld until age thirty. If we are serious about *sola Scriptura*, we might view such an age restriction as a prudent guideline.

Luther spoke of the Psalms in his Bible translation preface as a "small Bible reduced to the loveliest and most concise form so that the content of the whole Bible exists in them as a handbook." He recognized that all the great theological ideas of the Bible were found in its songbook, and, as a result, Lutheran hymnody of the Reformation brought the gospel to bear on every aspect of life.[3]

We no longer have the Levitical ceremonial law, and yet the larger teaching role of the Levitical musicians will not cease until the second coming of the Lord. The apostle Paul understood that well, when, under the inspiration of the Holy Spirit, he told us that the way the word of Christ richly dwells within us with all wisdom is that we teach and admonish one another with psalms, hymns, and spiritual songs. The word of Christ richly dwells within us with all wisdom when we sing with thankfulness in our hearts to God with psalms, hymns, and spiritual songs (Col. 3:16). Paul took the teaching of the Old Testament as so self-evident that he was not compelled to elaborate. Why should he? He had the "God-breathed" Psalms already in hand.

Most worship music traditions have failed miserably to see this teaching mandate. The revivalist music of the nineteenth and early twentieth centuries and contemporary Christian music have both been significant offenders on this score.

Consider the well-known chorus, *Bless His Holy Name*.

> Bless the Lord, O my soul,
> and all that is within me
> bless His holy name.
> He has done great things.
> He has done great things.
> He has done great things,
> bless His holy name.[4]

It is true that the opening sentence of the chorus is a verbatim quote of Psalm 103:1, and that is to be applauded. Beyond that, however, the remaining twenty-one verses of Psalm 103 are compressed into a scant eight words that give the vague notion that we should bless the Lord because of the great things He has done. What those great things are is left to the imagination, not the plain teaching of Scripture. The problem is that true, biblical gratitude must have its basis in objective facts or doctrine. If it doesn't, it is mere sentimentality.

Worship music teaches whether or not we want it to do so. It behooves us, therefore, to approach the writing of worship music texts with as much theological clarity and as much linguistic skill as possible. In the 150 psalms, we find all the great biblical doctrinal themes presented poetically—themes such as our depravity, the Atonement, our redemption, God's creation and providence, and so on. Whatever else Paul's admonition means, even a loose reading indicates that our worship music must regularly touch the entire superstructure of Christian doctrine.

BUT HOW DO WE WORK OUT THIS TRUTH?

The moment that we turn our thoughts to the fleshing out of this concept, we run into some huge style barriers. There are styles that simply cannot carry various texts, and often those individuals who are most fond of those styles will be the first to admit that the words do not fit their preferred style. Thus, the usual response is that the texts do not belong in worship because they do not *feel* "worshipful." It seldom occurs to the style adherent that perhaps there is actually something wrong with the style, not the words.

I would say axiomatically, *Any style that is not able to carry texts whose presence is demanded biblically is an inappropriate style for Christian worship.* Furthermore, encouraging diversity of styles merely allows individual worshipers to gratify their own appetites, dismissing those worship songs that are not in their preferred styles.

What is style? In order to apply biblical principles to style and worship music, we need to understand what the Bible says about style, as well as what style is. Style, per se, is something common to all humanity and, as such, belongs squarely in the realm of common grace. The sun and the rain come down on the good and the evil alike. All humans, all cultures, exhibit "style" or aesthetic behavior.

It is precisely at this point that Christians of all persuasions fall on their faces. We often confuse our theology with our style, resulting, in the end, in confused theology. It is a lack of alertness. To borrow a metaphor, it is not enough to be gentle as a dove; one needs to be as wise as a serpent too. Moses had the finest training of the Egyptians; Daniel had the finest training of the Chaldeans and the Medes. Their training was one of common grace, and the community of faith was richer for it.

Before unraveling this tangled web, I would raise two questions that must be in constant consideration during this whole discussion. First, is style good or bad due to some intrinsic beauty? Second, is style good or bad due to the ethical effect it has on humanity?

STYLE AND THE DOCTRINE OF CREATION

All issues of style and culture have their distinct seeds in Creation. Of course, they were not developed, but as the fertilized egg is fully human with all the essential information contained in forty-six chromosomes, so, in much the same way, all the essential details of human culture can be found in the first three chapters of Genesis.

First, we see God making tangible objects and enjoying them. He makes them, apparently, merely for His pleasure. We need to linger on this point a bit because it runs against the grain of American pragmatism, which is deeply entrenched in our intellectual presuppositions and in our methods of church life, even among those of us who repudiate the technique-oriented views of the church growth movement. We still tend to order our regular assembling together according to norms that are acceptable to our culture. And of all the various veins of philosophy, we need to remember that pragmatism is the only indigenous, uniquely American innovation.

God is self-sufficient. He needs nothing. Without the presence of necessity, there is no pragmatism. Pragmatism solves problems and fulfills needs. But God created the cosmos for His own pleasure. It was an act of undiluted aesthetic delight, a work of art. He did not have an unfulfilled need. He set the wild donkey free (Job 39:5). He made the ostrich with wings that "flap joyously" (v. 13). The heavens are the poetry[5] of His fingers (Ps. 8:3). Throughout the process of creation, we see God periodically taking a step backward to view His work, then noting, "It is good," not "That does what I need it to do," or "That functions well." If there is a human analogy to this aspect of God, it is not the engineer or the salesman but, rather, the artist.

"Then God said, 'Let Us make man in Our image, according to Our likeness; and let them rule over the fish of the sea and over the birds of the sky and over the cattle and over all the earth, and over every creeping thing that creeps on the earth'" (Gen. 1:26). I would suggest that we know only two things about the nature of God to this point and that these two features are equally significant for understanding human nature: first, He made things merely for the purpose of delighting in the process of making as well as in the completed object of that process; second, He is a singular being who, nonetheless, has some mysterious plurality to His nature.

When God brought man into the picture, the first thing Adam did was name the animals. Adam did not have to study grammar and spelling; he made up the rules and sounds just as they pleased him. Furthermore, he could just as easily have called a camel a *nahotsdowth* or a *stroile* if it seemed appropriate.[6] It appears that the names were merely a matter of Adam's pleasure: "And whatever the man called a living creature, that was its name" (Gen. 2:19). This is a variant on "and it was so" seen in the first chapter.

So we see both in God and in the man created after His image the tendency to make objects just for pleasure and beauty. In both cases, there is no apparent human audience; the audience seems to bring no bearing to what the aesthetic object shall be. The essence of the aesthetic object is based solely in the pleasurable intentions of the Creator (God) or of the maker (man).

This brings us to our first principle of style that is found in the creation: *There is style, culture, or art that has intrinsic goodness, a goodness based on beauty itself.* This principle has come down to us in the activity of high art, or high culture. This is "art for art's sake." In its most rarefied state, high art is art made simply for its beauty (as understood by the individual maker) without regard for any audience.

For the most part, high-art composers have been outside the church for about 250 years, since the death of J. S. Bach, who was the super-nova of the great Lutheran tradition of biblical church musicians. There are two reasons for this.

The first was that Pietism overwhelmed the church at that time, and Pietism put a premium on how one *felt* as a mark of orthodoxy. (Pietism is truly alive and well today!) If the music didn't make the worshiper *feel* worshipful, then it was not spiritual music. High-art composers, who delighted in using the minds God gave them, quickly found them-selves on the endangered-species list.

The second reason high-art composers ceased to be active in the church was that the church (especially in Europe) ceased to be a viable entity. Pietism, begun as an effort to strengthen the church, eventually so intellectually weakened it that the attack of the Enlightenment left the visible European church of the nineteenth century in a liberal cesspool.

With this divestiture of high culture, the church gave up leadership in the development of culture and has since tried, with tongue hanging out, to keep up with the world. Those who stand ready to cast asper-sions on contemporary Christian music should soberly and penitently consider the fact that such music actually filled a regrettable void.

STYLE AND THE NATURE OF GOD

The second principle of style is found in that mysterious plurality of God's nature. God further places His image on man in the words "It is not good for the man to be alone" (Gen. 2:18). He reveals His intention to make man mysteriously into a plural being. These words apply directly to human marriage, most specifically to the marriage of Adam and Eve, in which we have the beginnings of human society. God made us as communal beings. It is truly not good for us to be alone, and this creation imprint should call into question many of the forces contained in modernity that are making the world highly populated with lonely, disconnected people—people with few communal relationships in the present or meaningfully connected to the past.

Unlike high art, there is a type of art made by people who know each other for people who know each other, and this art is used to enhance their being together. It is an art or style presupposition that is ever conscious of the audience, with the well-being of that audience in mind. Whole-some community, not beauty, is the chief end of this type of art. There-fore, this should be spoken of as folk art.[7] Here, goodness could be described as "extrinsic." Plato is probably the chief proponent of this assessment of art. He maintained that anything that brought about undesirable behavior in the citizen should be censored by the republic. The early church Fathers, almost to a man, also held this view of style, most specifically of musical style.

When Paul tells us to think on those things that are true, honorable, right, pure, lovely, of good reputation, excellent, and worthy of praise, we are admonished to bring issues of style under this microscope. Certainly high art, with its root in the image of God, fits these categories. But so does folk art, because it is not good for the man to be alone. The wholesome community of folk art fits the model of creation as God intended it.

POP CULTURE: THE GREAT MODERN PARASITE

Before moving on, it is important to recognize that high culture has its roots in aesthetics; folk culture has its roots in sociology. Comparing them is like comparing apples and oranges. They are both good when done well, and the canons of what is "good" are quite different for the two types. The Bible has a good deal more to say about folk culture than high culture, because folk culture is inextricably based in interpersonal relationships. Indeed, the church is a folk culture that transcends national and ethnic boundaries through a divinely inspired printed word.

There is yet a third type of culture or style presupposition that borrows liberally from folk and high culture. It is an impostor and a parasite because it is based in deceit. Its creation root is found in that tragic event when "the woman saw that the tree was good for food, and that it was a delight to the eyes, and that the tree was desirable to make one wise" (Gen. 3:6).

There are two threads to be considered here: the first is that Eve coveted—she wanted something that was not rightfully hers; second, by eating of that tree, she opened the Pandora's box of ever-increasing knowledge resulting in technological wonders that we cannot control. And those technological wonders have had a profound and devastating effect on our ability to maintain cultural objects that cause us to think on things that are true, honorable, right, pure, lovely, of good reputation, excellent, and worthy of praise (Phil. 4:8).

This third type of culture, or art, is made by people who tend not to know one another for people they do not know at all and will probably never meet. This is made possible by magnetic recording and by broadcasting. Before the twentieth century, the effects of these technologies and the kind of culture they would create were unimaginable.

This third type of culture is not fundamentally concerned with beauty of form, as in high art, or in wholesomeness of community, as in folk art. It is concerned primarily with dollars and cents; therefore, it is not surprising to discover that several Christian music companies are publicly traded on the New York Stock Exchange.

The artist is not primarily held accountable to God for a transcendent standard of beauty, nor to a local community with ethical responsibility. Rather, the artist answers most directly to the shareholder. As the technology driving commercial music emerged, church leaders and seminary professors failed to realize how integral music was to the ministry of the Word. They left a gaping hole that business interests were all too ready to fill. In other words, music technology created a new entertainment market niche while ecclesiastical authorities stood by flat-footed.

COMMON OBJECTIONS

The first objection runs something like this: "But aren't all the people who work in these Christian music companies believers, and don't they want to serve the Lord with their music?" Yes, their intentions may be good. The problem is not with their intentions but with their lines of accountability. There is no potential for church discipline when these people spread marginal or outright false teaching. Whenever anyone teaches in the church, as Christian musicians certainly do, they display a low view of human depravity when their teaching ministry is accountable to shareholders rather than to ecclesiastical authorities. When such is the case, we have high-visibility moral lapses inside the Christian music industry that are handled with patchy results.[8] Has this crisis overtaken us because our church discipline is flaccid and because we are lax in protecting the doctrinal purity of the church through its music component of the ministry of the Word?

The second objection might run like this: "Isn't popular music just today's folk music?" This is, in reality, a good objection, since pop music forms often closely resemble folk music forms. If, however, we bear in mind that form and beauty are not the chief ends of folk music, the difference between folk and pop music will be clearer.[9] Our God is at least as concerned with *why* we do something as with *what* we do, for out of the heart "are the issues of life" (Prov. 4:23 KJV). It is a noble desire to "become all things to all men, that [we] may by all means save some" (1

Cor. 9:22). But I would caution that to "become all things" does not mean to embrace the world's culture uncritically.[10] Remember, folk culture is primarily communal. Pop culture is primarily profit driven. Contemporary Christian music is a half-billion-dollar-a-year industry.

There was a time when contemporary Christian music was folk music, a time when a bunch of hippies at Calvary Chapel and at Peninsula Bible Church bought guitars, learned a few chords, and then, out of the overflowing gratitude of their hearts, began to make up simple expressions of their faith. Their work was not especially strong, either musically or textually. Still, the movement was born in the wholesomeness of Christian community. The early Maranatha praise songs show the characteristic rough edges of music first made in the garage with little concern for future popular culture fame and wealth. It is regrettable that this simple sense of ministry and shepherding has been replaced in large measure by an ethos of stardom.

A similar movement occurred over a two-hundred-year period in Reformation Germany. During that time, nearly 100,000 hymns were written![11] Comparatively few of them are with us today, and most have graciously been forgotten. That time furnished us with "A Mighty Fortress," "Now Thank We All Our God," "When Morning Gilds the Skies," "All Praise to God, Who Reigns Above," and "Praise to the Lord, the Almighty." I would suggest that we might not have these exquisite hymns if there had not been the other 99,500 that quickly went into the wastebasket.

The point is that the good usually comes into being in the midst of necessary mediocrity. For this reason, we should encourage those who want to praise God and edify the saints by making new songs, even if those songs often seem vacuous and insipid. Music is not canonical. We can set aside something that is less than perfect later on. Inviolable traditions are idols. Traditions that keep the good and add the new are alive and healthy. We should view the music of the Jesus People in the late sixties and early seventies as a wholesome development, even though very little of it should be used in corporate worship today.

THE GREAT CONTEMPORARY
CHURCH MUSIC REVOLUTION

As the music of the 1970s Jesus People grew in popularity, its commercial viability ignited a metamorphosis, one that removed it from local control inside the community of a local church to corporate control.

How odd it is that the current visible church is embracing diversity and multiculturalism uncritically, completely setting aside the wisdom of the early church Fathers. There are congregations all around the country now that have multiple worship services, each in a different style to cater to the appetites of different target groups. What emerges is a conglomeration of separate congregations under one roof, each sub-congregation expecting that its felt needs be met. This often results in a group selfishness that does anything but integrate the whole body of Christ.

Moreover, the lyrics in many of the praise choruses often contradict Scripture. Consider the chorus "Highest Place" directly associated with Philippians 2:9: "Therefore God exalted Him to the highest place and gave Him the name that is above every name (NIV).

> We place You on the highest place,
> for You are the great High Priest;
> We place You high above all else,
> and we come to You and worship at your feet.[12]

The trouble is that these lyrics indicate it is Christians—not God—who exalt Jesus to the highest place, directly contradicting the Scripture on which the song is based.

The larger problem with much commercial Christian music is not what is said but *what is left unsaid.* Two of the common troubling types of music that emerge feature God as hero and God as felt-need meeter. In itself this is not wrong, but it is consistently done at the expense of other essential doctrines. Unfortunately, the gospel of the New Testament is offensive. It is a stumbling block. The fact that Christ died for sinners according to the Scriptures is the baseline article of our faith. And yet the blood sacrifice for sin, that doctrine that shows how disgusting our depravity really is, receives conspicuously short shrift in commercial Christian music.[13] It just plain doesn't sell.

There are many reasons why all sorts of churches are embracing commercial contemporary Christian music uncritically. High among them is this naive assumption that popular culture is really folk culture. It is trusting when it should be fleeing.

SO WHAT ARE WE TO DO?

Like David Wells, "I begin by reserving my deepest suspicions for those who want answers to the difficulties I have mentioned. The desire for answers is innocent enough, but the spirit in which they are demanded frequently is not."[14] The fact is, the problems in worship music are deep, and they are manifold. They have grown steadily over a quarter of a millennium, and they will not be solved overnight. Reformation is needed, and the process will not bring quick results. Indeed, the suggestions I am about to offer are merely the starting point, seen through the glass dimly.

We need to recognize that there is no present worship music tradition that inculcates the word of Christ musically to such a degree that His word dwells in us *richly*. Some traditions are worse than others, but we must concede that God will not bless us for confessing other Christians' sins. Therefore, *the first step is to repent and to cry out for God's mercy*. I would go so far as to say that if this step is not taken seriously and continuously, there is no reason to anticipate God's blessing on our efforts, nor is there any reason to take the measures I am about to propose.

The next step is to examine the entire corpus of worship music specific to the local congregation to see what sort of teaching, what sort of admonition, and what sort of gratitude to God we see in the worship music. There are all sorts of pre-formed grids that will help us in this work. Whether or not our congregations use them liturgically, or even if they are of different doctrinal persuasions, I think they are, nonetheless, useful in getting a comprehensive handle on our own specific practices. When we read the command to honor father and mother, certainly this extends to wise and faithful saints of the past. These forebears have produced many admirable comprehensive doctrinal teaching models that we would do well to employ in evaluating our own thoroughness. Such a set of tools might include the Apostles' Creed, the Nicene Creed, the Anglican Thirty-nine Articles, Luther's Shorter Catechism, the Westminster Confession of Faith, the Heidelberg Catechism, the church year, lectionaries, and Louis Berkhof's *Systematic Theology*, to name a few.

Prudential wisdom would encourage us to consider not buying and using commercial Christian music. On the face of it, this measure might seem Draconian, in part because it will force us to home-grow our own contemporary worship music, and the bald fact remains that music literacy has dropped to such a dismal level that skilled composers are not frequently to be found in local congregations. The local church will have to review its vision in light of this failing and take steps to remedy it. As worship music begins to flex its biblical muscles, we will quickly find that our general music literacy is woefully inadequate to the task.[15]

This will take a generation or two, thousands of hours of careful music study, and many dollars to remedy. The church has left the job of music education to the public school and to the whim of individuals. But public schools do not train very good worship musicians.

We will need to review the way we spend our time in corporate worship. Each Sunday, we will need to ask, "Did the music ministry today cause the word of Christ to dwell in us richly? Did we teach and admonish one another with psalms, hymns, and spiritual songs? Did we sing with gratitude in our hearts to God for Christ's finished work on the cross?" My guess is that we will quickly find that we do not sing together enough to accomplish these biblical demands. One of the canons of the church growth movement is that services that extend beyond an hour are not seeker sensitive and are, therefore, to be avoided at all costs. There are one hundred sixty-eight hours in a week. What do we say about the lordship of Christ when we spend only one of those in corporate worship?

A PRACTICAL RESPONSE

By now pastors might feel a bit withered. The assignment is reaching Herculean proportions. Some may be thinking, *How will Aunt Maude, who plays the piano voluntarily (and not very well), pull this off?* Others may think, *The college kids I've hired to do the worship band won't have a clue about this.* Still others may think, *I see my pastoral responsibility for oversight in this task, but I'm already overworked, and I do not have the budget to hire a real worship musician even if I could find one. Furthermore, what little music education I've had has not prepared me to deal with any of these problems.*

The worship music load I have described cannot, generally, be carried by a preacher. The biblical church musician has the ministry of the Word and prayer just like the pulpit preacher, but with musical means. He needs a training corollary to that of the preacher. He needs to operate under the same standards of accountability and scrutiny as the preacher. And like the ox and the preacher, he must not be muzzled while he is treading out the grain.

To the overwhelmed pastor I would say two things: Take the long view, and take heart. Here are some measures the pastor can take now.

First, retake ecclesiastical authority over the music and over every word sung in corporate worship and in small groups. When approached with a doctrinally inadequate special music project (usually an accompaniment track from some favorite commercial Christian artist), the pastor must be able to say, as Erik Routley did, "You can't have it because it is not good for you."[16] Remember, worship music is an issue of shepherding.

Second, vociferously denounce the widely held notion that entertainment is good whereas boredom is bad. Gene Edward Veith points out that the word "bored" did not enter English vocabulary until the Enlightenment of the eighteenth century.[17] Moreover, Veith shows that the corresponding biblical concept of boredom is sloth. In other words, boredom is primarily the hearer's problem, not the speaker's. Until this point is won, much biblical teaching and admonition will remain off limits.

Third, read Calvin Johansson's excellent book Discipling Music Ministry.[18] Recognizing that pastors' reading lists are already overburdened, I restrict my recommendation to one small book. A wise man once said, "with all thy getting, get understanding" (Prov. 4:7 KJV). Johansson's small volume catapults the pastor into understanding.

Fourth, register complaints with your seminaries over the minuscule and sometimes nonexistent place music holds within their Master of Divinity training.

Fifth, within congregational life foster children's choirs that have as a major goal the teaching of great hymn texts. Start early. Children are not born believing that they should like popular culture while disliking great old hymns. It is amazing how many children enjoy Mr. Rogers's operas. Children will acculturate to what is placed before them. Remember, worship music is an issue of shepherding.

Sixth, grow worship musicians from inside the four walls of the church under your theologically watchful eyes. It is true that the guitar can serve some limited use, but keyboard instruments present much greater musical versatility. Congregations should seriously invest in the continuing education of musicians. We should consider paying for piano lessons as well as instruction in music theory and counterpoint. Music theory is to music what hermeneutics is to theology. Counterpoint is to music what logic is to philosophy. We have a crisis in church music because these disciplines are not part of the life and breath of our musicians. Remember, worship music is part of the ministry of the Word. We would be appalled by a preacher who read at a third-grade level and did not understand grammar, yet we handicap the ministry of the Word when we leave our musicians unprepared.

Should all these measures be implemented, I would not expect overnight and glamorous results. Still, if we care about our children's children, we need to begin to take the tough, disciplined steps now. We need to seriously pray, "Your kingdom come. Your will be done, on earth as it is in heaven" (Matt. 6:10). Even better, we might consider singing it.[19]

NOTES

1. Ancient Gnosticism was a slippery heresy that evaded definition. At a minimum, however, Gnosticism embraces a secret knowledge derived more intuitively than objectively. For a good exposé of Gnosticism, see Peter Jones, *The Gnostic Empire Strikes Back* (Phillipsburg, N.J.: Presb. & Ref., 1992).

2. Kenneth A. Myers, *All God's Children & Blue Suede Shoes* (Wheaton, Ill.: Crossway, 1989), 186. Myers notes, somewhat wryly, that "evangelicals seem to have more in common concerning the sentimental trappings associated with faith than they do in defining what the nature of that faith is." In other words, what evangelicals have in common is a type of Gnosticism.

3. We need think only of Tobias Clausnitzer's "We All Believe in One True God, Father," Phillipp Nicolai's "Wake, Awake, for Night Is Flying," or Martin Luther's "Isaiah, Mighty Seer, in Spirit Soared."

4. Entry #33 in *Praise*, Maranatha Music (1983).

5. Martin Luther translated the word *work* as "poetry."

6. God made Adam with a specific design whereby some things would seem appropriate while others would not. Adam's artistic behavior should not be construed as relativistic or capricious.

7. By "folk" music, we should not automatically think of the style of James Taylor or Gordon Lightfoot or of guitars, tin whistles, and Celtic drums.

8. One is reminded of Nathan's comment to David: "By this deed you have given occasion to the enemies of the Lord to blaspheme" (2 Sam. 12:14). As with fallen pastors, the scope of the influence determines the necessary scope of the repentance. For further study, see John H. Armstrong, *Can Fallen Pastors Be Restored?* (Chicago: Moody, 1995).

9. John Styll ("The Christian Music Industry: Under New Ownership," *Worship Leader* [July/August 1995], 29) claims that "contemporary Christian music, generally speaking, is not church music." Yet the church is a folk unit because it is not good for the man to be alone. The irony here is that when our parishioners listen to many hours of commercial Christian music during the week, they come to expect and desire the same thing in corporate worship.

10. Many Christians who appropriate the goods of popular culture cite Luther as a precedent. A common claim is that Luther used tunes "from the bar." However, musicological research since 1923 is weighing in heavily for Luther as the composer of his own melodies. Luther did use a musical form called a "bar" form. But this is a technical term referring to the architecture of music, not, as would normally be expected, a place were alcoholic beverages are consumed. Others mistakenly cite Luther's famous question, "Why should the devil have all the good tunes?" When Luther spoke of the devil metaphorically, it was directed at the pope, not the pub. To rephrase what Luther was saying, "Why should we leave the great old hymns to the Roman Catholics?" It was an apology for the traditional, not for the contemporary!

11. Albert Edward Bailey, *The Gospel in Hymns* (New York: Scribner's Sons, 1952), 309.

12. Words and music by Ramon Pink, 1983, Scripture in Song, administered by Maranatha Music, c/o The Copyright Company, 40 Music Square East, Nashville, TN 37203.

13. When the blood of Jesus appears in praise and worship choruses, it is frequently unclear whether the blood is understood as a propitiation for our sins or as a talisman to protect us against physical catastrophes, such as auto wrecks and cancer. The lyrics of commercial Christian music are seldom refined in a doctrinal crucible, yielding rather to the demands of rigid rhyme schemes and popular musical/architectural forms. Such a practice inadvertently conveys the message that the exact words are not important; the listener is called upon to read between the lines and fill in the meaning as he or she wishes. As the queen said to Alice, "The word means what I say it means." *Sola scriptura* people must stand in oppostion to such practices, difficult though it might be.

14. David Wells, *God in the Wasteland: The Reality of Truth in a World of Fading Dreams* (Grand Rapids: Eerdmans, 1994), 29.

15. Full-orbed music literacy includes the ability to compose music from scratch, to perform that music or to conduct other performers, and to understand theologically and historically the place of that music.

16. As quoted in Calvin M. Johansson, *Discipling Music Ministry: Twenty-First Century Directions* (Peabody, Mass.: Hendrickson, 1992), 168.

17. *Tabletalk* (November 1995), 8.

18. Ibid.

19. There are many settings. The two that I consider especially good are John Fischer's "Holy Father, Hear Our Prayer" (F.E.L. Publications, 1969) and Martin Luther's "Our Father Who in Heaven Art."

CHAPTER
12
HOW SHALL WE CURE TROUBLED SOULS?

David Powlison

Sigmund Freud once described his work this way: "The words, 'secular pastoral worker,' might well serve as a general formula for describing the function which the analyst, whether he is a doctor or a layman, has to perform in his relation to the public."[1] Carl Jung, Freud's most famous disciple—and the most famous heretic from Freudian orthodoxy—further elaborated: "Patients force the psychotherapist into the role of a priest and expect and demand of him that he shall free them from their distress. That is why we psychotherapists must occupy ourselves with problems which, strictly speaking, belong to the theologian."[2] Psychotherapists are "secular priests" by the open admission of the more self-conscious among them.[3] Perhaps more pointedly, as a Christian looks at the phenomena of twentieth-century psychotherapeutics, the therapists are secular prophet-theologians who redefine human nature and the meaning of life to excise God; they are secular priest-pastors who shepherd the human soul to find refuge in itself; they are secular king-elders who administer the secular institutions of the modern cure of souls.

But how is the evangelical church responding to this massive redefinition of the ideas, practices, and institutions of "pastoral care" that are taking place around us? The approach to helping souls live in faith, love, joy, peace, and every other wisdom has largely changed from the use of Scripture's ideas, methods, and institutions to the use of almost everything except what Scripture actually teaches and models. What should be done to recover the centrality of Scripture for helping people to grow up into the image of Christ? How can face-to-face "helping" relationships be reconfigured to serve as instruments of the only enduring wisdom? How are we to face the ever-growing crisis of biblical authority that has become a major component of evangelical talk and life in the last twenty-five years?

To recover the centrality of Scripture for the cure of souls demands two things: *conviction* backed up with *content*. The conviction? Scripture is about understanding and helping people; the scope of Scripture's sufficiency includes those face-to-face relationships that our culture labels "counseling" or "psychotherapy." The content? The problems, needs, and struggles of real people—right down to the details—must be rationally explained by the categories with which the Bible teaches us to understand human life. Those problems must be addressed and re-dressed using means the Bible teaches us to use.

Conviction alone simply waves a flag and eventually degrades into sloganeering. But convictions demonstrated in action, convictions shown to be penetrating, comprehensive, and subtle, will edify the teachable and even persuade the skeptical. The church needs persuading that the conviction is true, and a key ingredient in such persuasion will be to parade the riches of Scripture for curing souls.

In the pages that follow we will look first at the conviction that Scripture is about what "problems in living" are about.[4] Then we will look in some detail at one piece of the Bible's content. We will seek to redeem the biblical term *the lusts of the flesh*, which has languished in near uselessness.

CONVICTION: SCRIPTURE IS SUFFICIENT

What is a genuinely biblical view of the problems of the human soul and the procedures of ministering grace? Such a view must establish a number of things.

First, we must answer whether or not Scripture gives us the materials and call to construct something that might fairly be called "systematic biblical counseling." I believe that we do have the goods for a coherent and comprehensive practical theology of face-to-face ministry.[5] Scripture is dense with explanations, with instructions, with implications.

In many places the Holy Spirit reflects on the sufficiency of the treasure that He has created through His prophets and apostles. For example, in one classic passage Scripture proclaims itself as that which makes us "wise unto salvation" (KJV), a comprehensive description of transforming human life from all that ails us (2 Tim. 3:15–17). This same passage goes on to speak of the Spirit's words as purposing to teach us. Both the utter simplicity and unsearchable complexity of Scripture enlighten us about God, about ourselves, about good and evil, true and false, grace and judgment, about the world that sur-rounds us with its many forms of suffering and beguilement, with its opportunities to shed light into darkness.

Through such teaching, riveted to particular people in particular situations, God exposes in specific detail what is wrong with human life. No deeper or truer or better analysis of the human condition can be concocted. God's words reconstruct and transform what they define as defective. He speaks as He acts, to straighten out wrongs through the corrective power of grace. To promote any solution but God's is to offer opiates to the masses, the stuff of dreams, not the stuff of real answers for real problems. And this God continues to speak, performing His wisdom-renewing work in an ongoing process. The net result? We begin to live like Jesus Christ Himself. Scripture accomplishes our renewal in the image of Him who is wisdom incarnate so that we are equipped for every good work. Second Timothy 3, reflecting on the inexhaustible riches of wisdom revealed in the Scriptures, makes a case for the sufficiency of the Word to cure souls.

Many conservative Protestants, however, do not believe in the "sufficiency of Scripture" for the cure of souls. Typically, "spiritual" matters are split off from "psychological, emotional, relational" matters. "Spiritual" matters include such things as commitment to God, prayer, ethics, doctrine, evangelism, assurance of salvation, the devil, and a mystical leading of the Spirit. Other matters—suffering, socialization dynamics, unpleasant emotions, interpersonal reconciliation, enslavement to sinful habits, patient and probing conversation, self-deception, motivation, and so on—are relegated to extrabiblical authorities. Scripture is not seen to offer the fundamental categories for interpreting and redressing human experience. Instead, wise and effective counseling is seen to emerge from grafting or "integrating" secular psychological systems into Christianity. In practice, the engrafted secularism inevitably predominates over an impoverished and impotent Scripture.

Continued debate must occur over the *scope* and *purposes* of Scripture's intended sufficiency and the consequent *use* of Scripture. Conservative Protestants on both sides of the question confess Scripture as an authoritative guide to "matters of faith and practice." But do those matters include understanding life's practical problems and ways to help? On the one hand, the "integrationist" paradigm proclaims the insufficiency of what God has revealed about Himself and us. Scripture is an inadequate guide for the counseling task. Though most integrationists view what they do as a form of "ministry" for Christ, in their view such ministry needs a *fundamental* contribution from outside biblical revelation. Scripture is not dense with explanations, instructions, and implications.

On the other hand, those committed to develop systematic biblical counseling believe that the task of articulating a coherently biblical practical theology is not only possible but necessary. For example, "spiritual matters" include the details of how we understand practical human problems. The contribution of extrabiblical sources is distinctly subordinate and secondary—often even contradictory in intent and interpretation—to the givens of the biblical model. Other sources may be informative and provocative, but they become constitutive to the peril of Christianity. We may learn from and be challenged by our own experience, popular fiction, history, the mass media, psychology, the idiosyncrasies of those we counsel, sociology, music theory, rock stars, rhetoric, comparative anthropology, Muslim immigrants who move in next door, medicine, and organizational management. But epistemologically, all these interesting things are on the same level: qualitatively subordinate to Scripture, inherently suspect, needing the reinterpretive gaze of the Spirit's wisdom.

Unless God lies, then we do have the goods for developing systematic biblical counseling. Any such system must provide four particulars: (1) a penetrating and comprehensive analysis of the human condition, (2) an effective solution, equally penetrating and comprehensive, (3) a wise pastoral methodology that engages the variety of persons and problems appropriately, and (4) a standpoint from which to discern the noetic effects of sin in other systems of counseling. If Scripture does offer these things, it is sufficient.

In this chapter, I will examine one facet of that first particular. The Bible's view of what is disordered in human motivation sharply challenges all secular pretenders to explanatory wisdom about why we do what we do.

"Why did I do that?"

"Why did you do that?"

The question "Why?" has launched a thousand theories of human nature. In fact, the way a theory of human life answers the question of motivation is the engine and rudder of that theory.

Why do people do what they do? Are you genetically hardwired toward aggression? Are raging hormones the culprit? Do your instinctual psychic impulses conflict with the dictates of society? Have your drives been reinforced by rewarding stimuli? Did you become fixated somewhere on the hierarchy of need? Are you an adult child of something unhappy and determinative? Are you compensating for some perceived inferiority? Did a demon named Addiction infiltrate a crevice in your personality? Is your temperament melancholic or sanguine? Are you an Aries with Jupiter rising? Did you have a failure of willpower? "I did that *because* . . ." What meets the eye—behavior—has reasons. And those reasons are up for debate. Scripture vigorously debates each of these contenders.

Theories of what makes people tick incarnate into counseling models. Explanations are signposts to solutions: take medication, experience reparenting, cast out a demon, get your needs met, don't make big decisions on bad star days. Counseling based on Scripture must do justice to what the Bible says about the whys and wherefores of the human heart. Scripture claims to search out the "thoughts and intentions of the heart" (Heb. 4:12) according to the criteria by which the Searcher of hearts explains and weighs.

In the pages that follow I will zero in on one particular family of questions: "What do you crave, want, desire, pursue, wish?" There are many ways to come at the topic of motivation biblically.[6] But this is one of the most fruitful. New Testament authors repeatedly allude to life-controlling cravings when they summarize the inward dimension of our struggle with sin. And they have the greatest confidence that the resources of the Gospel of Jesus Christ—the Word and the Spirit—are alone sufficient to change people in the way people most need changing.

LUST: THE NEW TESTAMENT WAY TO DESCRIBE WHAT'S WRONG

Lusts of the flesh (or cravings or pleasures) is a summary term for what is wrong with people in God's eyes. People turn *from* God in order to serve what they want. People turn *to* God from their cravings. According to the Lord's assessment, we all formerly lived in the lusts of our flesh, indulging the desires of the flesh and of the mind (Eph. 2:3). Non-Christians are thoroughly controlled by what they want. And the most significant inner conflict in Christians is between what the Spirit wants and what we want.

But "lust" has become almost useless to modern readers of the Bible. It is reduced to sexual desire. Take a poll of the people in your church, asking them the meaning of "lusts of the flesh." You will find that sex appears on every list. Greed, pride, or gluttonous craving might appear in the answers of a few of the more thoughtful believers. The marquee sins of the heart appear, but the subtleties and details are washed out. And a crucial biblical term for explaining human life languishes.

The New Testament writers, however, use this term as a comprehensive, summary category for the human dilemma! It will pay us to think carefully about its manifold meanings. We need to expand the meaning of terms that have been truncated and drained of significance. We need to learn to understand life through these lenses in order to use these categories skillfully.

The New Testament repeatedly focuses on the "lusts of the flesh" as a summary of what is wrong with the human heart that underlies bad behavior: Romans 13:14; Galatians 5:16–17; Ephesians 2:2 and 4:22; James 1:14–15 and 4:1–3; 1 Peter 1:14; 2 Peter 1:4; 1 John 2:16.[7] This does not mean that the New Testament is internalistic.[8] In each of the passages just cited behavior intimately connects to motive. Wise counselors follow the model of Scripture and move back and forth between lusts of the flesh and the tangible works of the flesh, between faith and the tangible fruit of the Spirit.

Lusts of the flesh is meant to answer the why question that is at the heart of any system of explaining human behavior. Specific ruling desires—lusts, cravings, or pleasures—create bad fruit. Inordinate desires explain and organize diverse bad fruit: words, deeds, emotions, thoughts, plans, attitudes, brooding memories, fantasies. For this intimate and pervasive connection between motive and fruit, see Galatians 5:16–6:10; James 1:13–16; 3:14–4:12. In modern language (both casual use by individuals and formalized in counseling theories), such sinful cravings often masquerade as expectations, goals, felt needs, wishes, demands, longings, drives, and so forth. People talk about their motives in ways that anesthetize themselves and others to the true significance of what they are describing.

What makes our desires wrong? This question becomes particularly perplexing to people when the object of their desires is a good thing. Notice some of the adjectives that get appended to our cravings: *evil, polluted* lusts (Col. 3:5; 2 Peter 2:10). Sometimes the object of desire itself is evil: e.g., to kill someone, to steal, to control the cocaine trade on the Eastern seaboard. But often the object of desire is good, and the evil lies in the lordship of the desire. Our will replaces God's as that which determines how we live. John Calvin put it this way: "We teach that all human desires are evil, and charge them with sin—not in that they are natural, but because they are inordinate."[9] In other words, the evil in our desires often lies not in what we want but that we want it too much. Natural affections (for any good thing) become inordinate, ruling cravings. We are meant to be ruled by godly passions and desires. Natural desires for good things are meant to exist subordinate to our desire to please the Giver of gifts. The fact that the evil lies in the ruling status of the desire, not the object, is frequently a turning point in counseling.

Consider this example. A woman commits adultery and repents. She and her husband rebuild the marriage, painstakingly, patiently. Eight months later the man finds himself plagued with subtle suspiciousness and irritability. The wife senses it and feels a bit like she lives under FBI surveillance. The husband is grieved by his suspiciousness because he has no objective reasons for suspicion: "I've forgiven her; we've rebuilt our marriage; we've never communicated better; why do I hold on to this mistrust?" It emerges that he is willing to forgive the past, but he attempts to control the future. His craving could be stated this way: "I want to guarantee that betrayal never, ever happens again."

The object of desire is good; its ruling status poisons his ability to love. The lust to ensure her fidelity places him in the stance of continually evaluating and judging his wife rather than loving her. What he wants cannot be guaranteed this side of heaven. He sees the point, sees his inordinate desire to ensure his marital future. But he bursts out, "What's wrong with wanting my wife to love me? What's wrong with wanting her to remain faithful to our marriage?" Here is where this truth is so sweet. There is nothing wrong with the object of desire; there is everything wrong when it rules his life. The process of restoring that marriage took him a long step forward as he grasped a lesson his Shepherd had for him.

Are preferences, wishes, desires, longings, hopes, expectations always sinful then? Of course not. What theologians used to call "natural affections" are part of our humanity. They are part of what makes humans different from stones, able to tell the difference between blessing and curse, between pleasure and pain. The moral issue always turns on whether the desire takes on a ruling status. If it does, it will produce visible sins: anger, grumbling, immorality, despair, what James so vividly termed "disorder and every evil thing" (James 3:16). If you wish your son to grow up to be a Christian, and he strays, it may break your heart, but it will not make you sin against either God or your son.

Consider a second adjective that Scripture attaches to the phrase lusts of the flesh: *deceitful* lusts (Eph. 4:22). Our desires deceive us because they present themselves as so plausible. Natural affections become warped and monstrous, and so blind us. Who wouldn't want good health, financial comfort, a loving spouse, good kids, success on the job, kind parents, tasty food, a life without traffic jams, control over circumstances? Yet cravings for these things lead to every sort of evil. The things people desire are delightful as blessings received from God but terrible as rulers. They beguile, promising blessing but delivering sin and death.

Some sins are "high-handed," done with full awareness of choice (Ps. 19:13). Other sins reflect the blind, dark, habitual, compulsive, hardened, ignorant, confused, instinctive insanity of sin (Gen. 6:5; Ps. 19:12; Eccl. 9:3; Jer. 17:9; Eph. 4:17–22; 1 Tim. 1:13; 2 Peter 2:10–22). One of the joys of biblical ministry comes when you are able to turn on the lights in another person's dark room. Souls are cured as the ignorant and self-deceived are disturbed by the light of God's analytic gaze and then comforted by the love that shed substitutionary blood to purchase the inexpressible gift.

"ROOT SINS" AND "INORDINATE DESIRES"

I have yet to meet a couple locked in hostility (and the concomitant fear, self-pity, hurt, self-righteousness) who really understood and reckoned with their motives. James 4:1–3 teaches that cravings underlie conflicts. Couples who see what rules them—cravings for affection, attention, power, vindication, control, comfort, a hassle-free life—can repent and begin to learn how to make peace.

Unpack the term into twentieth-century experience, redeeming the evasive language people use instead. People frequently talk about what they want, expect, wish for, desire, demand, need, long for. Pop psychologies typically validate these needs and longings as neutral givens. Little do people realize that much of the time they are describing sinful usurpers of God's rule over their lives: inordinate desires, lusts of the flesh, cravings. For example, listen to children talk when they are angry, disappointed, demanding, contrary: "But I want. . . . But I don't want to . . ." In our family we taught our children about the "I-wantsies" from the time they were less than two years old. We wanted them to grasp that sin was more than behavior.

Analyze any argument or outburst of anger and you will find ruling expectations and desires that are being frustrated (James 4:1–2). The street language gets you into the details of a person's life but comes with a distorted interpretation attached. Wise counseling must reinterpret that experience into biblical categories, taking the more pointed language of "lusts, cravings, pleasures" and mapping it onto the "felt needs" that underlie much sin and misery. The very unfamiliarity of the phrase is an advantage, if you explain it carefully and show its relevance and applicability. Behavioral sins demand a horizontal resolution—as well as vertical repentance. But motivational sins have first and foremost to do with God, and repentance quickens the awareness of relationship with the God of grace.

With good reason, the Bible usually refers to the "lusts" (plural) of the flesh. The human heart can generate a lust tailored to any situation. John Calvin powerfully described how cravings "boil up within us," how the human mind is a "factory of idols."[10] We are infested with lusts. Listen closely to any person given to complaining, and you will observe the creativity of our cravings. Certainly one particular craving may so frequently or habitually appear that it seems to be a "root sin": love of money, fear of people and craving for approval, love of preeminence, desire for pleasure, and so forth can dictate much of life. But all people have all the typical cravings.

Realizing the diversity in human lusts gives great flexibility and penetration to counseling. For example, one lust can generate very diverse sins, as 1 Timothy 6:10 states: "The love of money is a root of all sorts of evil." Every one of the Ten Commandments—and more—can be broken by someone who loves and serves money. The craving for money and material possessions is an organizing theme for symptomatic sins as diverse as anxiety, theft, compulsive shopping, murder, jealousy, marital discord, a sense of inferiority in comparing oneself with others, sexual immorality that trades sex for material advantage, and so on.

On the flip side, a single behavioral sin can emerge from very different lusts. For example, an act of sexual immorality might occur for many different reasons: erotic pleasure, financial advantage, revenge on a spouse or parent, fear of saying no to an authority figure, pursuit of approval and affirmation, enjoyment of power over another person's sexual response, the gaining of social status or career advancement, feeling sorry for someone and playing the savior, fear of losing a potential marriage partner, escape from a feeling of boredom, peer pressure. Wise biblical counselors dig for specifics. They don't assume that all people have the same characteristic flesh or that a person always does a certain thing for the same reasons. The flesh is creative in iniquity.

How can you tell if a desire is inordinate or natural? By their *fruit* you know them. Human motivation is not a theoretical mystery that we must speculate about. There is no need to engage in introspective archeological digs. Evil desires produce bad fruit that can be seen, heard, felt (James 1:15; 3:16). For example, a father who wants his child to grow up to become a Christian reveals the status of that desire by whether he is a good father or a manipulative, fearful, angry, suspicious father. In a good father, the desire is subordinate to God's will that he love his child. In a sinful father, the desire rules and produces moral and emotional chaos. Similarly, a wife who wants to be loved reveals the status of that desire by whether she loves and respects her husband. Visible fruit reveals whether God rules or a lust rules.

It is a serious mistake to engage in introspective "idol hunts," attempting to dig out and weigh every kink in the human soul. The Bible calls for a more straightforward form of self-examination: an outburst of anger invites a moment of reflection on what specific craving ruled the heart that our repentance might be intelligent. The Bible's purposes are "extrospective," not introspective: to move toward God in repentant faith (James 4:6–10) and then to move toward the one wronged by anger, making peace in repentance, humility, and love.

HUMAN MOTIVATIONS: A MISCELLANY OF FURTHER OBSERVATIONS

As we have seen, the term "lusts of the flesh" opens many doors for explaining the intricacies of human behavior. In this section we will answer five questions that frequently arise.

First, since the Bible teaches that the heart is unsearchable and unknowable to anyone but God (1 Sam. 16:7; Jer. 17:9–10), is it even legitimate to probe issues of motivation? Surely no one but God can see, explain, or control another person's heart and its choices. He is the only heart-knower and heart-changer. There is no underlying reason why a person serves a particular lust rather than God; sin is irrational and insane. And there is no therapeutic technique that can change hearts. But the Bible teaches us on every page that we can *describe* what rules the heart and speak the truth that convicts and liberates. Effective biblical ministry probes and addresses why people do things, as well as what they do.

For example, 1 Samuel 16:7 says that a person judges by externals while God judges the heart. Yet a few verses earlier, we are told that Saul visibly disobeyed God for a reason: he feared the people and listened to their voice instead of fearing God and listening to His voice (15:24). His motives are describable, even if inexplicable. There is no deeper cause for sin than sin. Jeremiah 17:9–10 says that the human heart is deceitful and incomprehensible to any but God. But the same passage describes how behavior evidences that people trust in idols, themselves, and others instead of trusting in God (17:1–8). Scripture is frank to tell us the causes of behavior: interpersonal conflicts, for example, arise because of lusts (James 4:1–2).

To search out motives demands no subtle psychotherapeutic technique. People can tell us what they want. The Israelites grumbled—a capital crime—when they had to subsist hand-to-mouth on boring food. Why? They craved flavor: fish, cucumbers, melons, leeks, onions, and garlic (Num. 11:5). Later they grumbled when they got thirsty and no oasis appeared. Why? They craved juicy foods, foods that demanded irrigation: grain, figs, vines, pomegranates, water (20:5). In each case the craving reflected their apostasy from God and expressed itself in visible, audible sins.

Second, does the word *lust* properly apply only to bodily appetites: the pleasures and comforts of food, sex, drink, rest, exercise, health? People follow the *desires of body and mind* (Eph. 2:3). Bodily appetites— the organism's hedonistic instinct to feel good—are certainly powerful masters unto sin. But desires of the mind—for power, human approval, success, preeminence, savings account ownership, and so forth—are also potent masters. The desires of the mind often present the most subtle and deceitful lusts because their outworkings are not always obvious.

Third, can cravings be habitual? Paul describes a *former manner of life* characterized by deceitful lusts. Peter tells his readers not to be conformed to their *former desires* (Eph. 4:22—cf. 4:17–19, which reinforces the notion of a characteristic lifestyle; 1 Peter 1:14). Like all other aspects of sin—beliefs, attitudes, words, deeds, emotions, thoughts, fantasies—desires can be habitual. You will counsel people who typically and repeatedly seek to control others or to indulge in the pleasures of sloth or to be seen as superior or to be liked. Jesus' call to die daily to self recognizes the inertia of sin. God is in the business of creating new habitual desires. An active concern for the well-being of others before God is one example.

Most contemporary counseling systems are obsessed with locating the reasons for current problems in the distant past. The Bible's worldview is much more straightforward. Sin emerges from within the person. The fact that a pattern of craving became established many years before—even that it was forged in a particular context, perhaps influenced by bad models or by experiences of being sinned against—only describes what happened. For example, past events do not cause a craving to be accepted by others any more than current events cause that craving. The occasions of a lust are never its cause.

Fourth, aren't fears as important in human motivation as are cravings? Fear and desire are two sides of a single coin. A sinful fear is a craving for something *not* to happen. If I want money, I fear poverty, with its deprivations and humiliations, and vice versa. If I long to be accepted, I'm terrified of rejection. If I fear pain or hardship, I crave comfort or pleasure. If I crave preeminence, I fear being subordinate to others. With some people the fear may be more pronounced than the corresponding desire, and wise counseling will work with what is pronounced. For example, a person who grew up during the Great Depression might manifest money worship through a fear of poverty that shows up in anxiety, hoarding, repeated calculations of financial worth, and so on. A 1980s yuppie might manifest money worship through unchecked consumer spending. With the former, address fear; with the latter, address greed. They are complementary expressions of craving treasure on earth.

Fifth, don't people sometimes have conflicting motives? Certainly. The conflict between sinful lusts and the Holy Spirit's desires is a given of the Christian life (Gal. 5:16–17). People often have mixed motives, some good, some bad. Most preachers and counselors will acknowledge that loving Christ and people battles with loving success and human approval.

People may have various sorts of conflicting motives. Two sinful cravings may conflict. For example, a businessman might want to steal something but will hold back out of fear of what his friends and clients would think of him if they found out. In this example, money worship and social approval both present themselves as options for the flesh; the heart inclines to the latter.

People often prioritize their cravings, and they may arrange the priorities differently in different situations. For example, that man who would never shoplift from a convenience store out of fear of social consequences might cheat on his taxes because he's not likely to get caught, and no one whose opinion matters would know even if he were caught. In this case, self-will and money worship seize the steering wheel, and social approval moves to the backseat. The "broad way" has a thousand creative variants!

LUSTS AND OTHER WAYS TO SPEAK OF SIN

How does thinking about lusts relate to other ways of talking about sin, such as "sin nature," "self," "pride," "autonomy," "unbelief," and "self-centeredness"? These words are general terms that summarize the problem of sin. One of the beauties of identifying ruling desires is that they are so specific and can enable more specific repentance and specific change. For example, a person who becomes angry in a traffic jam may later say, "I know the anger is sin and that it comes from self." That is true as far as it goes. But it helps to take self-knowledge a step further: "I cursed in anger because I craved to get to my appointment on time, I feared criticism from the person waiting for me, and I feared losing the profits from that sale." Repentance and change can become more specific when the person identifies these three lusts that particularly expressed the lordship of "self" in this particular incident.

The Bible discusses sin in an astonishing variety of ways, bringing out several nuances. Sometimes Scripture addresses sin at the general level: e.g., Luke 9:23–26 on "self" or Proverbs on the "fool." At other times Scripture increases the microscope's power and treats a particular theme of sin: e.g., Philippians 3 on the pursuit of self-righteousness; 1 Timothy 6 on love of money. In still other places, the Bible speaks of sinful desires that lead to sin, and invites us to make the specific application: e.g., James 1:14–15 and 4:1–2; Galatians 5:16–21; Romans 13:12–14. We could diagram this roughly as follows: (1) general terms, (2) midlevel typical patterns, and (3) detail-level specifics.

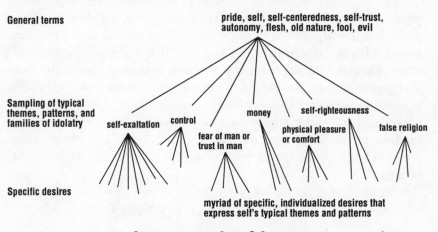

Confrontation and Sinful Cravings

Wise counselors will work at all three levels. The *general terms* keep one's worldview aligned properly, identifying characteristics of the "city" of human sin; the *typical themes* help locate the "neighborhood" in which a person lives; the detailed *desires* make truth personal, providing the "street address." In counseling do we simply confront a person with his sinful cravings? Wise counselors don't "just confront" anything. They do many different things that make confrontation timely and effective. Counselors don't see the heart, only the evidences, so a certain tentativeness is often appropriate to discussing motives.

But that doesn't mean we cannot tackle such issues. Second Timothy 3:16 begins with "teaching." Good teaching (for example, on how Galatians 5 and James 1 connect outward sins to inward cravings) helps people examine and come to know themselves. Good teaching invites self-knowledge and self-confrontation. Experience with people will make you "case wise" to typical connections. Probing questions— "What did you want or expect or fear when you blew up at your wife?"—help a person reveal his ruling lusts both to himself and to the counselor.

In the light of self-knowledge before God's face (Heb. 4:12–13), the gospel offers many promises: mercy, help, the Shepherd's care in a life of progressive sanctification (4:14–16). "The unfolding of Your words gives light" (Ps. 119:130). Repentance and faith can become vigorous and intelligent in a person who sees both his inner cravings and his outward sins.

The patterns, themes, or tendencies of the heart do not typically yield to a once-for-all repentance. Try dealing one mortal blow to your pride, fear of man, love of pleasure, or desire to control your world, and you will realize why Jesus spoke Luke 9:23! But genuine progress will occur where the Holy Spirit is at work. Understanding your motivational sins gives you a sense for the "themes" of your story, how your Father is at work in you over the long haul.

Work hard and carefully both on motivation issues (Rom. 13:14, the lusts of the flesh versus putting on Jesus Christ) and on behavioral issues (13:12–13, the varied deeds of darkness versus proper "daylight" behavior).

CHANGING WHAT YOU WANT

But can you change what you want? Really? Yes and Amen! This is central to the work of the Holy Spirit. You will always desire, love, trust, believe, fear, obey, long for, value, pursue, hope, and serve . . . SOMETHING. The Holy Spirit works to change the something, as He leads us with an intimate hand (Ps. 23:3; Rom. 6:16–18; 8:12–16; Gal. 5:16–25).

The desires of the heart are not unchangeable. Your cravings are not a given. God never promises to give you what you want, to meet your felt needs and longings. He tells you to be ruled by other, different desires. This is radical. God promises to change what you really want! God insists that He be first and all lesser loves be radically subordinate.

The best way to understand this is to think about prayer. Prayer means asking. And you ask because you *want* something. You ask God, because you believe He has power to accomplish some desired good. When Solomon prayed for a wise and discerning heart, God freely gave Solomon what he wanted (1 Kings 3). God was delighted that Solomon did not ask for a long life, riches, and success, the felt needs of most people of his day. Solomon had not treated God as a genie in a lamp who exists to grant three wishes. What we want by nature—the cravings of the flesh—expresses our sin nature. But Solomon had learned to know what he really needed. He had learned to pray according to the will of God, and it pleased God to answer him. We can change what we want and learn to pray for what delights God.

God challenges the things that everybody everywhere eagerly pursues (Matt. 6:32). What desires of body and mind (Eph. 2:3) *do* people naturally follow? Desires of the body include life itself, air, health, water, food, clothing, shelter, sexual pleasure, rest, and exercise. Desires of the mind include happiness, being loved, meaning, money and possessions, respect, status, accomplishment, self-esteem, success, control, power, self-righteousness, aesthetic pleasure, knowledge, marriage, and family. Must these rule our lives? They did not rule Jesus' life. Can these cravings really be changed? The Bible says yes and points us to the promises of God: to indwell us with power, to write truth on our hearts, to pour out His love in our hearts, to enable us to say "Abba, Father."

As we have seen, many of these things are not bad in themselves. The evil in our desires does not lie in what we want but that we want it too much. Our desires for good things seize the throne, becoming idols that replace the King. God refuses to serve our instinctive longings but commands us to be ruled by other longings. What God commands He provides the power to accomplish: He works in us both the willing and the doing of His good pleasure (Phil. 2:12–13).

Can you change what you want? Yes. Does the answer to this question surprise you? It counters very influential contemporary views of human motivation. Most Christian counseling books follow on the heels of secular psychologists and take your desires, your "felt needs," as givens. Many leading Christian psychologists make the unchangeability of what we long for the foundation of their systems.

For example, many teach that we have an "empty love tank" inside and our craving for love must be met or we are doomed to a life of sin and misery. Desires to feel good about ourselves ("self-esteem") or to accomplish something meaningful are similarly baptized. This creates the psychological equivalent of the "health and wealth" theology, which similarly selects certain common desires (in this case, the well-being of both body and wallet) and accepts them as givens that God is bound to fulfill. The psychological versions of health and wealth miss the fact that God is about the business of changing what people really long for. If felt needs are unchangeable, then it is impossible for us to learn how to pray the way Solomon did. This reinforces our tendency to pray for our cravings. It reinforces a sense of bottom victimization in those who were mistreated. It reinforces the tendency to press God into the service of our lusts.

The longings of the human heart must be changed if we are to become all that God designed us to be. Our longings are illegitimate masters; even where the object of desire is a good thing, the status of the desire usurps God. Our cravings should be recognized in order that we may more richly know God as the Savior, Lover, and Converter of the human soul. God would have us long for Him more than we long for His gifts. To make us truly human God must change what we want; we must learn to want the things Jesus wanted. It is no surprise that the psychologists can't find any biblical proof texts for their view of human motivation. The Bible teaches a different view.

The Christian life is a great paradox. Those who die to self find self. Those who die to their cravings will receive many times as much in this age and, in the age to come, eternal life (Luke 18:29–30). If I crave happiness, I will receive misery. If I crave to be loved, I will receive rejection. If I crave significance, I will receive futility. If I crave control, I will receive chaos. If I crave reputation, I will receive humiliation. But if I long for God and His wisdom, I will receive God and wisdom. Along the way, sooner or later, I will also receive happiness, love, meaning, order, and glory.

Every vital Christian testifies that the instinctive passions and desires of the flesh can be replaced with the new priorities of the Spirit. This reorientation is not instant and complete. But it is genuine and progressive. Two of the greatest books of practical Christian theology—Augustine's *Confessions* and Jonathan Edwards's *Treatise Concerning Religious Affections*—meditate on this transformation. So does the prayer of Francis of Assisi: "O Divine Master, grant that I may not so much seek to be consoled, as to console; to be understood, as to understand; to be loved, as to love." The need to learn how to love and understand replaces the craving for love and understanding.

Those who hunger and thirst for such righteousness will be satisfied—we have Jesus' word. We have no promise, however, that God will satisfy the instinctive cravings of the soul. The Bible teaches us to pray, to learn to ask for what we really need. Can we pray the petitions of the Lord's Prayer and really mean it? Yes. Can we long for God's glory, for His will to be obeyed, for daily material provision for all God's people, for sins to be forgiven, for aid in warfare with evil? Yes.

A wise Puritan pastor, Stephen Charnock, once wrote of "the expulsive power of a new affection." New ruling desires expel lesser masters from the throne. What are the new and different motives that rule in renewed hearts? What changed objects of desire characterize the master motives of the new, listening heart? How does God change what people want? The Bible treats these matters everywhere.[11]

Idolatrous cravings hijack the human heart. Both the Christian life and Christian ministry are by definition about the business of accomplishing a transformation in what people want. Such transformations lie at the very center of the Holy Spirit's purposes in working His Word into our lives. The lusts of the flesh lead somewhere bad: dead works. The lusts of the flesh have a specific solution: the Gospel of Jesus Christ, which replaces them. "He died for all, so that they who live might no longer live for themselves, but for Him who died and rose again on their behalf" (2 Cor. 5:15). The desires of the Lord lead somewhere good: good works. One key ingredient in reclaiming the cure of souls is to make this transformation central.

CONCLUSION

We have probed only one of the many terms by which the Bible explains the workings of the human heart in specific detail. This is only a down payment on a theme whose riches are inexhaustible. The human heart is an active verb. We do not "have needs"; we "do desires," just as we do love, fear, hope, trust, and all the rest. Here we have examined the verbs of desire. We could have examined any of scores of complementary verbs and metaphors that capture the fundamental activism of the human heart. The task of developing systematic biblical counseling, of reclaiming the cure of souls, lies before us.

Conviction backed up with content—God has given us both mandate and ingredients. If we listen to Him, we will construct a counseling system worthy of the name systematic biblical counseling. Such a system will stand in sharp contrast to the secular claimants that vie for legitimacy in the culture at large. Such a system will also stand in sharp contrast to the baptized versions of secular theory that vie for legitimacy within Christian culture. The Gospel of Jesus Christ is as wide as human diversity and as deep as human complexity. The Scriptures that bear witness to this Christ in the power of His Spirit are sufficient to cure souls.

NOTES

1. Sigmund Freud, *The Question of Lay Analysis*, trans. and ed. James Strachey (1927; trans., New York: W. W. Norton, 1959), 93. By "layman" Freud means a medical layman, someone who is not a physician. Freud recognized that psychotherapy was not strictly a medical activity. Many of Freud's followers, commentators, and critics have stated unambiguously that psychotherapy is a fundamentally "moral" or "spiritual" activity; that is, it fundamentally deals with belief, behavior, conscience, value, identity, meaning, and worldview.

2. Carl Jung, *Modern Man in Search of a Soul*, trans. W. S. Dell and Cary F. Baynes (San Diego: Harcourt Brace Jovanovich, 1933), 241.

3. Perry London, *The Modes and Morals of Psychotherapy* (New York: Holt, Rinehart & Winston, 1964), chapter 7.

4. In fact, Scripture is about even more than that, because it even redefines what a "problem" is. Scripture is as much about the problems of the self-satisfied, who never seek counseling, as it is about those who evidently struggle in their misery. A consistent biblical counseling ministry will both "comfort the disturbed and disturb the comfortable." The biblical model does not merely address the troubled and the troublemakers; it addresses everyone.

5. One characteristic of our times is that far more people believe in the sufficiency of Scripture for preaching or doctrinal teaching than believe in the sufficiency of Scripture for the tasks of counseling, discipleship, child rearing, and so forth. In effect, Scripture is fine for addressing crowds but inadequate for addressing individuals.

6. Companion pieces to this study might examine, to pick two examples, the mosaic of false beliefs that an individual embraces, or the varied functions and distortions of the self-evaluative gaze (questions of the conscience and identity). In fact, any of the verbs that relate human beings to God provide doors into what immediately and problematically motivates people. What do you love? fear? trust? hope in? take refuge in? seek? serve? obey? glorify? worship? Because human existence is "religious" down to the details, a biblical understanding will expose and dissect the "for God" or the "instead of God" that inhabits our behaviors, emotions, cognitions, choices, memories, anticipations, and attitudes. For a study of yet another door into human motivation, see David Powlison, "Idols of the Heart and 'Vanity Fair,'" *Journal of Biblical Counseling* 13, no. 2 (Winter 1995): 35–50.

7. The Old Testament typically focuses on idolatry as the way people go astray. This doesn't mean that the Old Testament is externalistic. Visible idolatry simply regis-

ters, for all to see, the failure to love the Lord God with heart, soul, mind, and might; it registers an internal defection. There are places where the problem of idolatry is turned into a metaphor for the most basic internal problem (e.g., Ezekiel 14). Visible idolatry always expressed a defection of heart from God. There are places where the human heart is described as insane (Eccl. 9:3), evil (Gen. 6:5), full of cravings and lies (Numbers 11–25), uncircumcised, hard, and blind. The New Testament also equates sinful desires with idolatry, metaphorically, on several occasions (e.g., Col. 3:5; Eph. 5:5). Idolatry can summarize every false, life-controlling master (1 John 5:21).

8. We often hear warnings against externalistic religion. But internalistic religion creates equally serious problems. Christians often seek some experience or feeling, some mystical high, some sense of total brokenness, some comprehensive inward transformation, and miss that biblical change is practical and progressive, both inside and out.

9. John Calvin, *Institutes of the Christian Religion*, trans. Ford Lewis Battles (Grand Rapids: Eerdmans, 1960), 604.

10. Ibid., 65, 108.

11. The following passages get a start on this question. For each passage ask, What does this person *really* want, long for, pursue, delight in? Psalms 42:1–2; 63:1–8; 73:25–28; 80; 90:8–17; Proverbs 2:1–6; 3:13–18; 8:11; Isaiah 26:8–9; Matthew 5:6; 6:9–13; 6:19–33; 13:45–46; Luke 11:9–13; Romans 5:1–11; 8:18–25; 9:1–3; 2 Corinthians 5:8–9; Philippians 1:18–25; 3:8–11; 3:20–21; 2 Timothy 2:22; 3:12; 1 Peter 1:13; 2:2; Revelation 22:20.

CHAPTER
13

HOW SHALL WE WAGE OUR WARFARE?

John H. Armstrong

D. Martyn Lloyd-Jones, perhaps our century's greatest biblical expositor, wrote several years ago: "There is nothing more urgently important for all who claim the name of Christian, than to grasp and to understand the teaching of [Ephesians 6:10–20]."[1] This is not overstated. In the face of growing citizen militia groups, committed to arming themselves in order to defend personal freedoms, it seems ironic that the church has forgotten that she is spiritually armed for an entirely different battle. As the church, in response to various culture wars, increasingly turns to numerous battles "with flesh and blood" rather than to the primary battle with "the spiritual forces of wickedness in the heavenly places" (Eph. 6:12), one must wonder if we have forgotten the teaching of the New Testament itself.

As the evangelical church becomes increasingly absorbed in a message less and less distinctly rooted in Scripture, a crisis of immense consequences looms. Believers are confused. Churches chase after techniques for growth and ministry, while Christian leaders rooted and grounded in the classic truths of Scripture seem harder and harder to find.

Two extremes regarding our spiritual warfare can be seen in the present climate. On the one hand, we have believers, and significant numbers of churches, who live as if there really is no enemy. They blithely ignore Satan, becoming embarrassed when anyone takes his existence seriously. For them, "out of sight is out of mind." They have been profoundly influenced by a scientific and rationalistic mind-set. At the other end of the spectrum is a new approach adopted by a growing number of evangelicals. This model threatens to overwhelm the church with its techniques. Desiring to help us wage warfare, these technique-centered materials take us away from Scripture in several important ways.

A NEW APPROACH TO SPIRITUAL WARFARE

Spiritual warfare ministries abound. They have various names, but all are ultimately related to *deliverance*. They generally speak of Chris-

227

tians being demonized.[2] Proponents of this approach tell us that Satan rules the lives of those who belong to Christ but does not possess them.

A recent visit to a local Christian bookshop revealed a whole section labeled "Spiritual Warfare." Here I discovered shelf after shelf of books, almost all published in the last five to ten years, dedicated to the subject of deliverance. This did not include similar books found in the huge counseling and psychology section. A simple perusal of titles revealed common terms such as *infest, attach, enter, inhabit, indwell, bind, enslave,* and even *control.*

The main emphasis of this approach is clear to see: Believers can be so affected by demons that a particular kind of *technique* or *method* is needed to stop them. The techniques needed for this battle must be learned. They are proven techniques mastered through firsthand experience. These authors, certain that they understand what they have experienced, disciple others with their techniques. When one reads this literature, the distinct impression is that *many* believers will have to overcome the work of demons at some point in their lives.

This movement is having an immense practical impact upon the church. It is hard to avoid its teaching. It is found repeatedly in sermons, as well as in popular seminars offered by almost every evangelical denomination and mission agency. Everywhere you turn, a testimony is being shared about someone's deliverance or of "territorial spirits" being driven out of an area so that the gospel can bear fruit.

The problem we face is not with the recognition of the enemy or even of his program. Biblical Christians all agree that Satan is both real and active in the world today. All evangelical Christians have much common ground in spiritual warfare. The central question, however, comes down to this: How does *Scripture* teach me (us) to engage in spiritual warfare?

This is not simply a matter of one group of believers believing in warfare whereas another group does not. It is, in reality, a matter of determining what we do and say according to the written Word itself. It is a matter of doctrine that takes us right back to the foundational truth of *sola Scriptura.*

The stated goal of this new model is deliverance, namely, to free all, especially Christian believers, from the influence of evil spirits who attach themselves to the human personality. David Powlison, in his immensely helpful book *Power Encounters*, sums up the issue well:

These ministries typically describe themselves using the words *deliverance, warfare,* or *spiritual warfare*. But all Bible-believing Christians believe in deliverance, warfare, and spiritual warfare, and many disagree with the distinctives of "deliverance" ministries. These ministries assert a particular version of spiritual warfare that has developed in recent years. Whether their version is correct or faulty is precisely the point of debate as we reclaim spiritual warfare. In doing so we should not relinquish good words whose meaning is at stake.[3]

Powlison coins the term "ekballistic encounter" to describe these new techniques. He derives this term from the New Testament itself. The word *ekballō* is the Greek compound word used to describe what Jesus did with evil spirits. It comes from two Greek words: *ek* ("out, or exit") and *ballō* ("to throw out, to cast out," from which we get "ballistic"). This term best captures what Jesus actually did in the Gospels. When He met someone suffering from the work of an unclean spirit, He directly cast it out. Powlison summarizes this new "ekballistic mode of ministry" clearly:

> The term EMM [Ekballistic Mode of Ministry] focuses on the mode of ministry, suggesting a particular form of pastoral activity: casting out demons. It is part of a grassroots practical theology—a way of addressing life problems—that finds varied expression both in pastoral ministry and in methods of personal growth. Ekballistic evangelism, for example, seeks to drive demons out of people and places so that individuals and groups can come to Christ who would otherwise be prevented. Ekballistic sanctification seeks to break demonic strongholds inside Christians; "when the demon goes, the Christian grows." EMM sanctification can be done to others as part of discipleship-counseling. And Christians can do it to themselves after being taught methods of ongoing self-deliverance. In sum, ekballistic spiritual warfare envisions the warfare of Christians as a *battle against invading demons*, either to repel them at the gates or eject them after they have taken up residence.[4] (italics added)

These contemporary approaches rely on the assumption that demons of sin reside in the human heart. It is assumed that people undergo a kind of moral demonization; that is, demons of pride, lewdness, rebellion, and so on actually infect, inhabit, or terrorize those who are in Christ. Demons take up residency and powerfully control, or at least strongly influence, the function of what the Bible calls the "heart." As Powlison puts it, "As squatters in the soul, they exert the power of a behind-the-scenes government."[5]

For this new model, if a person is having a spiritual problem, the distinct possibility exists that he or she also may have a "spirit" problem. I can illustrate this by a conversation I had with a pastor friend several years ago. He informed me that his son, who attended a well-known Christian school, was quite depressed. He had been struggling with doubts and had sought out a professor who engages in modern warfare counseling. The professor asked the young man a few questions and determined, to his satisfaction, that the boy was a believer. He then proceeded to say that a demon of doubt had most likely become attached to his spirit. The counseling followed this line for some weeks with not-so-helpful results.

Further, in this new model unclean spirits are often said to blind the mind, to enslave the will, and to make those affected unable, without the use of proper technique, to change their behavior. Perhaps the best description of the approach is this: Think of the human personality as a computer hard drive, with demons attacking it as a computer virus. This virus can infect the hard drive and corrupt its programs. This virus can rewrite programs, thus executing its own commands within this portion of the hard drive. To solve the problem, the computer specialist must remove the virus. Ekballistic ministries expel the virus, but they can also act as virus protection in the hard drive in order to keep it clear of future intrusions.[6]

BIBLICAL SPIRITUAL WARFARE

What is *biblical* spiritual warfare? And what have Christian authors and teachers prior to these contemporary movements said about this subject? More precisely, is the spiritual warfare model of these types helpful? Even more important, is it biblical?

For hundreds of years the church has understood that it was called to spiritual battle. The approach taken to this battle can be seen in the scores of valuable books written by Protestant Reformers, Puritans, and earlier evangelicals. Only in recent years has our preoccupation with techniques become so blatant.

Take the Puritans as an example. Here the older, classical approach is seen clearly. They wrote about warfare continually. They exposed Satan's deceptive wiles, analyzed the nature of how he utilized sinful hearts, and in general exposed his ways in order to help believers grow. They lived in an era when people still believed in the supernatural, and they took seriously the assaults of Satan. Puritan Thomas Brooks's classic *Precious Remedies Against Satan's Devices* helped to deliver more than one troubled soul from attack. William Gurnall's massive volume *The*

Christian in Complete Armour laid out the most complete systematic thinking of an era, while John Bunyan's two classic works, *Pilgrim's Progress* and *Holy War*, have influenced Spirit-filled Christians for centuries. It is my conviction that these classic volumes are far more reliable than any of the modern ekballistic approaches. (Some modern authors have addressed this issue from the older, classical approach with helpful emphasis upon the sufficiency of Scripture.[7])

I am struck, upon reading Ephesians 6:10–20, that nothing of the modern technique is to be found here. Though at times Puritan writers relied too heavily on their pastoral experience of Satan's wiles, they never developed techniques for expelling demons from within believers. What is found is reliance upon God, both His power and His grace, a clear and specific call to obedience, and fervent intercession guided by Scripture. These are the components of a biblically based response. All of this is in a corporate context: we are urged to fight in fellowship with other believers. (Note the "we," the "us," and the "our" of Ephesians 6:10–20.) If anything is remarkable about the approach taken by the apostle, it is that the weapons suggested here are not extraordinary. This passage, if exegeted carefully, will disappoint those seeking support for a deliverance model.

The classical model of spiritual warfare is grounded solidly in the written Scriptures and holds to the principle of *sola Scriptura*. The modern approach needs to be exposed for its inherent weakness.

DOES THE EVIDENCE SUPPORT THE NEW MODEL?

With stories of deliverance abounding in a growing genre of literature, it seems unbelieving to doubt this model. But is this warfare technique truly helpful? What is the evidence offered by these modern writers to defend this model of warfare?

1. THE PROBLEM OF DEEPLY ROOTED SINFUL BEHAVIOR

As already noted, this new model is directly concerned with sin in the life of the Christian. Modern warfare proponents are serious about the devil's part in causing us to sin. Poor eating habits, deviant sexual behavior, and much more are attributed to the devil.

Scripture takes an entirely different approach when it treats our own lusts as the reason for such sin (James 1:13–14), as David Powlison so plainly revealed in chapter 12. The responsibility for such sin lies with us. To blame forces outside of us is to run the risk of fighting the wrong battle with the wrong weapons. The ultimate source of such struggles is posited very clearly in Scripture—it is our own evil hearts that lead us into trouble (Mark 7:21–22).

But do believers ever succumb to the "flesh"? Do their hearts get them into trouble with sin? You bet! A perusal of Romans 7:18–21 will plainly reveal that the most earnest and godly still engage in such struggle. One might say, as the classic model has always taught, that the more godly you are, the more likely it is that you will become aware of the depth of your own heart's depravity. As you grow in grace, the battle will be waged on fronts you never imagined existed. Your heart's cry may often be, "Who will set me free from the body of this death?" (Rom. 7:24).

Our battle with sin within will not be over until we have a new, redeemed, glorified body (Rom. 8:23). An overrealized eschatology that seeks to press future things too much into present experience will always lead to trouble. To engage in even the most subtle form of blame-shifting spirituality that potentially passes off direct responsibility for my sin and seeks help in ways that do not correspond to the realities of the situation will only create greater problems for Christians.

2. THE PROBLEM OF DEMON POSSESSION AND THE CHRISTIAN

As previously noted, this approach generally prefers to speak of believers being "demonized" but not "demon possessed." Is this a distinction with a real difference?

There can be no doubt that demons controlled and used the human personalities of several individuals we read of in the Bible. The Greek term for "demons" is actually a broad one meaning "gods" (Acts 17:18) and supernatural beings. "Unclean spirits" (Matt. 10:1) brought with them incredible problems. Jesus cast them out (*ekballō*) by the word of His own power as a sign of the coming of His kingdom (12:28). These evil spirits work with Satan and were apparently cast out of heaven when he rebelled. They now await their final judgment (cf. 2 Peter 2:4; Jude 6). They are permanently opposed to God—and His goodness, mercy, and truth—to the kingdom of His Son, and to the well-being of His subjects, believers. They have real power, but it is *limited* power. (The Greek idea of dualism must be rejected completely—Satan is not a rival god with an agenda that can be carried out so that God is sometimes defeated by him.)

John Calvin summed up the biblical perspective well when he spoke of these spirits being used in God's larger purpose as those who "drag their chains wherever they go." Martin Luther captured the right sense of things when he called the devil "God's devil." Satan must always be subject to the sovereign will and power of the Almighty One. Paul concurs when he says that Satan's power is limited since he is a defeated foe (Col. 2:15).

These beings manifested *unique* and direct attack upon our Lord during His earthly sojourn. Nothing in the Old Testament, or in subsequent church history, compares to what we read in the Gospels. It seems quite obvious that demons feared the authority of Christ and were completely subject to Him (Mark 1:25; 3:11–12; 9:25). But what about today? Are believers in danger of being "demonized" in such a way that they lose control over themselves, their thoughts, actions, and choices? The modern teachers of spiritual warfare insist that this is exactly what happens.

Though these teachers insist that believers cannot be possessed, I find no comfort in the distinctions they make between demon possession and demonization. Perhaps it is because I can see no real difference. For some, Christians can never be totally free of demons. The demon's work is said to be one of *degree*. In this approach, the believer will need continual counsel, direction, and aid in having the right techniques, teaching, and ministry to remain free.

I believe that a straightforward reading of the Gospels reveals that being "demonized" and being "demon possessed" are virtually the same. A *demoniac* is one who was controlled, or possessed, by a demon spirit. The phrase is used thirteen times in the Gospels. The other term, used eight times, means simply "to have a demon." A simple reading reveals that those who were demonized were controlled by evil spirits. The category of believers invaded by demons but not possessed or controlled by them is not one Scripture warrants (cf. Matt. 8:16; 8:28; 9:32; Luke 8:2; etc.). Even these teachers admit that Scripture is inconclusive at best on the issue. Other evidence beyond the Bible is used for making their point.

I have one simple question: If we cannot be theologically precise and if the text is not conclusive at all, why build so much practice on what we have so little explicit biblical basis for in the first place? Further, if believers are truly God's property (1 Cor. 6:19) and the "temple of the Holy Spirit," what kind of salvation is it that allows the Evil One to "demonize" them? Paul says that Christ "gave Himself for us to redeem us from every lawless deed, and to purify for Himself a people for His own possession, zealous for good deeds" (Titus 2:14). This is not the description of a people controlled by demons one moment and by the Spirit the next. I fear that an entire doctrine of sanctification, itself defective, is behind this theology. It is a doctrine that does not adequately grasp the greatness of the Spirit's work in applying salvation to those who believe.

In addition, the writer of Hebrews says that the power of the Evil One has been broken for those who believe:

> Since then the children share in flesh and blood, He Himself likewise also partook of the same, so that through death He might render powerless him who had the power of death, that is, the devil, and might free those who through fear of death were subject to slavery all their lives. (2:14–15)

How can I fear ancestral demons if this is true? Why become concerned with breaking the hold of demonization if Christ has rendered Satan powerless by His death? Where do I get explicit biblical instruction to use any technique or counsel to break Satan's hold?

3. THE PROBLEM OF TERRITORIAL DEMONS

Perhaps no subject in the realm of spiritual warfare has caused such a stir as the doctrine of "territorial spirits." This theory maintains that demonic spirits rule geographical areas.

The thesis of this particular theme is simple: Fallen angelic beings (demons) control territory and operate behind, with, and in societal structures. God allows this to happen within His sovereign purpose (dualism is formally rejected), but we as believers must learn to discern, oppose, and resist these spirits. Much of the time it is something to be done in public as a kind of "power encounter," where strongholds are overtly and aggressively attacked. God, it is claimed, is leading the church into a new ministry as we bind demons so that villages, towns, and cities can be evangelized. We defeat "territorial spirits" through worship and praise, along with intercessory prayer. This loosens demonic strongholds, often evidenced in the presence of prostitution, pornography, fear, apathy, violence, and so on.

What is the real evidence for these "territorial spirits"? Mostly anecdotal stories, such as the following:

> Steve Nicholson has preached the gospel in the area for six years with virtually no fruit. Nicholson begins some serious prayer and fasting. A grotesque, unnatural being appears to him. It growls, "Why are you bothering me?" It identifies itself as a demon of witchcraft who has dominion

over the geographical area. In the heat of the warfare, Nicholson names the city streets in the surrounding area. The spirit retorts, "I don't want to give you that much." In the name of Jesus, Nicholson commands the spirit to give up the territory. During the next three months the church doubles in size from 70-150, mostly from new converts out of witchcraft. Nearly all of the new believers must be delivered from demons.[8]

There is really only one clear reference to Scripture in the material I have personally read. Where one might expect to find massive exposition of a passage like Ephesians 6 or references in the Great Commission to our dealing with demons in order to finish the task, what we find is a reference to the prince of Persia and the prince of Greece (Dan. 10:13, 20). Though there may be some reference here to Satan's assigning a certain area to a spirit being, this conclusion is far from certain. H. C. Leupold is extremely helpful when he comments upon this text:

> The sum of the matter is this: There are powerful forces of evil at work in and through the nations and their rulers to defeat and to overthrow the people of God. This may alarm and cause terror when one considers how powerful these demon potentates are. On the other hand, there are still more powerful agents of good at work who, by harmonious cooperation, will prevail over their wicked opponents. So the cause of the kingdom is in good hands, and its success is assured.
>
> This happens to be a truth that is considered too little in our day. Yet it throws light upon many a puzzling situation in the course of historical developments and helps God's children to keep a balanced judgment as well as a sure hope.[9]

This text does not provide us with input regarding the organization of Satan's kingdom or how he or demons actually oppose the kingdom of Christ. We are told certain things about his wiles (Ephesians 6) but little else. The only reason we can deduce for this silence is that God does not seem to think we really need to know more than what He plainly reveals (Deut. 29:29). Nothing in the Bible tells us to specifically identify "territorial spirits." Nothing is said about what technique we should use to expose them.

We pray as our Lord taught us: "Your kingdom come. Your will be done, on earth as it is done in heaven. . . . And do not lead us into temptation, but deliver us from evil" (Matt. 6:10, 13). We affirm that the church's prayer life is part and parcel of its biblical worldview and that the supernatural forces of darkness are arrayed against us. We believe that, as we pray, God's will is done both in things seen and unseen.

What is to be seriously questioned is the confusion created by stories and methods that have no biblical basis.

"RESIST THE DEVIL"

The clear counsel of the Word of God, regarding how the believer is to face the enemy, is found in passages such as the following:

Submit therefore to God. Resist the devil and he will flee from you. (James 4:7)

Your adversary, the devil, prowls around like a roaring lion, seeking someone to devour. But resist him, firm in your faith, knowing that the same experiences of suffering are being accomplished by your brethren who are in the world. (1 Peter 5:8–9)

Our *adversary*, which is the Greek term for an opponent in a lawsuit, goes about seeking to destroy or devour. He is the devil, adds Peter. Devil (*diabolos*) is the Greek translation of the Hebrew word *Satan*. Satan means "slanderer" or "accuser." This is his distinct work against us—to accuse or to slander our person before both God and man. We come against this work by remaining "firm in the faith," that is, by reminding ourselves of the gospel and of our standing in Christ and His grace. Our chief weapon is the Word of God (Eph. 6:17), especially as it reveals the gospel, which is the word of our redemption and our deliverance from Satan's kingdom into the kingdom of God's Son (2 Cor. 4:3–6).

Deliverance ministries can be seen in the life and ministry of our Lord Jesus. The question, however, is this: Where are we warranted to deal with Satan's kingdom in the same manner that our Lord dealt with the direct frontal assault upon His person and His message seen in the Gospels?

Jesus' power encounters are plainly *unique*. They are, as one has appropriately put it, "enacted parables."[10] He bound the strong man, and He plundered his kingdom. He did this in His death at Calvary, where the enemy made his biggest blunder of all time. Here the devil, whom Jonathan Edwards appropriately believed to be a "block head," overplayed his trump card, helping to stir up the crowd to crucify Jesus only to have his own kingdom routed and defeated once and for all through the death of the Savior (Matt. 12:29).

That is why we have no imperatives after the Cross to engage in the ministries of deliverance exactly like those historically seen in the life and ministry of the Messiah. This does not mean we shall never encounter the devil or demons, but we recognize that even Michael, the archangel of the Lord, did not rebuke the devil person to person but said to Satan, "The Lord rebuke you" (Jude 9; cf. also 2 Peter 2:9–11).

False teachers were warned of the dangers of falling into the trap of the Evil One if they mocked the devil's power (cf. 1 Cor. 5:5; 1 Tim. 1:20), thus demonstrating an opposite error from that of the modern warfare teaching. We must heed the warnings cited at the beginning of this chapter lest we do not take seriously the devil. If we do not, we may fall under his illusions, which appear particularly to be found in the area of false teaching resulting in a sensuous lifestyle.

When you read the Gospels, you discover that the purpose of Jesus' miracles is to reveal His kingdom and its purpose. Powlison is surely right when he concludes, "The deliverance mode served to attest, declare, accredit, bear witness, and confirm."[11] This same reality can be seen in Acts 2:43, where we read that "many wonders and signs were taking place *through the apostles*," who bore authoritative witness to the unique identity of Christ. By this we do not conclude that we shall never see power encounters at certain places and times but rather that we contextually understand the role these *biblical* signs and wonders had in relationship to the arrival of the kingdom. It is patently obvious that there are many things Jesus did that we are not told to do likewise.

The biblical way of dealing with the devil in this age is more simply stated: We are to "put on the full armor of God" (Eph. 6:11). We do not do this in our strength but "in the Lord." The very picture here is that we go to battle against an opponent who is outside us. As Jesus said, "The gates of hell shall not prevail." Gates signify a defensive posture. The church is on the march by the Word and prayer as it fights against the Evil One. We fight him by "standing firm." We do this with the truth.

THE SUFFICIENCY OF THE WORD OF GOD

This modern teaching on spiritual warfare leads to a number of significant problems. For one, it causes an undue reliance upon formula rather than Scripture. It causes the church to move further away from looking upon Jesus and His gospel as the true source for power. A more pressing problem can be seen in the counseling process. Here accountability for decisions and actions is shifted away from full human responsibility. But perhaps the most dangerous tendency of all is that this teaching and practice undermines the doctrine of the sufficiency of the written Scriptures.

First, we must note again that the proponents of these theories do not explicitly support their teaching with the Word of God. Their premises are simply not grounded in the plain didactic portions of Scripture. To appeal to the works of Jesus, as we have briefly shown, is not an adequate basis for saying that we too must do what He did. (In fact, much of what is claimed for this movement was not even done in Jesus' ministry.) Tom Austin summarizes this problem succinctly:

> Thus this teaching must be impressed upon Scripture, for Scripture clearly does not teach it. This is done through relating personal experiences and then drawing logical conclusions from them. . . . In this way, Scripture is not the authority for this teaching, rather personal experience is.[12]

In all this we see people who have, in Martyn Lloyd-Jones's terms, "capitulated to phenomena." This practice has become common in our time, as one Christian after another appeals to what they see, hear, or feel. Surely this counsel is helpful: "The Christian should seek to interpret the facts in the light of the teaching of Scripture. He must not allow phenomena to determine his belief."[13] B. B. Warfield, who defended the integrity of the written Scriptures in his own time, stated the problem well: "The real question, in a word, is not a new question but the perennial old question, whether the basis of our doctrine is to be what the Bible teaches, or what men teach."[14]

Second, many advocates of deliverance models admit that they are not always sure of what they are doing. They often appeal to *openness*—openness, they argue, to a bigger and better worldview, one that is supernatural. In the process, a working model is developed that cannot be tested rationally by "What saith the Scripture?" In the process a *super*-supernaturalism is developed that far exceeds the warrant of the Word of God.

What is always true is the Word of God. As Jesus said, "Sanctify them in the truth; Your word is truth" (John 17:17). The psalmist testifies, "The sum of Your word is truth, and every one of Your righteous ordinances is everlasting" (Ps. 119:160). If we begin to accept as truth what has happened, even to fellow believers, we have no basis for rejecting the truth claims of any other religious doctrine.

Third, according to this model, if we do not do this deliverance work in the right way, that is, with the correct and proven technique, then it may not work. Some even suggest that we must say "Jesus" the right way or we might be defeated. Or that we take Communion as a way to receive power when trying to rid ourselves of demonic infiltration. Surely this understanding of the Lord's Supper escaped the Reformers and subsequent evangelical commentators for the past five centuries.

Fourth, these techniques deny the whole counsel of God in a profound way. By saying that we do all that Jesus did, do we not teach that the whole of Scripture is not enough for us? With this approach we can only deduce that more revelation will be needed. Is the canon *really* closed? Has all that we need "for life and godliness" been revealed?

Sola Scriptura is a vital truth for the church in every age, especially in one that has closed its mind to doctrine and at the same time has opened its heart to the irrational and the bizarre. If we are not careful, we may really get demons—demons that will destroy the faith and confidence of the church in Scripture. "To the law and to the testimony! If they do not speak according to this word, it is because they have no dawn" (Isa. 8:20).

How should we respond to this explosion of interest in the demonic and in this new spiritual warfare model? I would suggest that a good dose of restraint would be a helpful starting point. Avoid going beyond the written Scripture. Avoid assuming too much about testimonies. Avoid the sensational and the fantastic. Satan is a deceiver who is not only a "roaring lion" (1 Peter 5:8) but also one who comes as an "angel of light" (2 Cor. 11:14). He can even reveal things about himself to confuse us.

Perhaps the most important issue goes even beyond the sufficiency of Scripture. This teaching directs believers inward to themselves and outward to an enemy, *rather than, historically, to the Cross.* Here victory was really won. The outcome is not in doubt. If we are not careful, modern warfare teaching will cause a whole generation to drift even further away from the doctrine of the Cross.

Professor John Bolt observes that here one must protest. Accenting "spiritual warfare as the fundamental description of the Christian life risks turning the 'Prince of Peace' into the 'Commander-in-chief,' a role that fits the messianic expectation of Jewish apocalyptic-eschatology more than the Christology of the Gospels and the Pauline corpus." Bolt concludes:

It also potentially diverts our attention away from the kingdom battles on earth—against unrighteousness, immorality, injustice, disease, and poverty—to a spiritual realm above the earth. Is there a war on for Christians? Undoubtedly! However, the weapons suggested by the apostle Paul in Ephesians 6 won't make the headlines of the *National Enquirer*; they include sound doctrine, evangelical readiness, obedience, and above all prayer.[15]

Martin Luther understood this well. He was engaged in a great battle for truth. His opposition was very visible. Preoccupation with the devil and mystical revelations was rampant in the church of his time. Because of his insistence on the finality and authority of Scripture he was considered a heretic. The whole world seemed to be against him. But more terrifying to Luther was the vast array of wicked spiritual forces *behind* the world system. He truly believed in a worldview based on Ephesians 6. But he would not give in to his human fears. And he would not resort to the mysticism of a church given to a kind of incantational response to the world of demons. His response can be seen in the powerful and familiar words of his oft-sung hymn:

> And tho' this world, with devils filled,
> Should threaten to undo us,
> We will not fear, for God hath willed
> His truth to triumph thro' us:
> The Prince of Darkness grim,
> We tremble not for him;
> His rage we can endure,
> For, lo, his doom is sure,
> One little word shall fell him.
>
> That word above all earthly pow'rs,
> No thanks to them, abideth;
> The spirit and the gifts are ours
> Thro' Him who with us sideth:
> Let goods and kindred go,
> This mortal life also;
> The body they may kill:
> God's truth abideth still,
> His kingdom is forever.

NOTES

1. D. Martyn Lloyd-Jones, *The Christian Soldier: An Exposition of Ephesians 6:10–20* (Grand Rapids: Baker, 1977), 11.

2. Tom Austin, "On the Demonization of Believers," *Reformation & Revival Journal* 4, no. 1 (1995): 11–12. This issue, given entirely to the theme "Spiritual Warfare," is a general survey of this modern movement. It is available from Reformation & Revival Ministries, Inc., P.O. Box 88216, Carol Stream, Illinois 60188.

3. David Powlison, *Power Encounters: Reclaiming Spiritual Warfare* (Grand Rapids: Baker, 1995), 28.

4. Ibid., 29.

5. Ibid., 29.

6. Ibid., 30. For an excellent history of this new model over the last thirty years, see pp. 32–33.

7. Cf. Frederick Leahy, *Satan Cast Out* (Edinburgh, Scotland: Banner of Truth, 1975), is far and away the best of this type of book. Also, James Bell recently compiled a 365-day devotional consisting of selections from Gurnall's work: *The Christian in Complete Armour: Daily Readings in Spiritual Warfare* (Chicago: Moody, 1994).

8. Steven Lawson, "Defeating Territorial Demons," *Charisma and the Christian Life* (April 1980): 48.

9. H. C. Leupold, *Exposition of Daniel* (Grand Rapids: Baker, 1949), 459–60.

10. Powlison, *Power Encounters*, 94.

11. Ibid., 95.

12. Austin, "On the Demonization of Believers," 18–19.

13. Leahy, *Satan Cast Out*, 166.

14. B. B. Warfield, *The Inspiration and Authority of the Bible* (Phillipsburg, N.J.: Presb. & Ref., 1948), 226.

15. John Bolt, "Satan Is Alive and Well in Contemporary Imagination: A Bibliographic Essay with Notes on 'Hell' and 'Spiritual Warfare,'" *Calvin Theological Journal* 29, no. 2 (November 1994): 506.

PART
5
RESPONDING TO THE CRISIS

CHAPTER
14
RECOVERING THE
PLUMB LINE

Michael S. Horton

We live in a fascinating time. Over the mere span of a few months in 1995, *Newsweek* magazine asked churches why sin and forgiveness have been thrown overboard for more psychological and "seeker-sensitive" themes; *Time* reminded us of the Resurrection and asked us why it is no longer central (or, for that matter, believed by all who call themselves Christians). Although the Reformation is perceived by many evangelicals as an irrelevant event somewhere in the foggy past, it was recently celebrated and sympathetically mined for its resources by the *Wall Street Journal*. And one cover story of *U.S. News and World Report* was on the commercialization of evangelical Christianity.

During this same span of time, I watched the ABC television special with Peter Jennings "In the Name of God," as the church growth movement and the signs and wonders movement (especially the so-called "laughing revival") were described by their own supporters. One entrepreneurial evangelical pastor announced that he did not "bore" people by telling them to turn to particular places in Scripture. Another parroted David Letterman's "Top Ten List" on Sunday morning, with the images of Letterman and other icons of pop culture facing the congregation (rather, audience) from the stage. Still another leading church growth pastor told Jennings that the reason he did not have a cross anywhere was because, as important as the cross is to the church, Christianity cannot be reduced to one message or symbol. On the signs and wonders side of things, it was utter bedlam, with men and women exhibiting the most astonishing hysteria. One leader, himself struggling with a terminal illness, said that he had to see miracles regularly and reminisced about his pre-signs and wonders days, during which he frequently asked himself, "I gave up drugs for this?" In his wrap-up, Jennings asked the viewing audience whether these bold enterprises are actually making Christianity relevant by abandoning the gospel.

My point in this litany is to observe that there seems to be more common sense in popular culture—even among some of those who may

245

not be Christian believers themselves—than one often discerns in the evangelical movement. The unregenerate may not understand the things of the Spirit of God (1 Cor. 2:14), but many certainly understand the things of the world, and they can tell when the church and the world are no longer distinguishable. As the lines continue to blur, a crisis looms on the near horizon. The church must be reminded that, when the text of Scripture is no longer regulating her doctrine, life, and worship, her authority and power, which is grounded in the Gospel of Christ revealed in Scripture, will soon be lost.

We must recover Scripture from the standpoint of that earlier recovery during the Protestant Reformation. To be sure, much has changed, and we live in a postmodern rather than a premodern context. Nevertheless, the church has a plumb line that transcends time and place, and we can always return to it in order to determine whether we are being faithful in our moment. When the Reformers reduced their message to its core, the results were a series of "*solas*" or "onlys" that became rallying points for the masses: Scripture only, Christ only, grace only, faith only, and to God alone be glory. By understanding what they meant by these slogans we can grasp something of the distance of today's supposed heirs of the Reformation from this center of gravity and our unfortunate proximity to the confused medieval church.

SCRIPTURE: OUR ONLY AUTHORITY

Since *sola Scriptura* is often misunderstood, let us begin by saying what it does *not* mean. Martin Luther once declared, "We may not deviate from the cause of truth, even if many, yes all are against it. . . . And though it is hard and difficult to bear such loneliness . . . we know God, who will be our judge, lives." But even more famous is his line at the Diet of Worms: "Here I stand, so help me, God." Many historians have interpreted Luther as though he set out to place the conscience above human authority and to set individual rights over against the community. A precursor of modern individualism, the Luther of popular high school lectures is made to sing a duet with Frank Sinatra: "I Did It My Way."

But this tells us more about our own age than about Luther's. Heiko Oberman observes how we came to misunderstand the Reformation as individualistic:

On the Protestant side the individualism of the nineteenth century and the personalism of the twentieth celebrated the Reformer as a fearless outsider and presented him as a prototype of modern man. Relying only on himself, he could assume and dared to assume the responsibility to act before God for the world in accordance with his own conscience and the dictates of the hour.[1]

On the Roman Catholic side, many interpreters have simply chalked Luther's revolution up to subjectivism. After all, was this not the Reformer's view of salvation: Redemption as a purely private affair, a personal relationship with God that had no reference to the communion of saints? While these Protestant and Roman Catholic interpretations may explain American sectarianism, they do not deal adequately with the actual writings of Luther and the other Reformers.

As a wave of contemporary historians are now pointing out, Luther and Calvin had a robust doctrine of the church—*catholic* in the best sense of that word. Calvin echoed the warning of Augustine—"He cannot have God for his father who does not take the church for his mother"—and reiterated the line of Cyprian—"Outside the church there is no salvation." The question for the Reformers was not whether "a church" but whether that particular assembly that calls itself the Church of Christ was in fact what it claimed to be. The Roman Catholic historical theologian Alexandre Ganoczy points out that Calvin referred to Rome as "the papal kingdom" rather than as "the Catholic Church," since he "does not think of reveling against the one, holy catholic and apostolic Church, but only against its distortions."[2]

The last thing on the mind of the Reformers was what we now call "the priesthood of all believers" and "the right to private interpretation" of the Bible. What we usually mean is that every believer is a minister and does not, therefore, require an authoritative creed, confession, catechism, or teachers to keep him or her in bounds. For the Reformers, the priesthood of all believers simply meant that laypeople could hear each other's confessions and pronounce absolution without a priest on the basis of James 5:16. And as for the right of private interpretation, Luther once quipped about such a notion, "That would mean that each man would go to hell in his own way."

No one has a "right" to interpret Scripture in isolation from the communion of saints. There is a "cloud of witnesses," from the patriarchs and apostles to the early fathers, doctors, and reformers, and the individual believer is responsible to this catholic community. In fact, it was because Rome had ceased to be faithful to this catholic community and its apostolic deposit that it had ceased to be "the Catholic Church."

However, it is true that the definition of the church did change with the Reformation when its leaders recognized that in Scripture the church was understood as referring to the entire number of those who are baptized—professing Christians and their children. While there are, as Augustine said, "many wolves within and many sheep without," the visible church consists of laypeople as well as pastors, teachers, and evangelists. Where Rome had referred to the Church as the Magisterium (the official teaching office—bishops, archbishops, and cardinals, with the pope as its head), the Scriptures everywhere assume that both clergy and laity are included together and are, therefore, bound by a certain equality before God.

At the same time, God had raised up pastors and teachers in the church, imbuing them with the learning, skills, and piety for a sacred calling to the ministry of Word and sacrament. The local government of all Protestant churches included laypeople, and the whole congregation elected those whom they considered aptly suited to such offices, based on the prescription of Paul to Timothy. When a minister had been suitably educated, he would be "called" by the congregation. This is far from the idea one finds in some evangelical and charismatic circles, in which an individual announces that he is "called" by God and begins to preach or teach without the permission of the church. In the Protestant understanding, one is not truly called by God to the ministry until he is called by the church, for it is through the mouth of the church that one hears the call of God.

Why all of this background for a discussion of "Scripture alone"? It is absolutely vital to understand that the Reformation did not set the individual against the church, as evangelicals often have in this century. We think so much of spiritual growth in terms of our personal relationship with Jesus Christ and very rarely consciously associate that with our relatedness to the body of Christ—not only those who are now living but those who have gone before us and who will come after us. The Reformers did make that connection. That is why they affirmed the ancient creeds, and that is why the Protestant churches drafted confessions of faith and officially adopted catechisms for the training of the young in the great truths of Scripture.

It was not a notion of the individual against the church but of every Christian (including the layperson) as included in the church that was recovered in the Reformation. Instead of the Magisterium confessing the faith of the church on behalf of the ignorant layperson, the layperson was taught sufficiently so that he or she could confess the faith of the church *with* the church gathered together for worship.

But ever since the beginning of the last century, the democratizing influence has bred a suspicion and outright hostility toward creeds, confessions, and catechisms. "Don't Fence Me In" is the egalitarian spirit of Romantic individualism that so characterizes our age and our churches. We criticize the liberals of the sixties for overthrowing authority, but it is endemic to the American frontier spirit. How far this is from the intention of our evangelical forebears and how disastrous to the cause of Christ when we are given permission to freely preach or teach our own whims and opinions even when they violate the consensus of the church.

It is this "freedom" and "no creed but Christ" emphasis that has contributed to the fragmentation of the body of Christ over the last two centuries. Far from bringing peace, unity, and freedom, it has invited discord, confusion, and bondage. Luther described the effects of this kind of individualism in the most merciless terms: Heretics all share a *philautos*, love of themselves,

> for they are wiser than the church and cannot err. But we who would be true Christians should be ready to be instructed by any child. A comet is also a star that moves about on the order of a planet, but it is [an illegitimate child] among planets. It is a proud star, occupies the entire heaven, and acts as if it were there alone. It has the nature of heretics, who also imagine that they are the only ones.

To defend "Scripture alone," therefore, we need to guard against its abuses. In our day, there are many popes instead of one. In fact, each man or woman has the capacity for becoming an infallible judge. Occasionally I will hear the objection to creeds, confessions, and catechisms with the assertion "I just go directly to the Bible." The assumption here is that those who drafted these documents that have stood the test of time did not go directly to the Bible.

But our forebears did go directly to the Bible when they drafted their confessions of faith and catechisms. In fact, the Puritans carefully included texts for every statement in the Westminster Larger and Shorter Catechisms. The minute one begins to explain what the Bible is saying in a particular place, he or she is doing precisely what these gifted pastors and teachers did: interpreting the Word of God. The only difference is that our own interpretations are limited by our own time, place, and circumstances, whereas these long-standing interpretations make available to us today the wisdom of centuries of biblical interpretation.

Forged in great upheavals and doctrinal controversy, the early creeds forced the church to carefully define the doctrines of the Trinity and the person of Christ. Today, most of the cults and sects that have arisen are champions of the "no creed but Christ" maxim—and with good reason. We have covered this ground before in the controversies of the past: the Mormons are Gnostics; the Jehovah's Witnesses are Arians; and so on. Why should we ignore the successes of the church in the past when facing the same heresies again and again in church history?

Beyond the creeds, the church needs to agree on a biblical understanding of the most important matters of faith and life. When we discover a lack of unity and a party spirit in the church, the last thing we turn to is doctrinal refinement. It is doctrine that divides, we often hear. But Paul saw it in just the opposite terms. Writing to a divided Corinthian church, he appealed to his brothers, "in the name of our Lord Jesus Christ, that all of you agree with one another so that there may be no divisions among you and that you may be perfectly united in mind and thought" (1 Cor. 1:10 NIV). So much for "agreeing to disagree agreeably." This did not mean, for Paul, that everything had to be nailed down, but it did mean that unity depended on a rather substantial consensus on the principal teachings of Scripture. It was by developing a common confession of faith that the divided church would achieve greater unity. It was not by avoiding doctrine but by discussing it that petty strife would be quenched.

Creeds, confessions, and catechisms are not, in the Protestant understanding, in competition with Scripture. They do not violate the principle of *sola Scriptura* but, rather, serve to strengthen it. After all, they are nothing more than the church's carefully thought-out interpretation of the infallible text. My own interpretations may be accurate and even occasionally insightful, but the accumulated wisdom of the church is far richer. We have something to learn about the Bible from those who lived before us, as, Lord willing, those who follow us will have something to learn from our mistakes, controversies, and conclusions.

Those who eschew these standards from the past are, in effect, declaring that they are so skilled in the Scriptures that there is nothing they can learn from teachers. One of the first signs of genuine wisdom and education is the recognition that one knows very little. It is this humility that drives one to ask questions, to probe, to read, to examine—in order to learn. But it is a sure sign of ignorance when one dismisses the need to learn from others. Such people are destined to live in a small, dark cell of solitary confinement.

What we need desperately right now is greater space, more light, and less confinement. We need to reconnect ourselves to the communion of the saints and to read the Bible with our spiritual ancestors again. The church must explain the Word of God. Its ministers must proclaim it in preaching, teaching, and pastoral ministry, but to do this responsibly they need to be accountable to the wider body. If creeds, confessions, and catechisms are merely the church's attempt to provide an agreed-upon interpretation of Scripture, we can recover *sola Scriptura* in some fundamental ways.

Scripture alone not only does not mean individualism or subjectivism; it must not be construed as saying that the Bible tells us everything. There is a particular purpose for Scripture, as Jesus said: "You search the Scriptures because you think that in them you have eternal life; it is these that bear witness of Me; and you are unwilling to come to Me so that you may have life" (John 5:39–40). Scripture is chiefly concerned with the unfolding of the drama of redemption, from the Garden of Eden to the New Jerusalem, and everything relates to Christ as prophet, priest, and king.

That means that the Bible is not principally concerned with organizing our schedule, giving us tips for winning in life and business, or with guiding us into self-fulfillment. It is a story about God and His saving acts leading up to the cross, the Resurrection, and our Lord's return in order to make all things new. It is not about us, and it is not about our daily lives. It is about God and His redemptive activity in the daily lives of wandering Hebrews and first-century Palestinian Jews who were eyewitnesses to the resurrection of the God-Man.

Very often these days, the demand is overpowering for the "practical." If the modern man or woman is going to take the time to get up, dress the kids, and make it to church, it had better be relevant. But is this great redemptive story irrelevant? Have we reversed our definition of the trivial and the grand? Is the greatest story ever told now boring, since we cannot see how it can possibly make us feel good or advance our self-fulfillment over the next seventy-two hours?

Many intend a high view of Scripture when they insist that it is a manual for life, but, in fact, treating the Bible as a manual ends up leading to a low view of Scripture by trivializing the message. We have auto manuals, cookbooks, and self-help guides for an endless spectrum of activities. What we do not have, besides the Bible, is an infallible self-revelation from God telling us how we, being sinners, can be reconciled to a holy God. There is a great deal that we can learn from philosophers, scientists, physicians, lawyers, artists, and other professionals that we cannot find in the Bible, and there is no reason to expect Scripture to answer questions that can be addressed by common sense, creativity, and education, whether the author is a believer or not. But psychology, sociology, marketing, politics, and all other secular disciplines have to take a backseat when we are forming our views of God, ourselves, and the meaning of life and history, salvation, and the nature, purpose, and methods of church growth, worship, and evangelism.

If "Scripture alone" does not mean private individualism or excluding all other books in order to make the Bible address every conceivable "practical" question, what does it mean and how can it be related to our present situation?

WHAT STANDS IN THE WAY OF THE SUFFICIENCY OF SCRIPTURE?

Throughout the Middle Ages there had been a "medieval synthesis" between Christianity and Greek philosophy. This was often a happy marriage, but it was frequently the case that Greek philosophy actually found a rather large area of overlap with theology, and, in those cases, the former had priority over the latter. In the late medieval period, the various philosophical schools were so busy warring over speculative positions that Scripture became an obscure, mysterious book whose secrets only the professionals could unlock. The Reformers referred to these theologians as "Sophists," after the ancient Greek school of relativists. The Sophists believed that there was no such thing as truth, only rhetorical brilliance. The winner of the argument was king, regardless of whether he was right.

When one reads the Scriptures, one is immediately impressed with the simplicity of its profound teachings. The straightforward character of the text is obvious, in sharp contrast to the philosophical speculations of the medieval schools. Consequently, the Bible—its doctrines and paradigms—did not rule the church; it was philosophical categories that occupied her greatest minds.

In our day we face a similar confusion. Many people today think that the Bible is a terribly obscure book as they look at all of the divisions and conclude that there could not possibly be one easily obtainable message in a book that has produced so many denominations. In addition to philosophy, the modern social and behavioral sciences have now claimed dominance in our society, and we often find evangelical sermons, books, broadcasts, and other resources parroting secular pop psychology, business, and marketing, while the biblical themes of sin and grace, wrath and redemption disappear from the vocabulary and diet of evangelical church life. We speak of peace of mind, emotional healing, recovery, dysfunction, self-talk, self-esteem, and so forth the way previous generations used to speak of original sin, atonement, justification, sanctification, and related biblical truths. Rather than a definitive source for all that we believe and teach, the Bible, in our present context, becomes a source of quotations for sermons and books that are essentially secular in their basic content and message. Just as the Bible was used to justify one philosophical school over another in the Middle Ages, in our day it is shaped like a wax nose to suit the latest fad.

The problem is that this happens in churches that claim fidelity to the inerrancy of Scripture. The unfaithfulness is difficult to mark objectively, since there is a high view of Scripture in theory, whatever the practice. While liberals of various stripes undercut biblical authority by direct assaults, evangelicals of various stripes are today undermining biblical authority by claiming one thing in theory (the authority of an inerrant Bible) while in practice giving priority to secular disciplines and popular culture in defining and shaping the spiritual diet. Theology is considered irrelevant, whereas "practical" tips for success in business, marriage, child rearing, and personal self-fulfillment seem to suddenly be the Bible's major preoccupation. In other words, the Bible is meant to say things that it does not actually say and to be interested in things it does not actually show a marked concern for, and all the while it is still touted as inerrant and inspired. But after it has been made "relevant" to our "felt needs," it is no longer the Bible; it is actually our culture that is speaking in the guise of Scripture. But, as many of our confessions put it, the Scriptures are our "sole rule for faith and practice." Let us try to unpack, in practical terms, what that means.

First, we could raise the subject of evangelism and church growth. Is the Bible really sufficient for the building of Christ's kingdom? In Acts 2 we learn that the early Christians devoted "themselves to the apostles' teaching and to fellowship, to the breaking of bread and to prayer" (v. 42). Note the nature of these activities, revolving around Word and sacrament. Should the church be more than this? The results were plain: "And the Lord was adding to their number day by day those who were being saved" (v. 47). The Lord builds the church, not we. As we devote ourselves to the apostles' teaching and to fellowship, to corporate prayer and Holy Communion, we are seeing Christ build His kingdom before our very eyes. He is incorporating unbelievers into the kingdom, brought to Christ through our witness, by making them devoted to the teaching and worship of the community. This is how God's new society grows and conquers.

The world knows a better way, of course. There are marketing strategies that can build a church as easily as they build a consumer base for a small business. Perhaps the ministry of the Word (the apostles' teaching proclaimed and explained) will have to be shortened and somewhat weakened in terms of the heavy concentration of doctrine. Instead, the minister should offer a ten- or fifteen-minute "meditation" or inspirational reflection explaining how Christ can better serve the audience's needs and wants than any other product out there. The prayers will also have to go, since they are too long and boring. We have to keep the horizontal attraction in place. After all, if one loses the audience's attention for more than two minutes, studies show that they will not stay with the worship leader.

As for Communion, it should not have a prominent and frequent place in the "worship celebration," since it takes too long and the unchurched do not want to be asked to get up and do anything when they are at church. It just doesn't keep things moving along very well, and people begin to feel self-conscious during the lulls (moments of silent prayer and self-examination). Heaven forbid that we should be brought face-to-face every Sunday with the law and our continuing sinfulness as believers and the need to confess our sins. Even if it is followed by the declaration of pardon, none of this is dealing with people's felt needs. It is all too much concerned with God's wrath and mercy rather than His help for me right now where I am most needy. And as for the "fellowship" part, unchurched Harry and Mary like to remain anonymous, as do most Christians, so instead of fellowship around the Word and the Lord's Table, we will let the visitors blend into the scenery. They can believe whatever they like or be engaged in a variety of unrepentant lifestyles, but we will make them feel at home and give them their anonymity.

By the time we are finished, we have entirely transformed the communion of saints. We did not even have to officially jettison the Bible, as the modernists did earlier this century. We did not have to say that Scripture failed to provide answers for the modern world or speak to the real needs of contemporary men and women, as the liberals said. All we had to do was to allow the world to define a church instead of allowing the Word to define it. Nobody had to deny anything publicly or officially in the process; in fact, one would not even have to be dishonest to transfer his allegiance to the secular authority (in this case, marketing) even while defending a high view of Scripture. He or she may insist on inerrancy even though, in practice, the Scriptures are being superseded.

Or we may take another example. What is the purpose of life? According to Scripture, it is—summarized in the words of the Westminster Shorter Catechism—"to glorify God and enjoy him forever." But according to pop psychology, self-fulfillment is the goal of life, and religion serves its role best when it assists in providing some useful service to one's felt needs. According to a leading pollster, more than half of the evangelicals agreed with the statement "The purpose of life is enjoyment and personal fulfillment."[3] Here we have another instance of the Bible being contradicted by human wisdom, and once more we do not even have to change our official position with regard to the Bible's authority. We can have our cake and eat it too by affirming biblical inerrancy while we decline its normative status. It is an infallible Word, but it either agrees with this particular tenet of popular narcissism (doesn't the Bible tell us to seek the abundant life?) or its message is not even remotely interested in, for instance, telling us how to organize our business while we ignore its voice of criticism when we are deciding answers to truly significant questions that will direct the course of our entire lives. In theory, we are orthodox; in practice, we are rewriting the Christian religion from a secular script.

Another example of a low view of Scripture in practice is the contemporary sermon one often hears. A text may be printed in the bulletin, but Jesus just happens to sound a lot like Oprah Winfrey, and Paul coincidentally says basically the same things as Carl Rogers and Carl Carcher. John sounds remarkably like Rush Limbaugh and, far from the traditional picture, Jeremiah is really concerned with offering us principles for handling stress. I realize that there is a bit of hyperbole here, but it makes the point. There is a familiar ring to everything we hear because, in fact, we are hearing the popular culture fed back to us as the Word of God. The lack of substance in the preaching, publishing, and broadcasting in American religion may well rival that of medieval times. John Calvin expressed sentiments to Cardinal Sadoleto that could easily be said today:

> Nay, what one sermon was there from which old wives might not carry off more whimsies than they could devise at their own fireside in a month? For as sermons were then usually divided, the first half was devoted to those misty questions of the schools which might astonish the rude populace, while the second contained sweet stories, or not amusing specula-

tions, by which the hearers might be kept alert. Only a few expressions were thrown in from the Word of God, that by their majesty they might procure credit for these frivolities. But as soon as our reformers raised the standard, all these absurdities, in one moment, disappeared from among us. Your preachers, again, partly profited by our books, and partly compelled by shame and the general murmur, conformed to our example, though they still, with open throat, exhale the old absurdity.[4]

The real losers in all this are the very people who were targeted by the religious marketing people. They came to hear a transcendent message that they couldn't get anywhere else—something to make sense of their confused and broken lives. Many of them came to church not to tell the church what should be preached or what should happen. After all, why should the patient give the doctor the prescription? They came looking for answers, but they found only a groveling church that attempted to win them by asking a different set of questions than the one the Bible happens to answer.

How we define the problem will define our gospel. If the "big problem" in the universe is my lack of self-esteem, the gospel will be "finding the neat person inside of yourself." If the great question is "How can we fix society?" the gospel will be a set of moral agendas complete with a list of approved candidates. But how often do we discuss the "big problem" as defined by Scripture? That problem is the wrath of God. God does not just hate the sin; He hates and punishes the sinner for all eternity. Apart from His saving work, His sacrifice, goodness, and love, every one of us would face a consuming fire. That is the problem: God's justice requires His hatred of sin and evil. It is because of His love that He chose and redeemed His people and continues to call, justify, and sanctify until the return of Christ. So, if the great question is "How can I, a sinner, be reconciled to a holy God?" then the gospel is substitutionary atonement and justification by faith alone. If we do not see divine wrath as a "felt need," we will not preach the biblical gospel. The problem defines the solution. The law leads us to Christ.

This is what the Reformation intended by *sola Scriptura*. To believe that the Scriptures alone were sufficient for our doctrine and life was to believe that Christ is sufficient. Only the gospel saves: that is the point of "Scripture alone." The Scriptures define the problem, and they also define the solution; nothing else has that privilege in the kingdom of Christ.

DARKER CLOUDS LOOMING ON THE HORIZON

But beyond the subtle subversion of biblical authority, there is also the outright rejection of biblical authority to contend with in our day. Up to this point, I have argued that even many conservative evangelicals today are committing the same fallacy as the medieval church: affording Scripture a place of official supremacy as an infallible, inerrant document, while in actual practice forcing Scripture to fit other shapes and sizes. However, even in evangelicalism today (never mind the liberal Protestant establishment) we see a growing willingness to jettison confidence in biblical authority.

In 1987, University of Virginia sociologist James D. Hunter published studies of evangelical college and seminary students that demonstrated a shift in this regard. What of Jonah's whale? An independent fundamentalist student replied, "It is not important to me that it happened historically," and this was, according to the author, a typical response.[5] Although there have been no great discoveries that would weaken our confidence in the historical accuracy of the biblical record (to the contrary), it seems that many evangelicals are adopting a dichotomy between real history and spiritual story or myth that one finds in the later German liberals and neoorthodox theologians. Of course, there is no great danger in overturning one's faith by a rejection of the historicity of Jonah and the whale on its own merit. But the justification for the position is about as dangerous to the Christian faith as one could pose: "It is not important to me that it happened historically." The fact is, Christianity is unlike every other major religion in that it is dependant on facts of history for its credibility and very existence. If it is the spiritual or moral lesson rather than the historical event that is important, why should the Resurrection not also share the same fate as Jonah? "You ask me how I know He lives? He lives within my heart." It seems that we are already prepared for the demythologization of the Resurrection by our Romantic, experimental, and subjective approach to truth.

Christianity does not rest on our testimonies of changed lives, for the Mormons, drug treatment centers, and psychotherapists can offer such examples. Nor is Christianity to be trusted because of a personal experience. How many times have we had personal experiences that turned out to be misunderstood? The Christian faith rests on the claim of its Founder that He was the Messiah, God incarnate, the Savior of the world, and the claim of its apostles that they were eyewitnesses to His resurrection. Christianity does not clasp hands with other religions in an effort to provide a general, universal understanding of support for morality, human goodness, and religious symbols. It is not looking for those universal religious principles that are held in common by the great religions of the world. Christianity stands or falls on the premise that Christ Jesus died for our sins and was raised for our justification in real time-and-space history, just as truly as the Battle of Waterloo took place.

As Hunter points out, evangelical theologian Bernard Ramm articulated the view held by a growing number who regard the inerrancy of Scripture as "exegetically improbable, hermeneutically defective, theologically dangerous, and educationally disastrous. . . . This theologian is not alone," Hunter tells us, "for nearly 40 percent of all Evangelical theologians have abandoned the belief in the inerrancy of Scripture."[6] Evangelicalism is "a theological tradition in disarray," and the movement's identity crisis leads one to wonder, "What does it mean to be an Evangelical?" Hunter concludes, "While there has always been a measure of imprecision and debate about this among Evangelicals, the imprecision is expanding. For what one finds is a brand of theology that for generations had been considered 'modernistic' being advocated by theologians who vigorously defend their right to use the name of evangelical."[7]

More recently, however, evangelical theologian David Wells reports the research on a sampling of seven evangelical seminaries. Thirty-three percent of the students are uncertain or disagree with the statement "Without theology, the rest of my life would not have much meaning to it." Only 22.5 percent strongly agreed with this statement. According to these recent studies, 53.8 percent of tomorrow's evangelical, seminary-trained pastors regard the Bible as accurate in its teachings, but its historical reporting is not always to be taken literally. As propositional revelation and history drift farther apart in the minds of many, so too do doctrine and life. "Longstanding church doctrines are the surest guide for knowing ultimate religious truth" is a statement with which only 3.7 percent could strongly agree, while 55.1 percent disagreed and strongly disagreed.[8]

If theology is not guiding the church, then the Bible is not guiding the church, for theology is the systematic study of the Bible and its relation to our beliefs. But, as we have seen, evangelicals are not only avoiding theology in practice while holding to a high doctrine of Scripture in theory; the schizophrenia inherent in this balancing act is leading what appears now to be the majority of evangelicals to abandon the theoretical affirmation as well. What becomes plain is that, when we downplay theology (i.e., creeds, confessions, catechisms), before long we lose the *content* of Scripture. And not long after our loss of biblical content follows the loss of the *authority* of Scripture altogether. In practice, it becomes a helpful resource for practical daily living, whose doctrines and historical details may or may not have a formative effect in shaping one's thought and life, and eventually it loses its supremacy in theory as well. Like Protestantism earlier this century, evangelicals are in precisely this state at present. To the question "Do you believe in absolute truth?" mainline Protestants are more likely than all other adults in America to answer negatively. But evangelicals are almost equally divided between those who "strongly agree" and "strongly disagree." One-third of the evangelicals agreed with this relativistic stance.[9]

Beyond the technical definitions of biblical authority, most Christians today simply do not seem to have a great interest in reading the Bible in order to shape their beliefs and worldview. But this is where the leaders seem to be also, as David Wells's report concerning evangelical seminarians makes plain. What is the most significant expected gain from Bible study? Only 9.3 percent answered that it "helps me to be more knowledgeable about my faith," while instructions for life won 58 percent, and 32.1 percent answered that it "helps discern God's speaking to me within."[10] Obviously, this says more about the pragmatic and subjective orientation of popular culture than anything else.

Ignorance is the result of this line of thinking. Many people today—including Christians—simply do not want to think. They want to be entertained, cajoled, soothed, and stimulated. But this was true at the time of the Reformation as well, when there was a famine of hearing the Word of the Lord. Luther opined, "The average man today says, 'I'm a layman, and no theologian. I go to church, hear what my priest says, and him I believe.'" In our day, George Gallup reports,

> Americans revere the Bible, but they don't read it. And because they don't read it, they have become a nation of biblical illiterates. Four Americans in five believe the Bible is the literal or inspired Word of God, and yet only 4 in 10 could tell you that it was Jesus who gave the Sermon on the Mount and fewer than half can name the Four Gospels. . . . The cycle of biblical illiteracy seems likely to continue—today's teenagers know even less about the Bible than do adults. The celebration of Easter . . . is central to the faith, yet 3 teenagers in 10—20% of regular churchgoing teens—do not even know why Easter is celebrated. The decline in Bible reading is due in part to the widely held conviction that the Bible is inaccessible and less emphasis on religious training in the churches."[11]

Apostasy begins harmlessly enough. First, we are told that we do not need creeds, confessions, and catechisms to reign us in—Scripture requires no such protection. The result is that the Scriptures go before long. Next, we are asked to tone down on our doctrinal distinctives and emphasize that which unites all religious people of goodwill. The result of this is the rejection of the gospel. Finally, we are told, "All we need is Jesus," and we are left with a moral crusader. The sufficiency of Scripture means that everything that we believe about God, ourselves, redemption, the meaning of life and history, the nature of evil and its solution must not simply be made to fit with Scripture; it must actually be shaped and given by Scripture. We can know that we are sinners without the Bible, simply by the law written on our conscience. But we can only know that we are redeemed and how we are redeemed by a gift of special revelation, namely, the Bible.

If *sola Scriptura* has fallen on hard times once again due to the church's conformity to the pattern of this world's way of thinking rather than being transformed by the Word of God (Rom. 12:2), by outright rejection of biblical authority, and by ignorance, there is still one more challenge to this truth in our day: fanaticism.

Coined during the Reformation, "fanaticism" was used to describe those who confused their own "spirits" with the Holy Spirit and preferred their own revelations to Scripture. Luther once quipped of these preachers, "They think they have swallowed the Holy Ghost, feathers and all!" Calvin sharply rebuked them: "The Fanaticism which discards the Scripture, under the pretense of resorting to immediate revelations is subversive of every principle of Christianity. For when they boast extravagantly of the Spirit, the tendency is always to bury the Word of God so they may make room for their own falsehoods." These fanatics contrasted the Spirit (which they took to be immediate revelations) to the "dead letter" (which they regarded as Scripture by itself). This simply gave the people several popes instead of one.

Against all pretensions of private revelation, whether Rome's claim to papal revelations or the fanatics', the Reformers demanded "Scripture alone!" In our day, we face a similar crisis. With the teaching office substituted by a prophetic office, many churches in the charismatic movement especially are prone to one fad after another, tossed back and forth with every wind of doctrine and experience. God's Word is indirectly subverted in many of these groups by attacks on "head-knowledge" over "heart-knowledge" and appeals to experience over doctrine. This is another way in which Scripture is overthrown in practice even while it is highly regarded in theory. After all, Scripture insists on informing our minds. It is the transformation of our minds that Scripture aims at (Rom. 12:2) precisely because our thoughts direct our emotions and together the two direct the body. There is no choice between head-knowledge and heart-knowledge, and those who opt for the latter over the former are simply saying that they do not need to be informed by Scripture; their own experience (perhaps confirmed by references from Scripture, in or out of context) will be sufficient.

HOW CAN WE RECOVER THE SUFFICIENCY OF SCRIPTURE?

There is a remedy for this situation, and, not surprisingly, the Bible itself offers the solution to the challenges to *sola Scriptura*.

First, we must recover the communal character of Bible reading in the church. After nearly two centuries of individualism leading to a multitude of sects, it is time we recovered the older evangelical, Protestant view of authority. Although each believer is involved in the process of confessing the faith, we are all responsible to each other for our interpretations. We have seen absolutely no reason to avoid creeds, confessions, and catechisms in this century and every reason to recover them. The creeds help us work through the precise definitions of the Trinity and the person of Christ so that we do not end up inadvertently advancing an ancient heresy. No comparable council of godly, wise, and well-instructed leaders has been gathered in the subsequent history of the church in order to challenge heresy than those of Nicea and Constantinople. Certainly there is no single individual today who possesses the wisdom, education, and understanding of the controversies that could rival the accumulated resources of those bodies. Therefore, when one goes to Scripture, he should go to the Scriptures with the Council of Nicea.

Furthermore, the period of the Reformation was a contest between two rival gospels of salvation—one offering Christ's merit alone, the other adding human merit. One promised assurance to every repentant sinner; the other called this assurance presumption. One gospel gave everything that Christ possesses to the believer the moment he trusted in Christ alone; the other made every "gift" after baptism conditional on good works. Again, controversy made the church think more clearly, and the cobwebs of the Middle Ages were removed to reveal the glory of Christ and His saving work.

Since religion always takes the same shape when it falls into disrepair (i.e., it is always human-centered, subjective, and moralistic), it should come as no surprise that the challenges to the biblical gospel today are similar to those faced by the Reformers. We would be irresponsible to disregard the gains made by God's Spirit, using the most brilliant and godly minds of two centuries to recover the ancient beauty of Christ's church. As W. Robert Godfrey is fond of saying, "We keep reinventing the wheel in this century, and it's never round." We are fools if we insist on "starting from scratch" every time we face a controversy that has been encountered before.

So the next time we go to the Scriptures, let us not only take along the Council of Nicea; let us bring with us the confessions and catechisms of the Reformation. Confessions (such as the Augsburg, the Belgic, the Westminster) declare the community's understanding of the main points of Scripture, whereas the catechisms (Luther's Smaller and Larger, the Heidelberg, Westminster's Shorter and Larger) explain these interpretations, especially for children and new believers. There is no easier way to walk through the main points of Scripture than by reading through a Protestant catechism. We are all confessing our faith; we are all interpreting the main points. Our confessional interpretation does not take away from Scripture's sufficiency but presupposes it. So all we are saying here is that this confession and interpretation of Scripture must take place *corporately*. We are part of the body of Christ, and none of us is qualified to interpret Scripture by ourselves. Nor is any church in any particular age qualified to interpret Scripture by itself. If Scripture is to be regarded with the highest degree of confidence and authority, we will make every effort to bring the greatest wisdom to bear on its interpretation, for the good of the church and the world.

The Scriptures themselves point us in this direction. For instance, Jude urges the church to "contend earnestly for the faith which was once for all handed down to the saints" (v. 3). It is not merely faith as your trust in Christ or my personal relationship with Jesus, though that is necessary. Scripture speaks regularly of *the* faith. There is something to confess, an objective summary of biblical teaching. In the early church this summary was the *Didache* (Manual of Instruction), so this pattern of handing down the faith to the next generation has been used by God to preserve His light in the world for nearly two thousand years, in spite of the challenges that we have encountered in the past and face at present.

Second, we must begin to allow ourselves once again to be transformed by the renewing of our minds. We must reject this anti-intellectualism that so marks our age and think more deeply than ever about the meaning of the biblical passages in an effort to gain a systematic understanding of their key teachings. We must come to terms with the fact that the alternative to systematic theology is not the simplicity of the Bible but the confusion that marks a generation that cannot rightly divide the Word of truth (2 Tim. 2:15). There is, the apostle tells us in that passage, not only a Word to be handled but a manner in which to handle that Word properly.

Third, we must allow the Bible to judge our thoughts, imaginations, opinions, and lifestyles. The *shibboleth* "worldliness" immediately creates impressions in our minds: immorality, lust, profanity, and so forth. And yet, there are more insidious forms of worldliness that seem to hold the church in captivity. Every church-growth scheme, every influence of pop psychology, every political ideology, and every sociological paradigm must be brought under the judgment of Scripture. The problem is that many of us are naively committed to these forms of worldliness. We do not even realize that we are committed to them because they are so much a part of the air that we breathe. This means that we will have to explain the "idols" so that our contemporaries can recognize them as something distinct. By "objectifying" them, we are able to analyze them in the light of Scripture. They must be named, and this requires some discussion of the problem of modernity. If we do not face it, we will be consumed by it. But beyond naming the idols, we must point people to the true God of revelation, and this means that we must know the Word of God thoroughly. We must read it not merely for the reasons most evangelical seminarians reportedly embrace but for the reason that only 9 percent of them favored: to understand what we believe and why we believe it.

Finally, we must recover the message of the Scriptures. In the Second Helvetic Confession, we are told that "the preached Word of God is, in a special sense, the Word of God." This is because preaching is a means of grace; by it, God creates a new life and gives the gift of faith to those who are "dead in . . . trespasses and sins" (Eph. 2:1). Miracles happen every time the Word is preached, accompanied as it is by the Spirit of God. But the preaching of the Word is not saving simply because it is a ritual; it is saving because it is preaching Christ. It is the message that is saving, for not everything in the Word is saving. The Scriptures are divided into two parts, the Reformers insisted: law and gospel. This is not the same as Old Testament and New Testament, for the gospel was present in the Old Testament and the law is present in the New. These are the categories that characterized all of Scripture.

Anything in Scripture that forbids, commands, exhorts, or admonishes is "law." It does not save but rather leads us to despair of being saved by fulfilling such demands. Anything in Scripture that promises, gives, invites, forgives, and assures is "gospel."

The Reformers—and the Protestants who were their heirs—were convinced that "preaching the Word" meant preaching the law and the gospel, without either confusing one with the other or doing away with one or the other. But in our day, many sermons focus on "daily principles" or "practical living." However nice and helpful, such sermons would fall into the category of "law-preaching." But it is not really law-preaching because it is not concerned with God's law; rather, it is our own insights as a result of reading some helpful books on the subject or seeing a talk show that inspired our thoughts for next Sunday's sermon. Thus, it does not really lead anyone to despair, giving the impression that Christianity is really quite an easy thing: If one simply will follow these principles, life will go much better, whereas Scripture declares, "Cursed is everyone who does not continue to do everything written in the Book of the Law" (Gal. 3:10 NIV; cf. Deut. 27:26). Therefore, all who rely on observing "the law are under a curse," Paul states (Gal. 3:10).

In law-gospel preaching, the believer is faced with his inability to satisfy God and God's solution to the problem in the person and work of Christ; in moralistic or "practical" preaching, the believer is encouraged to satisfy God (or, as is more often the case, himself) by imitating the example of David, Solomon, Jesus, or Paul. The law is not as deadly and the gospel is not as free in this kind of preaching, and it leaves believers trusting a little in themselves and a little in God, and largely unsure of the nature of their hope. By recovering a diet of guilt, grace, and gratitude as the pillars of biblical preaching and teaching, we will be restoring the sufficiency of Scripture as "the power of God unto salvation" (KJV) in the pulpit and pew.

Great days are ahead of us as we make use of these resources and firmly resolve to follow Paul's advice to Timothy:

> Preach the word; be ready in season and out of season; reprove, rebuke, exhort, with great patience and instruction. For the time will come when they will not endure sound doctrine; but wanting to have their ears tickled, they will accumulate for themselves teachers in accordance to their own desires [felt needs?], and will turn away their ears from the truth and will turn aside to myths. But you, be sober in all things, endure hardship, do the work of an evangelist, fulfill your ministry. (2 Tim. 4:2–5)

Although this is chiefly advice to ministers, it is the duty of all God's people. May He give us His grace to resist the pressures of our time and to grant to us an end to the famine of hearing the words of the Lord.

NOTES

1. Heiko Oberman, *Luther: The Man Between God and the Devil* (New York: Double-day, 1989), 247.

2. Alexandre Ganoczy, *The Young Calvin* (Philadelphia: Westminster Press, 1987), 216.

3. George Barna, *What Americans Believe* (Ventura: Regal, 1991), 112.

4. John Calvin and Cardinal Jacopo Sadoleto, *A Reformation Debate* (Grand Rapids: Baker, 1978), 65.

5. James D. Hunter, *Evangelicalism: The Coming Generation* (Chicago: Univ. of Chicago Press, 1987), 29.

6. Ibid., 31.

7. Ibid., 32.

8. David F. Wells, *God in the Wasteland: The Reality of Truth in a World of Fading Dreams* (Grand Rapids: Eerdmans, 1994), Appendix.

9. Barna, *What Americans Believe*, 83–84.

10. Wells, *God in the Wasteland*, 234.

11. George Gallup and James Castelli, *The People's Religion: American Faith in the 90's* (New York: Macmillan, 1989), 60.

GENERAL INDEX

Moody Press, a ministry of Moody Bible Institute,
is designed for education, evangelization, and edification.
If we may assist you in knowing more about Christ
and the Christian life, please write us without obligation:
Moody Press, c/o MLM, Chicago, Illinois 60610.